Better Homes and Gardens.

Christmas
all
through
the
house

crafts ✦ decorating ✦ food

Better Homes and Gardens® Books
Des Moines, Iowa

Better Homes and Gardens® Books
An imprint of Meredith® Books

Better Homes and Gardens®
CHRISTMAS All Through the House

Editor: Carol Field Dahlstrom
Technical Editor: Colleen Johnson
Contributing Writer: Susan M. Banker
Graphic Designer: Angela Haupert Hoogensen
Copy Chief: Catherine Hamrick
Copy and Production Editor: Terri Fredrickson
Contributing Copy Editor: Diane Doro
Contributing Proofreaders: Margaret Smith, JoEllyn Witke
Technical Illustrator: Chris Neubauer Graphics, Inc.
Electronic Production Coordinator: Paula Forest
Editorial and Design Assistants: Judy Bailey, Mary Lee Gavin, Karen Schirm
Production Director: Douglas M. Johnston
Production Manager: Pam Kvitne
Assistant Prepress Manager: Marjorie J. Schenkelberg

Meredith® Books
Editor in Chief: James D. Blume
Design Director: Matt Strelecki
Managing Editor: Gregory H. Kayko

Director, Sales & Marketing, Retail: Michael A. Peterson
Director, Sales & Marketing, Special Markets: Rita McMullen
Director, Sales & Marketing, Home & Garden Center Channel: Ray Wolf
Director, Operations: George A. Susral

Vice President, General Manager: Jamie L. Martin

Better Homes and Gardens® Magazine
Editor in Chief: Jean LemMon

Meredith Publishing Group
President, Publishing Group: Christopher M. Little
Vice President, Consumer Marketing & Development: Hal Oringer

Meredith Corporation
President and Chief Executive Officer: William T. Kerr

Chairman of the Executive Committee: E. T. Meredith III

Cover photography: Andy Lyons Cameraworks, Peter Krumhardt

All of us at Better Homes and Gardens® Books are dedicated to providing you with information and ideas to create
beautiful and useful projects. We welcome your comments and suggestions. Write to us at: Better Homes and Gardens®
Books, Crafts Editorial Department, 1716 Locust St., Des Moines, IA 50309-3023.

If you would like to purchase any of our books, check wherever quality books are sold.

To find instructions for the blue snowflake trim and the beaded candle shown on the cover, turn to page 320.
Turn to page 187 for the mitten cookie recipe.

the magic
of the season

All year long we anticipate Christmas, a season wrapped generously with caring, warmth, and love—a time when we renew our spirits and remember that gathering together is a blessing. It's a magical holiday— voices chorus in harmony, children delight in stories of wonder, and we savor every precious moment.

Better Homes and Gardens® Christmas All Through the House captures this spirit with hundreds of make-it-yourself crafts and decorating ideas. Look for wonderful ways to trim the tree and deck your house in holiday finery. Prepare special recipes—kitchen-tested to guarantee spectacular results—from casual munchies to just-for-company dishes. You'll also find inspired gifts to make for family and friends.

So share your talents and love with all those dear to you. Whether adorning the perfect wreath for your front door, creating a cherub doll for your own little angel, or baking dozens of goodies for your neighbors, you'll create sights, sounds, and aromas that will linger in loved ones' memories long after the New Year has passed. Christmas All Through the House—what better way to celebrate the most beloved of all holidays!

table of contents

welcome
home

Join us as we share a bounty of crafts brimming with holiday warmth. From lovely entry accents to unforgettable mantel trims, these special decorating treasures will help you welcome your loved ones home this Christmas.

elegant holiday wreath

Greet holiday visitors at the door with this regally adorned wreath. Created using a pineapple, purple grape clusters made from tiny Christmas balls, and satin ribbons, the wreath will say "Merry Christmas to all" during the holiday season. Instructions for the wreath and the grape clusters are on page 24.

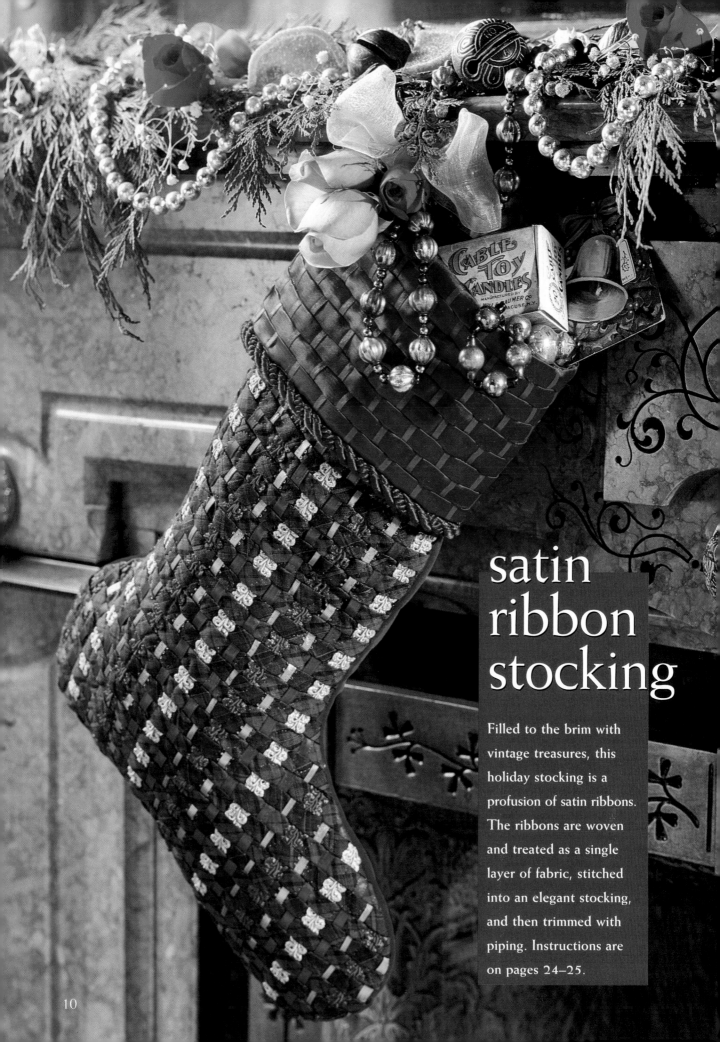

satin ribbon stocking

Filled to the brim with vintage treasures, this holiday stocking is a profusion of satin ribbons. The ribbons are woven and treated as a single layer of fabric, stitched into an elegant stocking, and then trimmed with piping. Instructions are on pages 24–25.

welcome sampler

Show off your talents at Christmastime by displaying your needlework for all to enjoy. Our Welcome Sampler can be quickly cross-stitched on 16-count Aida cloth and embellished with gold blending filament and beads. The instructions and the chart are on page 26.

country luminarias

Clear canning jars spread holiday cheer when they're transformed into luminarias. Filled with sand, red berries, and a votive candle, these vessels look beautiful reflecting in a mantel mirror. Or, as shown here, make enough to line the walkway and welcome all who come to call. The instructions are on page 27.

happy
lighted
snowman

This life-size snowman
lights up the backyard
and the holiday season
with an everlasting smile.
Cut from sturdy fiberboard,
the self-standing figure is
outlined in strings of
Christmas-tree lights.
A coffee-can top hat and
a hand-me-down scarf
make him as joyful as
can be. The instructions
and patterns are on
pages 27–28.

13

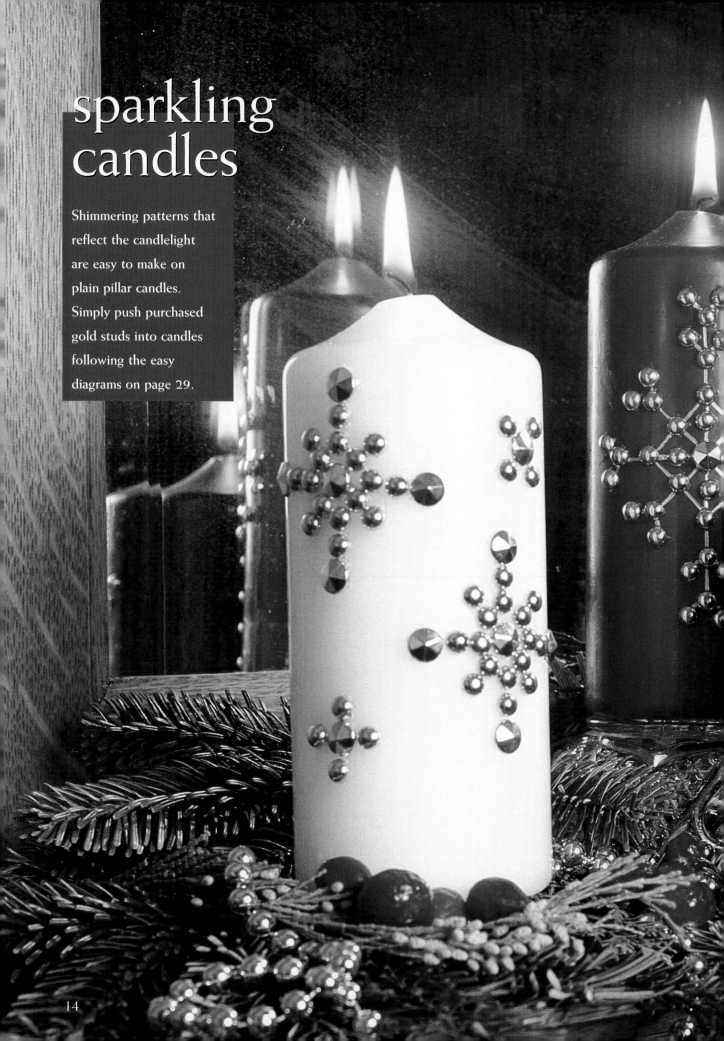

sparkling candles

Shimmering patterns that reflect the candlelight are easy to make on plain pillar candles. Simply push purchased gold studs into candles following the easy diagrams on page 29.

smiling snowman family

Pleased to be propped upon the mantel, or any spot in the house, our snowman family will bring smiles from wintertime guests of all ages. Made from gourds, fabric, a bit of clay, and paint, each snow person has a playful personality. The step-by-step instructions for the bunch are on pages 30–31.

16

crocheted candy-cane stocking

Stripes of red and white combine to create this sweet candy-cane stocking crocheted with soft acrylic yarn. The cozy stocking, worked in half double crochet stitches, can be passed down for generations to come. The instructions begin on page 32.

Our whimsical banner sets the stage for a happy holiday. The pieces are all cut from colorful felt, then sewn to a background. Simple stitches express the cheerful saying. The instructions and patterns are on pages 33–37.

jolly felt banner

Just like the old peddler with his Christmas pack, this aromatic snowman carries his own collection of goodies. Draped over cinnamon-stick arms, his herbs-and-spice showcase includes dried wheat, eucalyptus, and other garden delights. The elongated snow figure is a stitch-and-stuff construction that's fashioned from tea-dyed muslin. He's a dapper fellow, too, dressed in a woolly scarf and stocking cap. The instructions and patterns are on pages 38–39.

herbal snowman

flannel tree quilt

Simple and stunning, our country Christmas tree quilt is made using warm and cozy flannel. The quilt uses recycled flannel shirts for many of the blocks. The colorful pieces are sewn into tree blocks, then connected with sashing strips of red and gold. The instructions and patterns for this bold piece begin on page 40.

21

st. nick
stocking

Constructed from muted tones of felt, our St. Nick stocking is sure to be a holiday favorite. The country-colored Santa motif is sewn onto the stocking using blanket stitches and cross-stitches with contrasting embroidery floss. For complete instructions and full-size pattern, see pages 42–44.

Stitched on plastic canvas, our sprightly Santas bring festive holiday fun as door decorations or package ties. Because you can quickly stitch and finish them, you'll have plenty of time to create a Santa for everyone on your shopping list. The instructions and chart for these cheery fellows are on pages 44–45.

sprightly santas

elegant holiday wreath

As shown on pages 8–9.

Materials

One pineapple; knife
Liquid floor wax; floral picks
26-inch-diameter evergreen wreath
7 yards 2-inch-wide periwinkle
 satin-center organdy ribbon
3 yards 1-inch-wide burgundy
 reversible-stripe satin ribbon
17 dried red roses
14 pieces of dried purple stock
12 pieces of dried white statice
Four pieces of reindeer moss
Four 4-inch-long pinecones
Nine lemon leaves; paintbrush
White spray paint; gold metallic paint
24 peacock feathers
Hot-glue gun; hot glue

For grape clusters

Nine ½- to ¾-inch-diameter glass
 Christmas balls on wires
Purple flat spray paint; silk leaves
Floral wire; green floral tape

Instructions

Slice a ¾-inch-thick section from one side of the pineapple. Dip both sections into floor wax to seal; let dry. Position large pineapple section at the bottom of the wreath slightly left of center. Secure with picks. Fasten remaining section to the top right of wreath in the same manner.

Make an 11-loop bow from periwinkle ribbon. Secure center of the bow with floral wire. Wire the bow to the bottom center of the wreath.

For each grape cluster, paint balls purple; let dry. Tape two balls together with floral tape. Tape balls to the cluster, one at a time, until nine are joined. Add silk leaves. Poke wire end of cluster into wreath.

Arrange the burgundy ribbon on the wreath as desired. Glue all the remaining materials to the wreath, beginning with the roses then adding the stock, statice, reindeer moss, and pinecones. Space each type of material evenly around wreath for a well-balanced arrangement.

Spray-paint lemon leaves white; let dry. Accent edges and veins of the leaves with gold metallic paint; let dry. Glue peacock feathers and lemon leaves onto the wreath.

satin ribbon stocking

As shown on page 10, stocking measures 17 inches long.

Materials

Graph paper
½ yard of sheer black lightweight
 fusible interfacing
½ yard of small
 burgundy-and-green plaid
¾ yard of burgundy satin
Size 12 bias tape maker for a
 ½-inch finished width
Grid paper for ribbon pin-weaving
16×21-inch piece of cardboard
Quilting pins
12 yards of ¼-inch-wide burgundy
 satin ribbon
1⅞ yards of ⅛-inch-wide
 mauve ribbon
1⅞ yards of ½-inch-wide
 burgundy upholstery gimp
1⅞ yards of ¼-inch-wide mauve
 satin picot ribbon
1⅞ yards of ½-inch-wide mauve
 upholstery gimp
Nylon sewing thread
Burgundy sewing thread
⅝ yard of burgundy velveteen
½ yard of ½-inch-diameter
 burgundy upholstery cording

Instructions

Enlarge stocking pattern, *below,* onto graph paper. Mark right side of stocking "front;" cut out the pattern piece. With wrong side of pattern facing fusible side of interfacing, cut interfacing ½ inch larger than the pattern all around. Cut a 6×19-inch rectangle of interfacing for cuff.

Cut plaid fabric into 1-inch-wide strips, cutting with the straight grain. Cut 1-inch-wide strips of burgundy satin, cutting from selvage to selvage. Use bias tape maker to fold and press long cut edges to wrong side, creating ½-inch-wide strips for weaving.

Lay grid paper on top of cardboard. Position the interfacing stocking, fusible side up, on the grid paper. Pin the stocking to the board at the edge of the toe, heel, and the top edge.

To lay warp (lengthwise ribbons), pin ¼-inch-wide burgundy ribbon on far left vertical grid line, starting at top left edge of interfacing stocking. Smooth ribbon down interfacing stocking; pin in place at bottom. Cut ribbon just beyond pin. Repeat with ⅛-inch-wide mauve ribbon on next vertical grid line. Continue across interfacing, using burgundy gimp, ¼-inch mauve picot ribbon, ¼-inch burgundy ribbon, mauve gimp, and ¼-inch burgundy ribbon. Repeat sequence across interfacing stocking until covered. Pins must be on the edge of interfacing, on vertical grid line, and follow the contour of pattern as shown on pinning diagram, *far right.*

Weave plaid fabric strips over and under warp, working from left to right and from top to bottom. Extend strips at sides to cover entire fusible surface. Keep strips close together and level, using grid lines as guides.

With pins still in board, press entire piece according to manufacturer's instructions for interfacing. Remove pins, turn weaving over, and press from back.

Repeat pinning and weaving for cuff, using ¼-inch-wide burgundy ribbon for warp and weaving with burgundy satin fabric strips.

Stitch in a random wavy pattern over stocking using nylon thread in top of machine and burgundy thread in bobbin. For cuff, stitch across weaving "in the ditch" between fabric strips. Lay paper stocking pattern over woven stocking; cut out. Cut cuff 12 strips high by 18 inches wide. Straight-stitch around woven pieces close to edge.

Cut stocking back from burgundy velveteen. Cut two more stockings (reversing one) from burgundy satin for lining. Cut cuff lining from satin using woven cuff for pattern. Cut a 2¼×7-inch hanging loop from burgundy satin.

Unless otherwise indicated, sew fabric shapes together with right sides facing, using ½-inch seams.

Sew stocking front to back leaving top edge open; trim seam and clip curves. Repeat for lining. Turn stocking right side out; press. Slip lining inside stocking with wrong sides facing. Set aside.

Using zipper foot, stitch cording to the right side of one long edge of woven cuff. With right sides facing, place cuff lining atop woven cuff and sew along cording seam line.

Open piece out, then fold it crosswise, with right sides facing and matching short sides. Sew sides together, forming a tube. Turn cuff right side out, then fold lining to inside. Baste raw edges together.

Fold hanging loop strip in half lengthwise with right sides facing; sew long edges together. Turn and press. Fold strip in half crosswise and pin to back seam on inside of stocking, matching raw edges. Slip cuff into stocking with right side of cuff facing stocking lining. Sew cuff to stocking, matching raw edges; turn cuff to outside.

SATIN RIBBON STOCKING

1 Square = 1 Inch

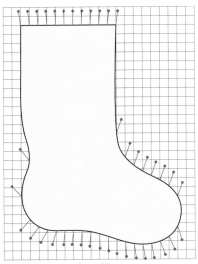

PINNING DIAGRAM

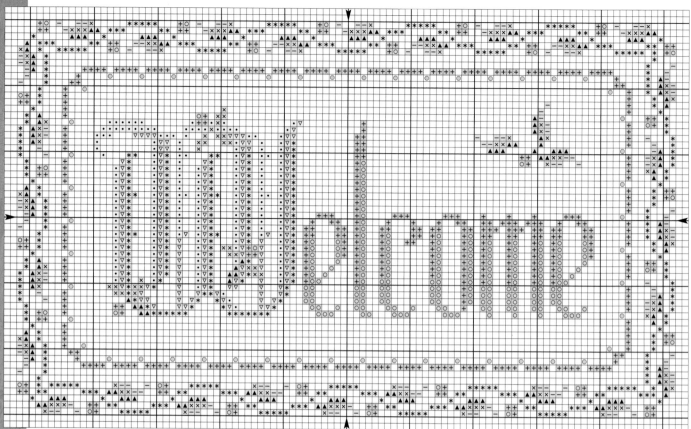

WELCOME SAMPLER

welcome sampler

As shown on page 11.

Materials

Fabric

9×12-inch piece of
16-count white Aida cloth

Threads

Cotton embroidery floss in
colors listed in key
Blending filament in color
listed in key

Supplies

Needle; embroidery hoop
Seed beads in color listed
in key
Desired frame and mat

WELCOME SAMPLER		
ANCHOR		**DMC**
860	☒	522 Dark olive drab
859	⊟	523 Medium olive drab
102	⊙	550 Violet
861	▲	935 Pine green
1028	⊞	3685 Mauve
BLENDED NEEDLE		
886	•	677 Old gold (1X) and
		002 Kreinik gold blending filament (1X)
888	✳	3045 Dark yellow beige (1X) and
		002 Kreinik gold blending filament (1X)
887	▽	3046 Medium yellow beige (1X) and
		002 Kreinik gold blending filament (1X)
BEADS		
	○	00557 Gold Mill Hill seed bead

Stitch count: 60 high x 104 wide
Finished design sizes:
16-count fabric – 3³/₄ x 6¹/₂ inches
14-count fabric – 4¹/₄ x 7³/₈ inches
18-count fabric – 3¹/₃ x 5³/₄ inches

Instructions

Zigzag edges of Aida
cloth to prevent fraying.
Find center of chart,
above, and center of
fabric; begin stitching
there. Use two plies of
floss for cross-stitches.
Work the blended needle
as specified in key.
Attach beads with old
gold (DMC 677) floss.
Press stitchery and frame
as desired.

country luminarias

As shown on page 12.

Materials

Quart- or pint-size Mason jars; sand

Sugar scoop or gardener's hand
   trowel

Candle in glass votive cups, one
   for each jar

Real or artificial evergreen sprigs
   and holly berries

Red-and-green plaid ribbon

Red and green tinsel

Instructions

For each luminary, fill the bottom of the jar ¼ to ⅓ with sand. Firmly press a candle into sand. Drop small bits of greenery or berries into the jar. Tie the ribbon around the top of the jar and tuck tinsel around the bow.

happy lighted snowman

As shown on page 13, snowman without hat measures 24×48 inches.

Materials

4×8-foot piece of ¾-inch
   particleboard

Tape measure; pencil; jigsaw

12-inch piece of 1-inch-diameter
   dowel

5-inch piece of ½-inch-diameter
   dowel

Drill; ½- and 1-inch drill bits

Sharp knife

39-ounce coffee can (6¾ inches
   tall with a 7⅛-inch diameter)

White, black, and orange
   spray paints

Three white Christmas light strings

Grapevine branches; scarf

Artificial greens and berry stems

Construction adhesive; caulk gun

Instructions

For snowman front/back, measure 12½ inches from edge on one 8-foot side of board; lightly draw a line the entire length of the

particleboard, referring to the diagram, *page 28*. Beginning at the 4-foot side (the bottom edge) of the board, measure along the marked line at 10½-, 29½-, and 42-inch intervals, and mark each with a dot.

Beginning at the bottom of the board and using the 10½-inch

mark as the center point, draw a 24-inch-diameter circle. Draw an 18- and 12-inch circle in the same manner using dots as center of the circles. *Note:* The circles will overlap.

For slot-cutting lines, measure and mark a dot along the center line 24 inches from the bottom of the board. Draw a parallel line ⅜ inch from the center line on each side of the line to create a ¾-inch-wide slot.

For snowman sides, measure 34 inches from the opposite 8-foot edge of the particleboard and draw another center line the full length of the particleboard. Measure and draw 24-inch and 18-inch-diameter circles in the same manner as directed above for the snowman shape. Measure and mark all the cutting lines for the slot as directed above.

happy lighted snowman — *continued*

Draw two 2½-inch-diameter eyes, three 3½-inch-diameter buttons, and one 10-inch-diameter hat brim circle in an open area of particleboard. Cut out all of the pieces, including slots.

For nose, drill a 1-inch-diameter hole ¾-inch-deep along center line of snowman front/back 6 inches from top of the head. For buttons, mark and cut a ¾-inch strip from center of each of the 3½-inch-diameter button circles. Set aside half-circle shapes. Drill a ½-inch-diameter hole 1-inch-deep into top center of snowman's head and in center of hat brim. Drill a ½-inch-diameter hole in each side of snowman front/back 6 inches from neck for inserting arms.

For light sockets, measure and drill ⅜-inch holes every 2 inches around perimeter of snowman front/back and side pieces. Drill a ½-inch hole in the neck to pass light string through to the front. For mouth, cut seven ⅜-inch-thick discs from 1-inch-diameter dowel.

For nose, use a sharp knife to shave end of 1-inch dowel until it resembles a carrot. Center the coffee-can container on hat brim; adhere in place using construction adhesive. Push ½-inch dowel into hat brim, adhering in place with construction adhesive. Paint snowman body pieces white; eyes, buttons, hat brim, mouth

pieces, and coffee-can black; and nose orange. Assemble snowman front/back and snowman side pieces together, matching slots and slipping pieces together. Cement eyes, nose, mouth, both button circles, and bottom button half-circles in place with adhesive. Beginning at bottom of

snowman front/back, insert lights into drilled openings around body. Repeat for snowman side, passing light string through the opening in neck to front.

Insert dowel on hat into the opening at the top of head. Insert grapevine arms into armholes; tie scarf around snowman's neck.

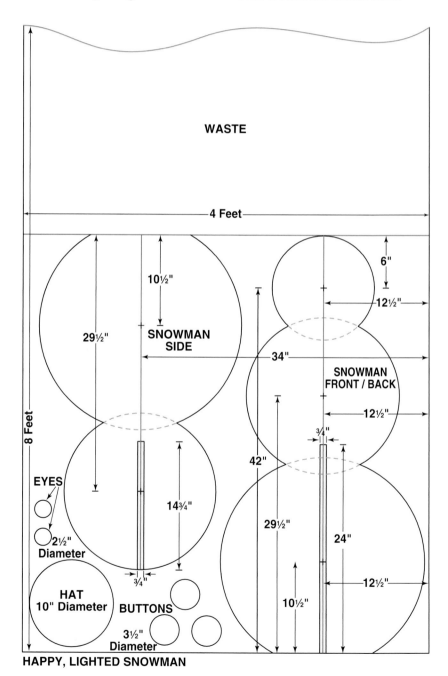

HAPPY, LIGHTED SNOWMAN

sparkling candles

As shown on pages 14–15.

Materials

Tracing paper; pencil
Three 6-inch-tall plain pillar candles
Masking tape; tapestry needle
One hundred and seventy
    ¼-inch-diameter gold
    nailhead studs
One ⅝-inch gold star-shaped stud
Gold metallic paint marker
Thirteen ⅜-inch-diameter gold
    nailhead studs

Instructions

For starburst design (shown on green candle), fold a 4½-inch square of tracing paper in half. Aligning the fold with dotted line on the pattern, trace starburst pattern, *above right.* Turn the folded tracing paper over and trace pattern on the opposite side of the fold; unfold. Center pattern on candle and tape in place. With needle, make a small hole in center of each paper circle and a light indentation on candle. Remove pattern and press ¼-inch studs into candle at each indentation. Press star-shaped stud into center.

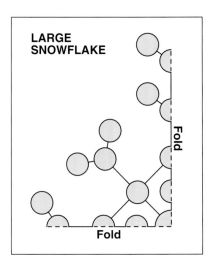

LARGE SNOWFLAKE

Fold
Fold

For large snowflake design (shown on red candle), fold a 4½-inch square of tracing paper in half; repeat, bringing the folded edges together. Matching folds, trace pattern, *below left,* onto tracing paper. Turn folded tracing paper over and trace pattern on opposite side of fold; unfold once and trace pattern on remaining two quarters of paper. Unfold pattern and tape to the candle, centering from top to bottom. Trace lines and

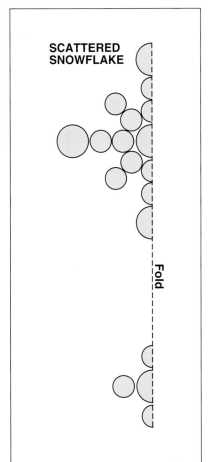

SCATTERED SNOWFLAKE

Fold

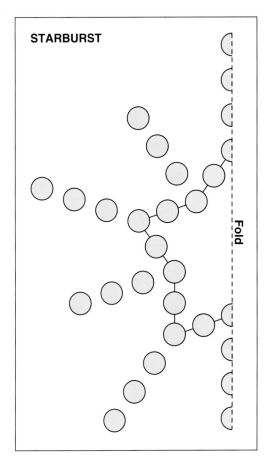

STARBURST

Fold

make indentations for the stud placement with needle. Remove pattern and draw over lines using gold marker. Press a ⅜-inch stud into center and ¼-inch studs into remaining indentations.

For scattered snowflake design (shown on white candles), fold 4½-inch square of tracing paper in half. Align fold with dotted line on pattern, *left;* trace. Turn folded tracing paper over and trace pattern on opposite side of fold; unfold. Center the pattern on candle and tape. With needle, make a small hole in the center of each paper circle and a light indentation on the candle. Remove pattern and press ⅜-inch and ¼-inch studs into appropriate positions as shown on pattern.

29

smiling snowman family

As shown on pages 16–17, snowmen range from 9½ to 12 inches tall.

Materials for one snowman

Hardened light-brown hollow dried gourd in snowman shape

Sharp non-serrated knife

8×30-inch strip of burlap

Mod Podge decoupage medium; bowl

Cotton sock or doll's black hat to fit head; small decorative bird

White sewing thread; needle

Acrylic paints: deep blue, white, black, orange, and desired colors for scarf and cap

Small sponge; artists' and 1- and 2-inch paintbrushes

Crayola Model Magic clay

Gel Superglue; black paint pen

Acrylic satin spray varnish; buttons

Embroidery floss; large jingle bell

Instructions

Clean gourd as shown in Step 1, *below*, and dry the surface.

Cut burlap for the scarf (see Step 2, *below*). Remove several threads along the edges to make ½-inch-long fringe. Wet scarf and wring out excess water. Dip scarf into the Mod Podge as shown in

Soak gourd in warm soapy water several hours. Using a knife held at an angle, scrape off outer layer of skin. Use a kitchen scrubber to remove any remaining skin.

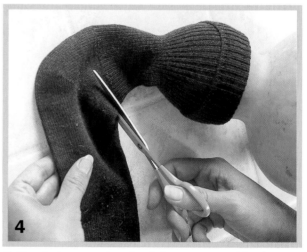

Cut burlap strip to measure three times the circumference of neck area on gourd. Fold strip in half lengthwise. Tie around neck and trim to desired length; remove scarf.

Pour Mod Podge into bowl. Dip scarf into bowl, working Mod Podge thoroughly into fabric. Let dry. Tie scarf around snowman, arranging fabric as desired.

Cuff sock about 1 inch and pull down over gourd head. Determine desired length, and cut off excess. Remove sock, turn inside out, and sew cut end closed.

Step 3, *below opposite*. Tie scarf around snowman's neck.

To make stocking cap, cut stocking as shown in Step 4, *below opposite*. Soak cap in water, wring out excess, and work Mod Podge into cap as for scarf. Position cap on head; cuff bottom edge and shape as desired.

Allow scarf and cap to dry several hours or overnight until hard.

Paint snowman as shown in Steps 5–7, *below*. Paint cap and scarf with desired pattern, using paint thinned to consistency of cream. Apply paint lightly to allow fabric texture to show. Follow direction of ribbing or threads of fabric as a guide for pattern, referring to photograph, *pages 16–17*, for ideas.

Make eyes and nose as shown in Step 8, *below*. When dry, highlight eyes with white; wipe nose with blue paint, removing excess for an antiqued effect. Glue eyes and nose in place. Using paint pen, draw a large curved mouth beneath the nose. Allow all glue and paint to dry.

Spray the entire snowman with varnish and allow it to dry. If desired, glue a jingle bell to the end of the stocking cap.

For snowman with black hat, glue hat to head at an angle. Glue bird to top of hat.

Layer colorful buttons by sewing one atop the other using scraps of embroidery floss. Glue buttons down the center front of the snowman.

5

Put the hat on the snowman; let dry. Paint the entire snowman blue, working paint well into the stiffened fabric of scarf and cap. Allow paint to dry thoroughly.

6

Thin white paint until transparent. Using sponge, apply layers of thinned paint to gourd surface. Use caution near edges of scarf and cap, allowing blue to remain.

7

To finish, use water to thin white paint, and paint open areas of the body. Thin colored paints, and paint cap and scarf with desired pattern.

8

Mold clay into two ½-inch-diameter round or oval eyes and one 1⅛-inch-long nose and allow to dry until hard. Paint eyes black and nose orange; allow to dry.

crocheted candy-cane stocking

As shown on page 18, stocking measures about 20 inches long.
Crochet abbreviations are on page 320.

Materials

Berella "4," "100% Monsanto acrylic" worsted-weight yarn (3.5-oz/100-gm. skein): one skein each of geranium (8929) and winter white (8941)

Size 8/H (5.00 mm) aluminum crochet hook or size to obtain gauge

GAUGE: In hdc stripes, 13 sts and 9 rows = 4 inches.

Instructions

Note: Striped pat is worked in hdc. To change color in hdc, yo and draw up a lp with present color in last st before change, with new color, yo and draw through all 3 lps on hook. Checked cuff is worked in dc; to change color in dc, with present color make a dc in last st before change until 2 lps rem on hook; with new color, yo and draw through both lps on hook.

STOCKING: Beginning at top and below cuff, with red, ch 49. Sc in second ch from hook and each ch across = 48 sts; join with sl st in first sc.

Rnd 1: With red, ch 2 (counts as hdc), hdc in each of next 2 sts changing to white; * (1 white hdc, 1 red hdc) twice, 1 white hdc **, (3 red hdc); rep from * around, ending last rep at **; join with sl st in second ch of beg ch-2.

Rep Rnd 1 for candy cane pat until it measures 9 inches. Fasten off.

HEEL: With RS facing, join red with sl st in tenth st to right of joining. Ch 1, sc in same st as join and in each of next 19 sts; turn.

Row 2: Ch 1, sc in 13 sts; turn.
Row 3: Ch 1, sc in 6 sts; turn.
Row 4: Ch 1, sc in 7 sts; turn.
Row 5: Ch 1, sc in 8 sts; turn.
Row 6: Ch 1, sc in 9 sts; turn.
Rows 7–17: Cont as est, working one more sc at end of every row = 20 sts after Row 17. Fasten off.

SOLE: With RS facing, join red with sl st in fifteenth sc from right edge of heel. Ch 2 (counts as hdc), with red, hdc in next 2 sts and change to white; 1 white hdc, 1 red hdc, 1 white hdc; sk first 4 sts along side of stocking, then work hdc around as follows: (1 red, 1 white, 3 red, 1 white, 1 red, 1 white) twice, 1 red, 1 white, 2 red, sk 4 sts along side of stocking, working on rem heel sts work 1 red, (1 white, 1 red) twice, 1 white, 3 red, (1 white, 1 red) twice, 1 white; join = 40 sts.

Rnds 2-12: Work in striped pat. After Rnd 12, fasten off white.

TOE: Ch 1, sc in each hdc around, dec 4 sts evenly spaced = 36 sts; join.

Rnd 2: Ch 1, (sc in 4 sc, sc 2 tog) around = 30 sts; join.

Rnd 3: Ch 1, (sc in 3 sc, sc 2 tog) around = 24 sts; join.

Rnd 4: Rep Rnd 2 = 20 sts.
Rnd 5: Rep Rnd 3 = 16 sts.
Rnd 6: Ch 1, (sc in 2 sc, sc 2 tog) around = 12 sts; join.

Rnd 7: Ch 1, (sc in sc, sc 2 tog) around = 8 sts; join.

Rnd 8: (Sc 2 tog) around = 4 sts.

Leaving an 8-inch tail, fasten off. Weave tail through sts and pull up to close opening. Secure in place.

CUFF: With RS facing and working along opposite edge of foundation ch, join red with sl st in first ch. Ch 3 (counts as dc), 1 red dc in each of next 2 ch and change to white; * 1 white dc in each of next 3 ch ** and change to red, 1 red dc in each of next 3 ch and change to white; rep from * around, ending last rep at **; join with sl st in third ch of beg ch-3.

Rnd 2: With white, ch 3 (counts as dc), 1 white dc in each of next 2 dc; * 3 red dc, 3 white dc; rep from * around, ending with 3 red dc; join.

Rnd 3: With red, ch 3 (counts as dc), 1 red dc in each of next 2 dc; * 3 white dc, 3 red dc; rep from * around, ending with 3 white dc; join. Fasten off white.

Rnd 4: With red, ch 1, sc in each dc around; join.

Rnd 5: Ch 1, sl st in each sc around and fasten off.

FINISHING: Close openings at heel and cuff. For loops; join white with sl st at top seam; ch 20; remove hook. Join red with sl st at top seam; ch 20; remove hook. Twist chs around each other; insert hook into last ch of each color, join to top of cuff with sl st; fasten off.

POM-POMS (make two): Holding red and white yarns tog, wrap around palm of hand 15 times. Tie separate strand tightly around center, clip lps at each edge; trim.

With RS facing, join white near hanging lp, ch 20; fasten off. Rep with red. Tie pom-pom to each ch; twist chs around one another.

jolly felt banner

As shown on page 19, banner measures 15¾×18½ inches.

Materials

Tracing paper

15×18-inch piece black felt

9×12-inch piece each of light ivory, cream, gold, light blue, turquoise, green, bright pink, lavender, purple, orchid, and dusty blue felt; scrap each of gold, light brown, dark brown, and tan felts

17×18¼-inch piece of light blue felt; pins

Cotton embroidery floss to match felt, including navy blue

Tapestry needle

14¾×5-inch piece of light blue broadcloth

14¾×5-inch piece of fusible web

Transfer paper and pen suitable for embroidery patterns

21-inch-long, ⅜-inch-diameter wood wallhanging dowel

Black acrylic paint; paintbrush

27 inches of black nylon cord

Instructions

Trace numbered pattern pieces, *pages 34–37,* onto tracing paper; cut out. From ivory felt, cut pieces 14, 28, 29, 32, 33, 34, 38, and 45; from cream, cut 8, 24, 26, and 35; from gold, cut 31; from light blue, cut 12, 23, 37, and 47; from turquoise, cut 1, 11, and 13; from green, cut 5, 6, and 7; from bright pink, cut 30, 36, 39, 40, 41, 42, and 44; from lavender, cut 21, 22, and 25; from purple, cut 2, 9, 10, 48, 49, and 50; from orchid, cut 3, 18, 43, and 46; from dusty blue, cut 4; from light brown, cut 15, 19, and 20; from dark brown, cut 16 and 17; and from tan, cut 27.

Pin piece 1 in place on black felt, following placement diagram, *below.* Sew using appliqué stitch and one ply of floss. Pin and stitch pieces 2–50, in numerical sequence.

Fuse broadcloth rectangle on felt following manufacturer's instructions for fusible web. Trace lettering and heart from pattern onto tracing paper. Turn tracing upside down and trace onto transfer paper using transfer pen. Transfer lettering to broadcloth.

Backstitch, then whipstitch lettering using three plies of navy blue floss. Using three plies of bright pink floss, satin stitch heart. Work blanket stitch around edges using three plies of light blue floss.

Center entire design on top of light blue felt rectangle with top edge of black felt 1½ inches from top edge of blue felt. Sew pieces together around perimeter ¾ inch from outer edges of black felt using running stitch and two plies of black floss. Cut free-hand scallop pattern around edges of black felt.

Cut notches in top of light blue felt according to notch diagram, *below.* Turn resulting three tabs to back; whipstitch edges to running stitch seam line.

Cut two ½×13-inch strips each from bright pink, lavender, purple, and orchid felt. Align one strip of each color; knot in center. Repeat to make two tassels. Tack one tassel to each bottom corner; trim ends.

Paint dowel black; allow to dry. Slide dowel through tabs. Knot each end of cord around one end of dowel to hang.

**JOLLY FELT BANNER
PLACEMENT DIAGRAM**

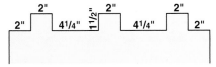

**JOLLY FELT BANNER
NOTCH DIAGRAM**

33

JOLLY FELT BANNER

8

6

7

5

16

17

4

A

B

JOLLY FELT
BANNER

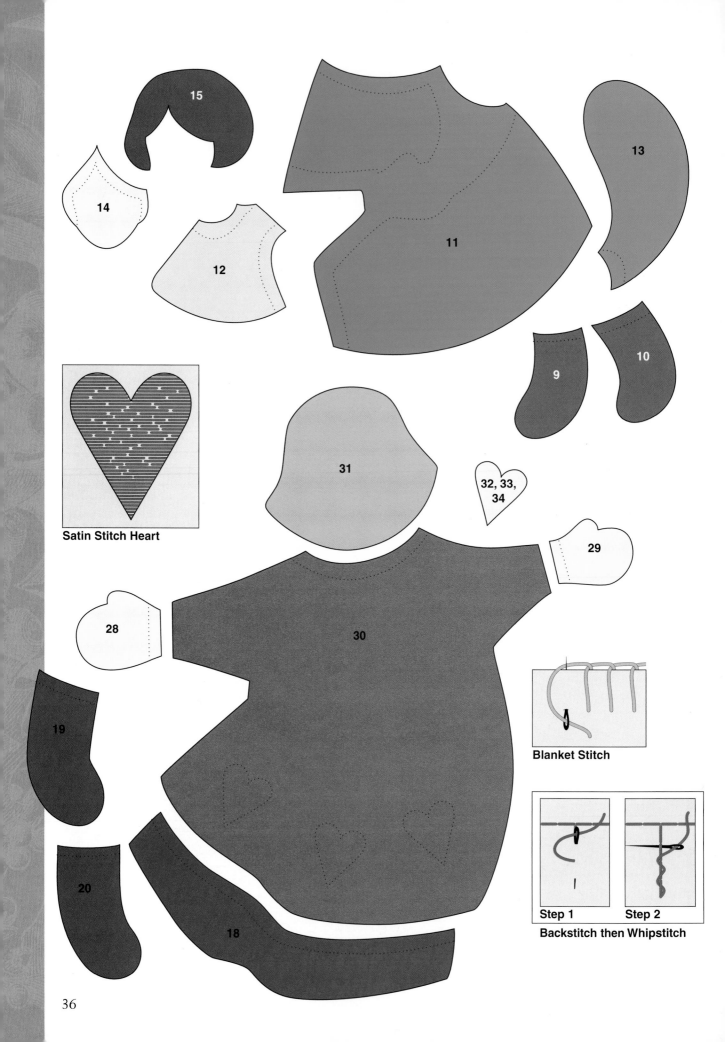

15

14

11

13

12

9

10

31

32, 33, 34

29

Satin Stitch Heart

28

30

Blanket Stitch

19

Step 1 | Step 2

Backstitch then Whipstitch

20

18

36

JOLLY FELT BANNER

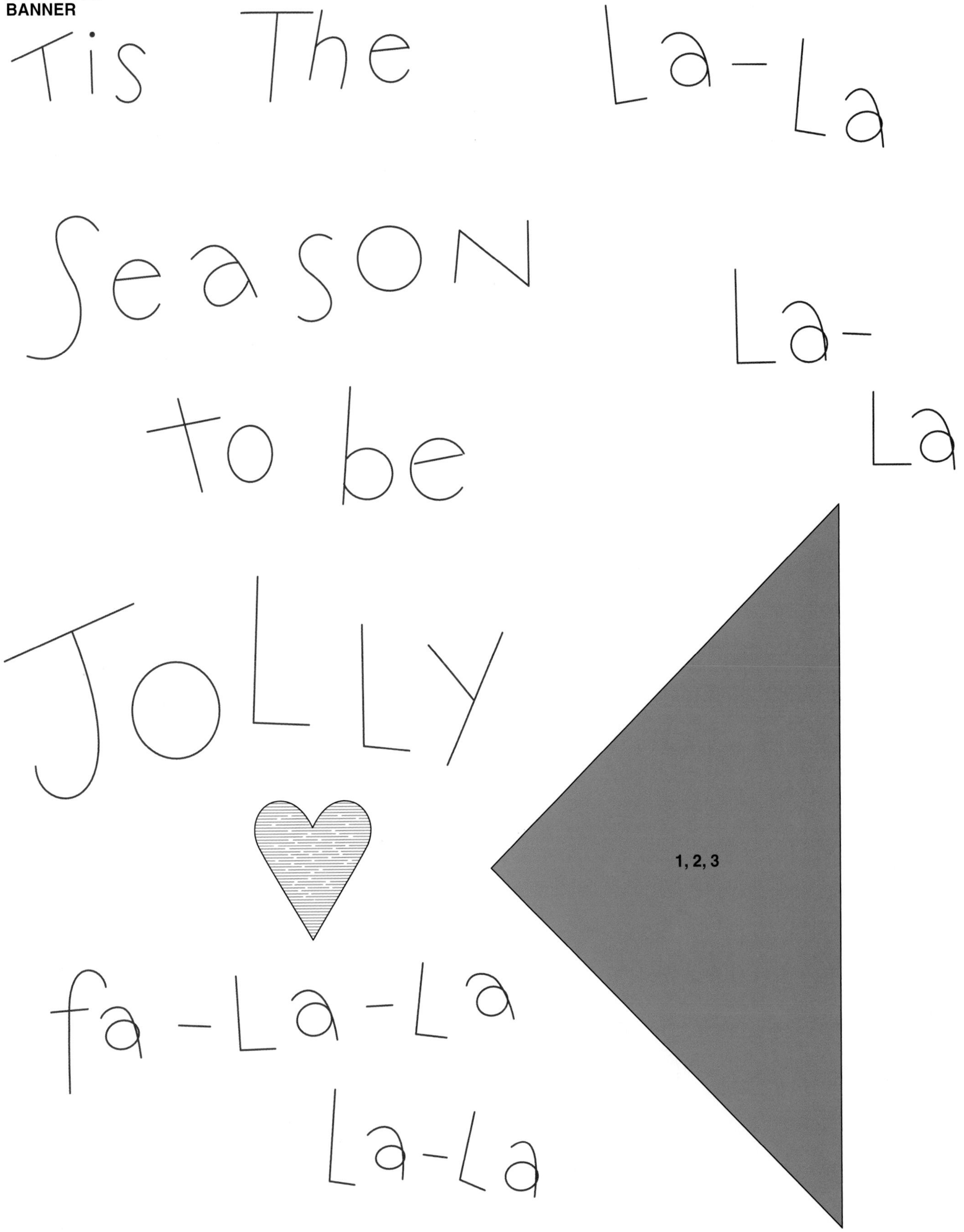
Tis The
La-La
Season
La-
La
to be
JoLLy
fa-La-La
La-La
1, 2, 3

herbal snowman

As shown on page 20, snowman measures 12 inches tall.

Materials

Four tea bags
15×12-inch piece of muslin
Tracing paper
Water-erasable fabric marker
6×12-inch piece of dark red print
Sewing thread: ecru and dark red
Polyester fiberfill
13-inch-long cinnamon stick
Thick white crafts glue
Hot-glue gun; hot glue
Black permanent artist's pen,
    size 03
Nine ½-inch-diameter
    brown buttons
Orange bakable modeling clay
Crafts knife
Kite string
Springerii (air fern) for carrot tops
72 inches of 18-gauge dark
    annealed stovepipe wire
⅜-inch-diameter dowel, 5 inches
    long (or pencil)
1⅛×20-inch strip of wool (scarf)
Small package of red potpourri
Six small bay leaves
Black buttonhole thread
Three ¾-inch-diameter pinecones
One star-shaped anise seed
3-inch-diameter grapevine wreath
Small sprigs of blue lavendula,
    red pepper berries, black
    spruce, blue delphinium,
    wheat, and eucalyptus
Two miniature pinecones
7-inch-tall miniature broom

Instructions

To tea-dye muslin, prepare a strong tea solution by steeping tea bags in 3 cups of hot water. Soak fabric in tea until it is slightly darker than desired color. Squeeze out excess liquid and place on a flat surface to dry. When dry, press on medium heat.

Enlarge patterns, *opposite*, and trace onto tracing paper; cut out. Use fabric marker to draw around body pattern onto a double thickness of muslin (transfer facial features, also). Trace mitten pattern two times on a double thickness of dark red print; do not cut out. Cut hat pieces from remaining dark red print.

Sew around body outline using ½-inch seam allowance, leaving open as marked on pattern. Trim body ¼ inch beyond stitching; clip curves. Cut 1¼-inch-long slit in neck back and turn body right side out. Stuff head with fiberfill. Insert cinnamon stick through arm holes and stuff remainder of body. Whipstitch neck opening closed. Use a small amount of crafts glue to secure cinnamon stick near bottom of each arm hole. Draw face in place using permanent pen.

Sew three buttons down the lower front section of snowman. Hot-glue anise seed pod to right side of waist.

For carrot nose, roll orange clay into a ¼-inch-diameter ball. Shape into a ¾-inch-long carrot.

Rotating carrot, score carrot-like ridges with a crafts knife. Cut the carrot top flat for ease in attaching to body.

Make five more carrots from ⅜-inch-diameter balls of clay (leave carrot tops rounded); make hole with needle in each carrot top to receive greenery stem. Pierce another hole through center of each carrot so they can be strung together after baking.

Bake carrots in 225° oven for 10 minutes; cool. Glue carrot nose to face. String remaining carrots onto 6 inches of kite string, knotting between carrots. Glue a bit of Springerii into top of each carrot. Set strung carrots aside.

Wrap wire around dowel, beginning 3½ inches from end of wire; referring to photograph, *page 20*, create a coil about 3 inches long. Thread a button onto the wire. Continue wrapping the wire and threading buttons; end with a 3-inch coil. Remove the wire from dowel. Twist the straight ends around the cinnamon-stick arms.

Fringe ends of wool scarf. Wrap around snowman's neck, drape over cinnamon stick, and glue to secure.

Sew long sides of hat pieces together using ¼-inch seams; turn right side out. Glue to head; tack point to right side of head.

For mittens, stitch along curved outlines drawn on fabric, leaving the cuff opening unstitched. Cut out ⅛ inch beyond sewing lines. Clip curves and turn right side out. Knot one end of a 5-inch length of string through dots on each mitten pair. Set aside.

String 6 inches of black buttonhole thread with red potpourri pieces, pinecones, two buttons, and bay leaves. Tie each end of thread onto cinnamon-stick arms 2 inches from body so strand drapes in front.

Hot-glue pepper berries and small pinecones to front of miniature broom. Glue string to top of handle for hanging. Knot a length of buttonhole thread to the wreath, blue lavendula, black spruce, blue delphinium, wheat, and eucalyptus for hanging. Hang the embellishments from the cinnamon-stick arms, referring to photograph, *page 20,* for placement.

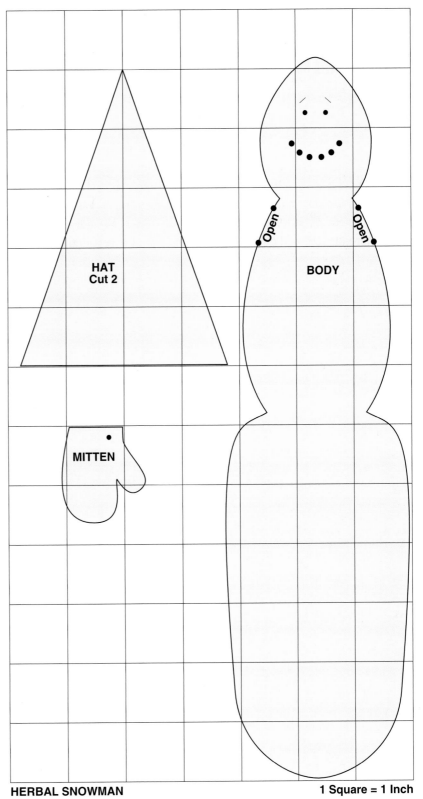

HERBAL SNOWMAN

1 Square = 1 Inch

flannel tree quilt

As shown on page 21, quilt measures 90×78 inches.

Materials

Graph paper

Quilters' template material

6 yards of 45-inch-wide green and red plaid flannel backing fabric

4 yards of 45-inch-wide solid cream flannel

3 yards of 45-inch-wide solid green flannel

3 yards of 45-inch-wide solid red flannel

1½ yards of 45-inch-wide gold cotton fabric

½ yard of 45-inch-wide brown plaid flannel

¼ yard each of sixteen 45-inch-wide different plaid flannel fabrics, in blues, reds, and greens

Polyester batting

#3 pearl cotton: gold and green to match fabrics

Instructions

Enlarge quilt patterns, *right*, onto graph paper; cut apart on solid lines. Draw around pieces on template material, adding ¼-inch seam allowances. From solid green flannel, cut 16 As. Using blue, red, and green plaids at random, cut 16 Bs, 16 Cs, 16 Ds, and 16 Es. From cream flannel, cut 16 Fs. Reverse template and cut 16 more Fs. Also from cream, cut 32 Hs. From brown plaid, cut 16 Gs. From gold cotton fabric, cut 25 Is and 100 Js. Reverse

template and cut 100 more Js. From solid red flannel, cut 20 Ks, 20 Ls, and 20 Ms.

In addition, from cream flannel cut eight 6½×12½-inch top and bottom row rectangles, eight 15½×6½-inch side edge rectangles, and four 6½×6½-inch-square corner blocks. From remaining solid green flannel, cut 3½-inch-wide binding strips to fit around outside edge of quilt. Measurements include ¼-inch seam allowances.

For each block, referring to the assembly diagram, *below,* sew B to A, C to AB, D to BC, and E to CD. Sew F to each side of plaid tree triangle. Next, sew one H to each long side of G. To finish block, sew HGH strip to bottom edge of plaid tree triangle. Make 16 blocks.

For sashing, sew the diagonal side of J to each angled edge of M. Repeat for 20 pieces. In the same manner, sew Js to all the Ks and Ls.

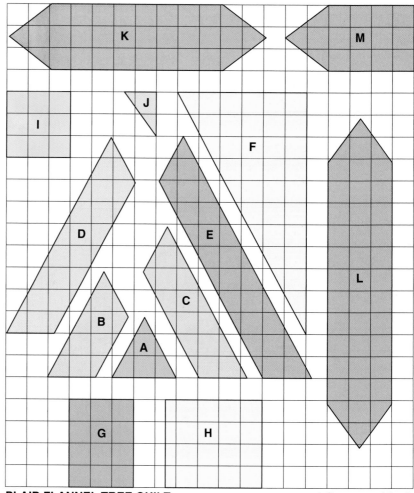

PLAID FLANNEL TREE QUILT   **1 Square = 1 Inch**

For top row, sew a 6½×6½-inch cream corner block to left side of MJ piece with point down. Working left to right, sew short side of 6½×12½-inch rectangle to right side of MJ, add another MJ, a second rectangle, third MJ, third rectangle, fourth MJ, fourth rectangle, fifth MJ, and finally a cream corner block. Repeat for bottom row, turning points up.

Arrange the trees in four rows of four blocks each. For each tree row, sew the long side of a 15½×6½-inch cream rectangle to the long edge of LJ, tree block to right side, LJ to right side of tree block, continuing left to right in the same manner, ending with a 15½×6½-inch cream rectangle sewn to the right side of the fourth tree block. Repeat for all four tree rows.

For horizontal sashing, sew one gold end of MJ to gold center block. Working from left to right, sew KJ to right side of gold block, second gold block to KJ, and so forth, using four KJ pieces and ending with an MJ piece, all separated by gold center blocks. Make five horizontal sashing strips.

Sew horizontal sashing between all rows, as shown on assembly diagram, *left*, matching seam lines. Layer quilt top, batting, and back (pieced as necessary). Baste. Tie the corners of the gold blocks using gold pearl cotton. Using green pearl cotton, tie the trees at the top point and at the two center points below.

Trim batting and back pieces 1 inch beyond quilt top. Sew enough 3½-inch-wide strips together to fit around edge of quilt. Pin the binding to the quilt top, right sides together; stitch through all layers, using a ¼-inch seam and mitering the corners. Turn binding to the back of the quilt and turn under ¼ inch along raw edge. Blindstitch in place.

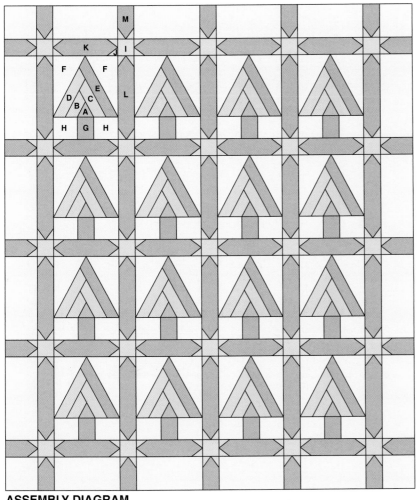

ASSEMBLY DIAGRAM

st. nick stocking

As shown on page 22, stocking measures 14½×7½ inches.

Materials

Tracing paper
½ yard of 45-inch-wide cream felt
5×11-inch piece of hunter green felt
5×6-inch piece of ivory felt
3½×8-inch piece of cranberry
   red felt

2×2½-inch piece of tan felt
5×5-inch piece of cranberry red
   print fabric
5×5-inch piece of blue and black
   print fabric
Paper-backed iron-on adhesive
Cotton embroidery floss: dark
   brown, ivory, and red

Embroidery needle
Three ½-inch-diameter
   ivory buttons
Two ⅝-inch-diameter
   brown buttons

Instructions

Trace one full stocking and each
individual piece from the pattern,
below and *opposite*, onto tracing paper.

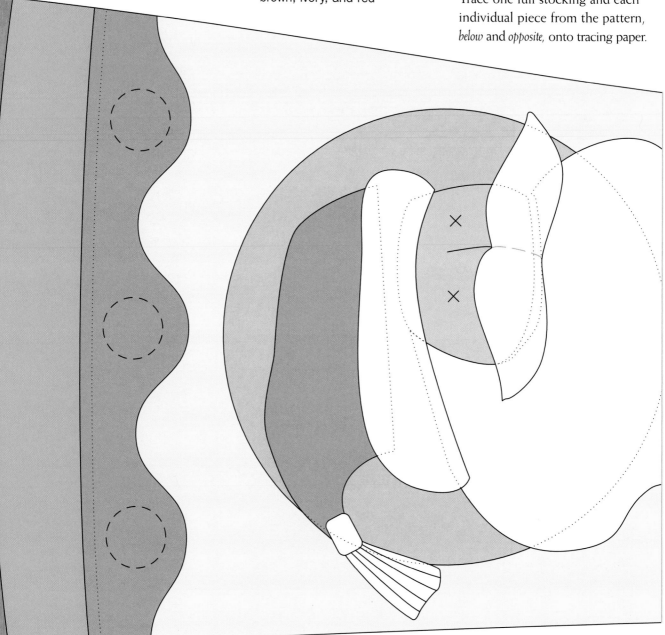

tan felt. Also, cut a 1½×1-inch tassel strip from ivory felt.

Draw around circle, hat, and toe patterns onto paper side of iron-on adhesive. Reverse hat and toe patterns to allow for proper direction after fusing. Following manufacturer's instructions, fuse double-sided adhesive to backs of blue with black and red print fabrics. Cut out the toe piece.

Remove paper backing from circle, hat, and toe pieces. Referring to stocking pattern, center circle 2½ inches below stocking top; fuse. Fuse toe piece over toe of stocking and hat in place atop circle.

Pin face, beard, and then hat trim in place. Using two plies of red embroidery floss and blanket

Cut two stockings from cream felt. Cut heel and top border from green felt; scallop border and hearts from red felt; beard, mustache, and brim from ivory felt; and face from

FELT ST. NICK STOCKING

43

stitches, see diagram on *page 36*, sew brim to stocking. Space the stitches approximately ³⁄₁₆ inches apart. Use brown embroidery floss and blanket stitches to secure the outside edge of the beard and the edge to the left of the face. Also using brown floss, work the eyes with large cross-stitches, and backstitch the nose.

Attach mustache with ivory floss running stitch through vertical center.

For tassel, cut ⅛-inch-wide fringe 1-inch deep across one long edge of tassel strip. Roll the strip, and wrap with ivory floss ¼ inch down from the uncut rolled edge. Tack the tassel to the tip of the hat.

Pin the top border and scallop border in place, allowing scallop border to overlap bottom of top border. Using two strands of brown floss, sew along sides and tops of both borders using running stitches. Using ivory floss, sew one cream button to each scallop at the dot.

Work large cross-stitches along the top edge of the toe piece using two plies of brown floss. Tack the hearts in place using brown buttons sewn with brown floss.

Cut two 12×¼-inch strips from green felt and one 12×¼-inch strip from red felt. Braid strips to make a hanging loop. Fold strip in half, stack ends, and tack to backside of stocking front at the outer top corner. Pin stocking front to back, wrong sides facing. Using the blanket stitch and two plies of brown floss, sew the front to the back, securing the hanging loop.

sprightly santas

As shown on page 23.

Materials for one Santa
Fabrics
8×4½-inch piece of 14-count clear perforated plastic
8×4-inch piece of red felt
8×4-inch piece of green felt
Threads
Cotton embroidery floss and #8 metallic braid in colors listed in key

Supplies
Needle
Pencil; thick white crafts glue
Scissors
⅔ yard of ⅞-inch-wide green grosgrain ribbon (optional)
1 yard of ⅛-inch-wide red satin ribbon (optional)
Three ½-inch-diameter jingle bells (optional)

Instructions
Find center of chart, *opposite*, and center of plastic; begin stitching there. Use two plies of floss or one strand of braid to work the cross-stitches. Use one ply to work backstitches.

Trim away the excess plastic one square beyond the stitching line. Center and glue the stitched piece on red felt. Trim away the excess felt a scant ⅛ inch beyond plastic. Center and glue atop green felt. Trim away excess felt a scant ⅛ inch beyond red felt.

Cut a 4-inch piece of braid and thread into needle. Take a small stitch in green felt ¼ inch below top of ornament. Knot ends together. Or, fold green ribbon in half, forming a loop at fold by crossing the ends 4 inches below fold. Stitch felt behind the hat to point where ribbon ends cross. Fold red ribbon into a multi-looped bow. Tack red ribbon and jingle bells to green ribbon just above hat.

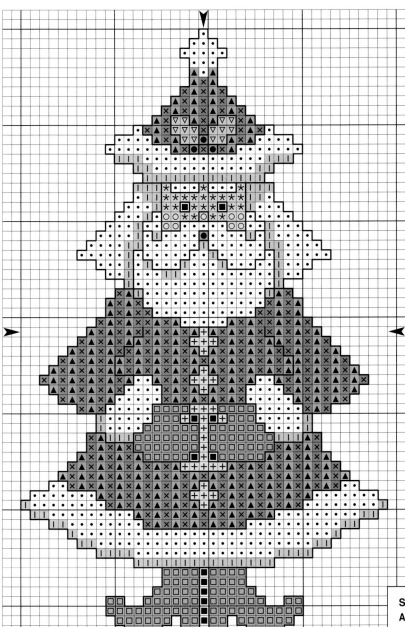

SPRIGHTLY SANTA

SPRIGHTLY SANTA		
ANCHOR		**DMC**
002	⊡	000 White
352	▣	300 Mahogany
403	■	310 Black
9046	●	321 Christmas red
398	▯	415 Pearl gray
923	▲	699 Dark Christmas green
228	▽	700 Medium Christmas green
024	◯	776 Pink
043	⊠	815 Garnet
1011	✴	948 Peach
	⊞	002 Kreinik gold metallic #8 braid

BACKSTITCH

403	╱	310 Black – all stitches

Stitch count: 63 high x 39 wide

Finished design sizes:
14-count fabric – 4½ x 2¾ inches

45

simple gifts

You can always find time to make that perfect gift for a friend who is dear to your heart—even if you have only an hour or two to spare. Choose any of these quick-to-make gifts for the special people on your Christmas list this year.

country christmas paper bags

Paper bags with handles become favorite wraps when a little felt, buttons, and a few quick stitches are added. Fill the bags with candles or other holiday items or treats. The full-size patterns and instructions are on pages 68–69.

49

christmas kitchen trims

Flea market finds, such as kitchen gadgets, take on new life when decorated with artificial evergreen and red berries. Cinnamon sticks bring the scent of the season alive. The instructions are on page 68.

These little gingerbread babies are sure to be everyone's favorites. Made from flannel and filled with birdseed, these posable friends will please young and old alike. The full-size patterns and instructions are on pages 69–70.

gingerbread babies

simple santa jewelry

Spread good cheer this holiday season by sporting Santa on a necklace, pin, or hair bow—
just right for either mother or daughter. Our Santa head is made from bakable clay
using basic shapes and simple instructions. After the clay is baked, it's ready to become
a favorite Christmas accessory by attaching it to a bow or jewelry finding.
The instructions for this jolly jewelry are on page 71.

dear st. nick pin

This wood pin with its jingle bell pom-pom makes a
much-appreciated gift. A scrap of wood and just a touch
of paint are all it takes to create this playful piece of
jewelry. The instructions are on page 72.

dainty welcome towel

Making your guests feel comfortable at the holiday season is a real gift. What better way to make them feel at home than to display welcome wishes on a lovely guest towel. Embroidered with floss and ribbons, this towel is quick to stitch. The instructions and chart are on pages 72–73.

stars in the chimney centerpiece

Star shapes etched onto a hurricane lamp create a stunning centerpiece when combined with a purple candle. Perfect for a hostess gift (or to display yourself), the centerpiece is surrounded with greens and sparkling beads. The instructions are on page 73.

For that serious music devotee on your list, fill a basket with musical gifts. Compact discs, cassette tapes, a tiny cassette tape player, or even a collectible record can be tucked inside. What better way to share the sounds of the season!

music lover's gift basket

A mitten cut from felt becomes a holiday holder for silverware—and a perfect gift for a little one. Embellished with blanket stitches, this tiny mitten can also hold other holiday surprises. The full-size patterns and instructions are on page 74.

playful felt mittens

snappy
button
snowman

Tiny white buttons
resemble glistening snow,
bringing this snowman to
life. This frosty fellow has
a jaunty ribbon scarf and
stacked buttons for a hat,
giving him personality
plus. The instructions are
on pages 74–75.

button-tree trims

Buttons and a variety of Christmas-colored fabrics combine to make our easy-to-craft tree trims. The pieces are lightly stuffed and edged with blanket stitches. The instructions and patterns are on page 75.

58

Just big enough for a tiny treasure and a lot of love, these felt stockings work up quickly. Use them as a centerpiece filled with something special for everyone at the table. Hung on a banister or on the tree, these fun felt stockings are at home almost anywhere. The instructions and full-size patterns are on pages 75–77.

tiny felt stockings

tiny clever packages

Big things come in small packages, but sometimes they are a challenge to wrap! These tiny treasures are fun from the inside out with clever wraps. From the *top left*: Santa's belt is the inspiration for this wrap made with a small belt buckle and black satin ribbon. Everyone loves to get money for Christmas—even when it is on the outside of the package (we've used white glue so the money comes off easily). Green ribbon and black-and-white dice make this package a high roller. For the tiniest of presents, just add a holiday button on ⅛-inch ribbon for a festive touch. Self-stick stars form a tree shape with a tiny 3-D bow on top.

Dress up your gifts this year with these simple eye-catching trimmings. From *left*, the four quick wraps are: A tiny jar of jelly and golden tinsel will impress that sweet tooth on your list; a beautiful peacock feather tucked in among iridescent teal ribbon is a touch that only takes a minute; a rhinestone-covered circle (available from the bridal section of your fabric store) is the dazzling secret to this sparkling gift; and there will be kisses all around after you've glued our wrapped-candy variety to a favorite gift package.

simply wrapped gifts

personalized festive bows

Handsome bows—created all by yourself—are easy to do and add a special touch to your packages. We've shown you how to make that perfect bow, step-by-step, using a dowel and floral oasis to help secure the ribbon as it's being fashioned. To make each bow one-of-a-kind, add a jingle bell, button, silver bell, or other tie-on after completing the bow.

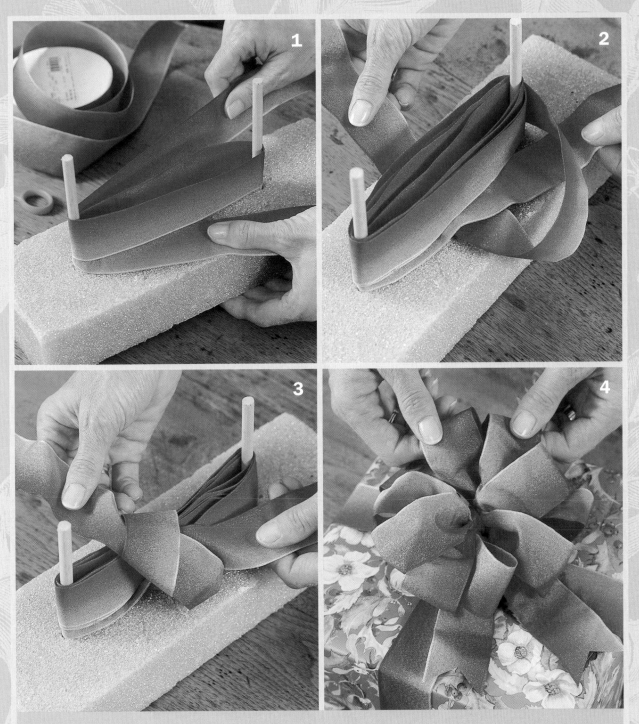

1 Push dowels into floral oasis about 5 inches apart. Holding ribbon end on top of oasis, wrap dowels at least 3 times. For larger bows, wrap 4–6 times. **2** After wrapping dowels, cut the ribbon, leaving about an 8-inch tail. Slip tail of ribbon underneath loops, continuing to hold the starting end of the ribbon. **3** Secure the loops by tying the ribbon ends firmly into a knot in the center of the loops. Carefully slide the bow loops off the dowels. **4** Tie the bow atop intersecting ribbons that wrap around the package. Separate and fluff the bow loops. Fold ribbon ends in half and trim on the diagonal.

step-by-step bow making

ribbon scrap wraps

Every scrap of ribbon has a special place when you combine them to create a pleasant mixture of color and texture atop your favorite gift papers. Small snippets of ribbon form a tiny tree and layers of ribbon combine to make a plain wrap oh-so-fancy.

oh-so-fun package toppers

1 Golden jingle bells sing when tied to the ends of our curling ribbon bow. **2** Black and white make a happy holiday statement when trimmed with buttons and curling ribbon. **3** Ponytail holders and ribbons combine for delightful doodad gift toppers! **4** Dress up a silver doily with a real or candy coin and glue atop a favorite paper.

Here is a pinwheel bow made just as if it was meant to go round and round in the wind. To make this fun bow: **1** Cut an 8-inch square of wrapping paper. On the back of the square, draw pencil lines from corner to corner to make a big "X". Place a penny in the center of the "X" and draw around it. Fold all four corners to the center. **2** Using scissors, cut between the folded triangles as shown in the photo, *above*, being careful to cut up to, but not through, the center circle. **3** Bend (do not fold) every other point to the center of the square as shown above. Secure with a pin, and poke the pin into the center of the pinwheel through the box. Glue a tiny ornament to the center of the pinwheel, if desired.

pinwheel bow making

gold and silver button bow

This dazzling button topper is both quick to make and elegantly charming. Shimmering gold and silver buttons found at an antiques shop are grouped into a pleasing arrangement and glued to gold-trimmed ribbon and paper using white crafts glue.

country christmas paper bags

As shown on pages 48–49, designs measure between 5 and 5½ inches high.

Materials for set of three bags

Tracing paper

Three 5¼×8¼-inch craft
   paper bags

Three 9×12-inch sheets of felt:
   white, red, and green

Cotton embroidery floss in desired
   colors

Assorted buttons: red, green,
   cream, taupe, and blue

Black Mill Hill pebble beads

No. 22 chenille needle or
   embroidery needle

White crafts glue; pencil

Instructions

Trace patterns, *right and opposite,* onto tracing paper; cut out. Cut one of each shape from felt.

Lay felt shapes on bags to determine placement of words as indicated on patterns. Lightly pencil the words on the bags. Remove felt shapes. Backstitch words using three plies of floss as indicated on patterns. Glue felt shapes on bags; let dry.

Lightly draw the snowman's arms. Stitch the arms with long stitches using six plies of brown floss. Sew on black beads for the snowman's buttons and eyes. Stitch a mouth using three plies of red floss.

Stitch buttons on the star, tree, and all three bags, referring to photograph, *pages 48–49.* Stitch around the edges of the felt shapes using three plies of floss and straight stitches in random lengths.

christmas kitchen trims

As shown on page 50, finished trim measures 9 inches high.

Materials

Old kitchen grater or other
   old utensil

Hot-glue gun; hot glue

Spanish moss; artificial greens

Cinnamon sticks; pinecones

Red berries

Spray-on artificial snow (optional)

¼-inch-wide plaid ribbon piece

Instructions

Glue a small bunch of moss to front of grater. Add small pieces of greens, cinnamon sticks, pinecones, and berries; glue in place.

Spray a light coating of artificial snow over front of decorated grater, if desired. Tie ribbon into a bow on the handle.

68

gingerbread babies

As shown on page 51, gingerbread babies measure 9×7 inches.

SEASONS GREETINGS

Materials for two babies

Tracing paper
⅓ yard of tan flannel
Thread to match fabric
Birdseed
Small funnel
Shiny paint pens: white, black,
    red, and green

**COUNTRY CHRISTMAS
PAPER BAGS PATTERNS**

PEACE

JOY

LOVE

Instructions

Trace the pattern, *page 70,* onto tracing paper; cut out. Cut four body pieces from flannel.

With right sides facing, sew the body pieces together in pairs, using ¼-inch seam allowances. Leave a 2-inch-long opening along an inner leg seam for stuffing. Turn each gingerbread baby right side out. Using a funnel, fill each body with birdseed; sew openings closed.

Outline each body front with white paint pen to resemble piped frosting. Add white

gingerbread babies — *continued*

eyebrows, noses, and mouths. Use black paint pen to make round eyes. Finish decorating the gingerbread babies with red and green paint pens as desired, using the pattern, *right,* and the photograph, *page 51,* for ideas.

GINGERBREAD BABIES

simple santa jewelry

As shown on page 52, Santa measures 2¾×1⅜ inches.

Materials

Fimo or Sculpey oven-bakable clay:
   pale peach, red, and white
Paring knife; garlic press
Powdered blush
Small artist's brush
Fine point permanent black marker
Hot-glue gun; hot glue

For necklace

Paper clip; wire cutters
1 yard of ⅛-inch-diameter green
   and gold cord
Small holly sprig
Two ¾-inch-diameter gold
   jingle bells

For pin

1-inch-long pin back
⅜-inch-diameter gold jingle bell

For hair bow

½ yard of 1½-inch-wide green,
   gold, and red striped ribbon
2¼-inch-long French barrette back

Instructions

Knead clay until it is pliable. For each Santa face, roll a piece of peach clay into a ball the size of a large pea. Flatten ball to measure ¾ inch in diameter. Also from peach, roll a ⅛-inch-diameter nose; center on face and press gently to secure.

Cut a ½×½×½-inch cube of red clay for hat. Roll cube into a ball. Flatten and shape clay with fingers into a flat triangle measuring 2¼ inches across bottom, 1¼ inches tall, and approximately 1¼ inches along each side. Join sides to form a cone. Slightly flatten cone and slide it over the top of face circle. (Hat will appear too large for face and should stick out on each side.)

Shape hat so point curves to left. Roll a ball of white clay to the size of a pea; press it to point of hat. Roll a piece of white clay into a ⅛-inch-diameter rope; flatten and wrap around the bottom of hat for trim. Use tip of paring knife to add texture to the white ball and trim.

Press white clay through garlic press to make whiskers and hair. Arrange hair on each side of head, attaching it under edges of hat. Press gently to hat and face to secure. Arrange whiskers to make a beard across face below nose. Press two longer strands horizontally under nose for a mustache. Use two ¼-inch-long strands for eyebrows.

Bake clay heads in a 225° oven for 20 minutes; allow to cool. Color cheeks and nose with a small brush rubbed across powdered blush. Dot eyes using fine point marker.

For Santa necklace, before baking, use wire cutters to cut a ½-inch-long U-shape from a paper clip. Press cut ends into clay at back of hat near top. Tilt loop away from clay so a cord can be threaded through loop. Bake as directed.

Knot cord through loop in Santa. Thread a ¾-inch-diameter jingle bell onto each end of cord. Tie a square knot in cord, securing bells next to Santa's hat. Hot-glue holly sprig to top of hat.

For pin, after baking, hot-glue pin back to back of Santa. Glue jingle bell to white ball on hat.

For hair bow, tie the ribbon into a bow and hot-glue to French barrette. After baking, glue Santa to center front of bow.

71

dear st. nick pin

As shown on page 52, pin measures 3½×2¾ inches.

DEAR ST. NICK PIN

Materials

Tracing paper
Carbon paper
Ballpoint pen
4×3½-inch piece of ¼-inch poplar
  or pine
Scroll saw
Fine grit sandpaper
Delta Ceramcoat acrylic paints:
  Santa's flesh, bouquet pink,
  berry red, barn red, liberty
  blue, sandstone, white, lichen
  gray, black, and Quaker gray,
Artists' brushes
Polyurethane spray
6 inches of ¹⁄₁₆-inch-wide red
  satin ribbon
⅜-inch-diameter green jingle bell
1-inch-long pin back
Hot-glue gun; hot glue

Instructions

Trace pattern, *right,* onto tracing
paper. Place carbon paper
between pattern and wood;
transfer pattern, tracing over
all but fine detail lines using
ballpoint pen. Cut out
ornament with scroll saw.
Sand edges smooth.

Paint Santa's face with
Santa's flesh; blend bouquet pink
into nose and cheeks. Paint hat
and back of pin berry red. Shade
hat with barn red. Dot eyes
liberty blue. Paint hat fur lichen
gray and beard, mustache, and
eyebrows Quaker gray. Shade
Santa's nose with Quaker gray.

Referring to pattern for detail,
add tiny slashes of white to hat
fur, grouping slashes as shown.
Use longer slashes of sandstone
to detail hair on beard and

eyebrows; top with white slashes.
Detail mustache with strokes of
white. Add tiny white highlights
to eyes and nose.

Spray entire pin with
polyurethane. Tie ribbon into
bow; glue to tip of hat. Glue
jingle bell atop bow and pin back
to center back of face.

dainty welcome towel

As shown on page 53.

Materials

Fabric

White fingertip towel with
  14-count Aida insert

Threads

Bucilla embroidery ribbon in the
  colors listed in key, opposite
Cotton embroidery floss in colors
  listed in key, opposite

Green sewing thread
Red sewing thread

Supplies

Tapestry, chenille, and beading
  needles
Embroidery hoop
Seed beads in colors listed in
  key, opposite

Instructions

Find center of chart, *opposite,* and
center of Aida insert; begin
stitching there.

Use three plies of embroidery
floss to work all stitches.

Work ribbon embroidery
stitches using the chenille needle.
Attach the seed beads using
coordinating thread.

stars in the chimney centerpiece

As shown on page 54, chimney measures 8 inches tall.

Materials

Hurricane lamp; white vinegar
¼-inch-wide masking tape
Burnishing tool (wooden orange
   stick or tongue depressor)
Armour glass etching cream
Paintbrush; plastic gloves
Adhesive star stickers in two sizes
   or contact paper
Tulip Slick paint in any color

Instructions

Wash hurricane lamp with vinegar to remove any fingerprints; let dry.

Wrap a strip of masking tape 1¼ inches up from the bottom edge of the hurricane lamp. Fill the section below the tape with vertical strips of masking tape placed ¼ inch apart. Rub all tape edges with the burnishing tool.

Follow the manufacturer's directions on etching cream jar to etch glass. Wear plastic gloves when washing off the cream.

Clean off all fingerprints with the vinegar.

To etch the stars, remove the stars from the strip and place on waxed paper. Peel the backing off the leftover portion, creating a star stencil, and stick this onto the hurricane lamp. Repeat with more stars, using both sizes of stars and placing them randomly around the hurricane lamp. Rub down the edges with the burnishing tool. (*Note:* If the star points are too close to the edge of the paper, surround the star stencil with strips of masking tape.) If desired, cut the star shapes from squares of contact paper instead of using purchased star stickers.

Etch all of the star stencils. Wearing plastic gloves, wash off etching cream with warm water.

Use the paint to make dots between the stripes at the bottom edge of the hurricane lamp.

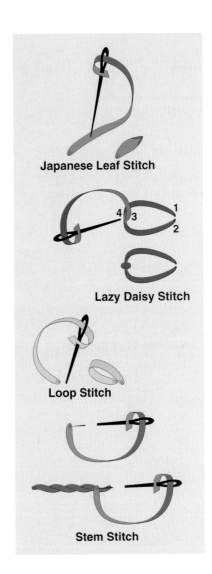

Japanese Leaf Stitch

Lazy Daisy Stitch

Loop Stitch

Stem Stitch

DAINTY WELCOME TOWEL

ANCHOR	DMC	
212	☒ 561	Dark seafoam

JAPANESE LEAF STITCH
539 Red Bucilla 4mm embroidery ribbon
628 Forest green Bucilla 4mm embroidery ribbon

LAZY DAISY STITCH
539 Red Bucilla 4mm embroidery ribbon
628 Forest green Bucilla 4mm embroidery ribbon

LOOP STITCH
503 Pale honey yellow Bucilla 7mm embroidery ribbon

STEM STITCH
628 Forest green Bucilla 4mm embroidery ribbon

MILL HILL BEADS
● 02013 Red red seed bead
● 00332 Emerald seed bead

Stitch count: 33 high x 56 wide
Finished design sizes:
14-count fabric – 2³⁄₈ x 4 inches
16-count fabric – 2¹⁄₈ x 3½ inches
18-count fabric – 1⁷⁄₈ x 3¹⁄₈ inches

DAINTY WELCOME TOWEL

playful felt mittens

As shown on page 56, mitten measures 6¼×4 inches.

Materials for one mitten

Tracing paper; 9×12-inch piece of
  felt in desired color
3×3-inch piece of white felt
White cotton embroidery floss
Tapestry needle
Two 1×3-inch strips of white fleece
Five ½-inch-diameter buttons
Two ⅜-inch-diameter silver
  jingle bells

Instructions

Trace mitten and star patterns, *right*, onto tracing paper; cut out. Cut two mitten pieces from colored felt and one star

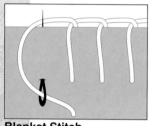

Blanket Stitch

from white felt. Sew the star to one mitten as shown in photograph, *page 56*, using two plies of white floss and small straight stitches.

Sew mitten pieces together, wrong sides facing, using six plies of floss and the blanket stitch (see diagram, *left*). Leave the wrist edges open.

Glue fleece strip to the wrist edges. Glue button to tip of thumb; glue four buttons around curved edge of mitten. Tack jingle bell to each side of mitten at fleece edge. Add floss loop at wrist edge for hanging.

snappy button snowman

As shown on page 57, snowman stands 10½ inches tall.

Materials

4-inch-diameter plastic-foam ball,
  3-inch-diameter plastic foam
  ball, and a 2-inch-diameter
  plastic foam ball
Assorted white buttons, up to 1 inch
  in diameter; 2-inch black button
Five 1- or 1½-inch-diameter black
  buttons or checkers
Five ½-inch-diameter black buttons
¼-inch-diameter black button
Hot-glue gun; hot glue
⅛-inch-diameter dowel; needle

Black cotton embroidery floss
3 small twigs; round toothpick; small
  paintbrush; orange acrylic paint
Small bunch of natural broom
  straw, cut to 7 inches long
Fine gauge wire; 24 inches of
  1½-inch-wide red plaid ribbon
6-inch-diameter plastic foam circle

Instructions

Hot glue enough white buttons to each foam ball to cover, reserving two ¼-inch four-hole white

buttons for eyes. Stack and glue checkers or larger black buttons in order of size to make hat. Glue hat to top of 2-inch-diameter ball.

Cut dowel into two 2-inch-long pieces. Use dowels to connect balls in a snowman configuration. Glue as necessary. Push twig arms into place on medium-size ball. Glue ½-inch-diameter black buttons down front as shown in photograph.

Sew a floss X through holes in white eye buttons; glue in place on face. Glue ¼-inch-diameter black button to face for mouth. Paint toothpick orange; push into face for nose.

For broom, wire broom straw around the base of remaining twig. Hot-glue broom handle to one arm.

Wrap and tie ribbon around neck for scarf. Glue completed snowman to the circular plastic foam base.

button-tree trims

As shown on page 58, finished ornaments measure 4½×7 inches.

Materials for one tree

Tracing paper
5½×9-inch piece of green solid or plaid quilted fabric
15-inch-long piece of brown twisted paper wire
Ecru embroidery floss
Tapestry needle
Polyester fiberfill
9 assorted buttons
Two ¾×6-inch strips of fabric in different red, green, or gold prints
⅜-inch-diameter gold jingle bell

Instructions

Trace pattern, *right*, flipping along dotted line to complete; cut out. Cut two trees from quilted fabric.

Bend twisted paper wire to form a three-quarter circle. Bend a small loop into each end. Pin quilted trees

together with wrong sides facing. At each X, shown on pattern, insert one end of twisted paper wire and pin in place. Thread tapestry needle with six plies of embroidery floss. Begin working blanket stitches, see diagram *opposite*, around perimeter, spacing stitches ¼ inch apart and ¼ inch deep, securing ends of wire. Before completing stitching, stuff tree lightly with polyester fiberfill. Hide floss ends between layers.

Use floss to sew eight buttons to ornament front, referring to photograph, *page 58*, as a guide. Using a half knot, tie fabric strips onto handle, one atop the other. Sew a button to knot leaving a 6-inch-long floss tail. Thread jingle bell onto floss end and knot in place, 1¼ inches from button.

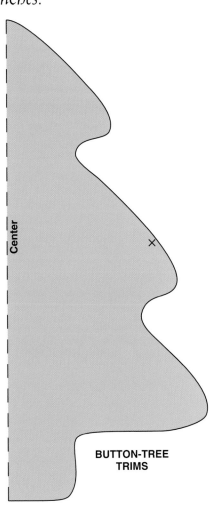

Center

×

BUTTON-TREE TRIMS

tiny felt stockings

As shown on page 59, each stocking measures 4½×3½ inches.

Materials

Tracing paper
10×12-inch piece of antique white felt
8×10-inch piece of dark denim blue felt
8×10-inch piece of mustard yellow felt

6×6-inch piece of cranberry red felt
3½×5-inch piece of hunter green felt
3×2½-inch piece of cinnamon brown felt
Cotton embroidery floss: mustard yellow, brick red, hunter green, medium brown, ecru, and black
Size 20 chenille needle

Nine ¼-inch-diameter white 4-hole buttons; hot-glue gun; hot glue
Two 16 millimeter gold acrylic stars
12 inches of ⅛-inch-wide green metallic ribbon
Paint pens: gold glitter, dark green, and dark red
1½ yards of ivory rattail cord

tiny felt stockings — *continued*

Instructions

Trace one stocking and each piece from patterns, *below* and *opposite*, onto tracing paper; cut out.

For Starry Night Stocking, cut two blue stockings, cuff and bottom large star from antique white, top large star from yellow, and small star from red felt.

For Snowperson Stocking, cut two blue stockings, large snowman from yellow; and cuff, snow, and small snowman from antique white.

For Present Under the Tree Stocking, cut two antique white stockings, large tree from yellow, small tree from green, and cuff and present from red.

For Gingerbread Stocking, cut two yellow stockings, cuff from antique white; gingerbread from brown.

For Stars and Stripes Stocking, cut two red stockings, stripes from green, stars from yellow, and cuff from antique white.

Use six plies of floss for all stitching. Refer to patterns as a guide for positioning the pieces on stocking fronts.

For Starry Night Stocking, stitch top yellow star in place using ecru straight stitches. Stitch antique white star in place with red blanket stitch, diagram *page 74*. Secure red star with yellow French knot in each point. Sew button at each X, using green. Work green running stitch circle around each button. Work yellow French knots over remainder of stocking front at dots. Position stocking front to back, with cuff in place. Use ecru to sew pieces together, leaving

stocking top open. Personalize cuff with paint pen. Glue rattail ends together inside top right edge of stocking for hanging loop.

For Snowperson Stocking, decorate white snowman with green French knot eyes and buttons and a red straight stitch mouth. Sew figure to larger yellow snowman using evenly spaced ecru straight stitches. Sew snow to stocking front bottom using green running stitches along top edge only. Blanket-stitch snowman to front with red. Make straight stitch arms and hands using red. Work ecru French knots at dots for snowflakes. Sew cuff, bottom edge of snow, stocking front, and back together using yellow blanket stitches; add hanging loop as for Starry Night Stocking. Personalize cuff with paint pen.

For Present Under the Tree Stocking, affix small tree atop

STARRY NIGHT STOCKING

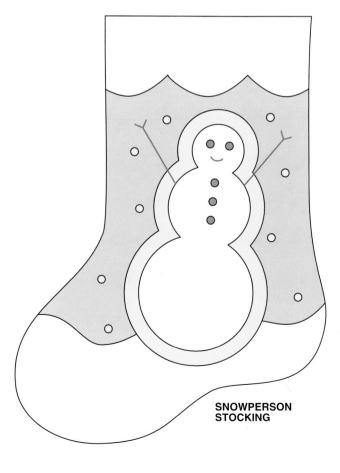

SNOWPERSON STOCKING

76

large tree by stitching buttons in place at Xs, using red. Add red, white, and yellow French knots at dots, using colors randomly. Sew tree to stocking front using evenly spaced red straight stitches. Attach present with running stitches up through center; tie floss bow at top. Sew cuff, front, and back together using green blanket stitches and add hanging loop as for Starry Night Stocking. Glue gold acrylic star to tree top. Personalize cuff with paint pen.

For Gingerbread Stocking, decorate gingerbread man with black French knot eyes, red straight stitch mouth, yellow French knot buttons, and yellow straight stitches across feet and hands. Sew figure to stocking front using evenly spaced ecru straight stitches. Sew button at each X, using brown. Work green running stitch circle around each

button. Sew cuff, front, and back together using brown blanket stitches; add hanging loop as for Starry Night Stocking. Personalize cuff with paint pen.

For Stars and Stripes Stocking, sew green stripes in place using evenly spaced yellow straight stitches. Affix stars by stitching a button to each center at X, using green. Work a red French knot in each point. Blanket stitch top and bottom of cuff to stocking front using green. Sew front to back using yellow blanket stitches, making sure to catch sides of cuff. Add hanging loop as for other stockings. Personalize cuff with paint pen.

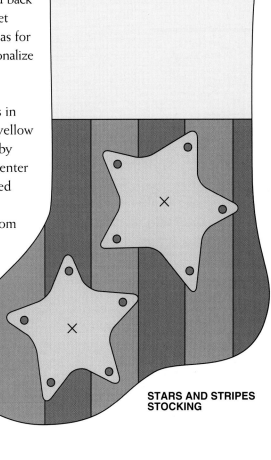

STARS AND STRIPES STOCKING

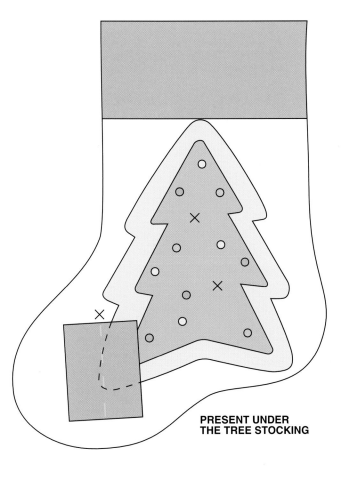

PRESENT UNDER THE TREE STOCKING

GINGERBREAD STOCKING

deck the halls

We anticipate it with excitement each year—decorating the house for Christmas! From the tree to the mantel, each part of the house can be dressed up for the season. Let this chapter inspire you to create a holiday home you'll always remember.

Dried gardenias, silver pinecones, and sparkling Christmas balls mirror the beauty of the season as they adorn this holiday wreath. The embellishments are added to a purchased wreath and topped with an ivory wire-edged ribbon. The instructions are on page 106.

white gardenia wreath

elegant hardanger doily

Stitches of cream and metallic gold combine to create this heirloom-quality Hardanger doily. This lovely 12-inch-square piece is worked on 20-count ivory Jobelan fabric. The instructions, chart, and stitching diagrams are on pages 106–107.

To build these cheery folks, start with a quick construction made of plastic-foam balls, jar lids, and wire. Add a touch of purchased white snow paste and dress them up in colorful fleece accessories. Set the trio on your mantel or share them with a friend, and hearts will melt away. The instructions are on pages 108–109.

frosty, no-sew snow family

snowman banner and doll

This collection of frolicking snowmen will add the magic of Christmas to any room in the house. The banner stitches up quickly using colorful felts and flosses, and the cute-as-a-button fleece doll is trimmed with buttons, sticks, felt, and fabric paint pens. The instructions for both of these lighthearted projects begin on page 110.

Make Grandma's lovely antique soup tureen the center of attention at your holiday gathering. Fill it with shelled calico popcorn and press votive candles into the corn at different heights. Complete this easy homespun centerpiece by adding a few ears of unshelled corn, a sprinkling of popped popcorn, and sprigs of bright Christmas greenery.

calico corn candles

clever canning jar candles

Gather a few old-time canning jars and fill them with Christmas candies, pretty buttons, colorful marbles, or unpopped popcorn. Position a tea candle in a metal cup atop the contents of each jar. Group several jars together and surround them with fresh holiday greens.

yo-yo stocking

Old-fashioned yo-yos dressed up in fancy fabrics and buttons adorn this rich velvet stocking. Hang it from your mantel early in the season so you can enjoy its elegance long before Santa's visit. The instructions are on pages 116–117.

vintage hankie tree

Antique poinsettia handkerchiefs (or brand-new ones) are displayed on a covered cork board, creating a three-dimensional fabric tree. Use pins and favorite buttons to attach the hankies to the board. The instructions for making this clever tree are on page 117.

What a wonderful way to keep the door ajar and to welcome guests inside! This festive fellow is painted on muslin using an array of acrylic paints. Re-create this doorstop masterpiece using the easy-to-follow instructions and painting pattern beginning on page 118.

painted santa doorstop

chenille snowflake afghan

Cuddle up with the luxurious feel of chenille in our ivory-and-white snowflake afghan. Crocheted with lush acrylic worsted-weight yarn, this piece works up quickly and is sure to keep out the winter chills. The instructions are on page 120.

shining ornament candles

To create a sparkling and delicate centerpiece, gently arrange small, colorful glass ornaments around a pillar candle in an antique pedestal dish. If you don't have an antique dish, simply use any pretty footed or pedestal dish that will hold the candle and ornaments. In no time at all, you'll have a bright and shining holiday display. For a warm reflected glow, place the dish in front of a mirror.

romantic candles and roses

To create a glowing Christmas centerpiece, try this quick and elegant idea. Fill a crystal bowl with water. Stir in ten drops of green food coloring to create a festive effect. Place white floating candles, a sprig of holly, and two or three roses in the green water. Sprinkle the water with gold or silver glitter and light the candles. In the blink of an eye, you have created a sparkling focal point for your holiday entertaining.

colonial apple candleholders

This traditional-looking holiday centerpiece uses real apples as candleholders. Cut a small plug from the top of each apple using an apple corer and insert a small taper candle. Embellish the tops of the apples with orange peel curls and group the candles on a pewter muffin pan or tray. Add a bed of holiday greens for that special Christmas touch.

whimsical painted chair

This lonely chair had a happy ending with playful winter motifs painted upon it. Tiny purchased wood shapes were painted, strung, and tied to the back of the chair to make it a favorite. The instructions and tips are on page 121.

buttons
the bear

Create a playful red
mohair bear to fascinate
a child or delight a
collector. This adorable
friend has a head that
turns and a lovable
personality. Pearl buttons
in a variety of sizes and a
lacy bow trim this cuddly
creature. The pattern and
instructions are on pages
122–124.

splendid hardanger stocking

Hardanger and appliqué combine to create this one-of-a-kind stocking. Tiny symbols of the season are embroidered on the stocking, and the open work of the Hardanger cuff displays a satin lining. The instructions and chart for this elegant piece begin on page 125.

bear-paw quilt

Cuddle under your very own Christmas bear-paw quilt, and read some favorite holiday stories to the ones you love. This classic design complements the season with its bright red and white color. The complete instructions to make this favorite quilt using full-size templates are found on pages 129–130.

nature lover's candles and leaves

Positioned in natural wood holders, hand-dipped candles and natural waxed leaves create a feeling of Christmas past. Carefully hand-dipped in pairs, each has its own personality. The holders are made by drilling a hole in a small piece of natural wood. Step-by-step instructions for dipping the candles and leaves are on pages 130–131.

Glittering silver garland and painted hydrangeas combine to create a festive table setting. The centerpiece features a sparkling hydrangea topiary arranged in a silver-and-white marbleized pot. The quick-to-make antique paper napkin ring is trimmed in tinsel. A pewter charger and tableware complement the shimmering tinsel accents. The complete instructions for these projects are on page 131.

silvery hydrangea tabletop

country patchwork stocking

Pieced with calicoes, this handsome stocking is sure to add a touch of country to your holiday decor. The evenweave cuff and toe are perfectly suited for daintily stitched accents. An alphabet is provided to personalize your own homespun stocking. The instructions are on pages 132–135.

vintage music cases

A tired suitcase will sing again covered with vintage music. Use sheet music of Christmas carols to decoupage the suitcase, and line it in red velvet. Fill with greens, cards, gifts, or musical instruments. The instructions are on page 136.

christmas rose chair

A flea-market chair with a common rose pattern takes on a new life with some special painting techniques. Coated with layers of color and spattered with tiny dots of paint, the piece is transformed into a holiday work of art. The step-by-step instructions are on pages 136–137.

103

glittering
goblets

Dip the rims of crystal-clear
goblets into glue and
sparkling glitter, and you
have a pretty effect. But
fill the goblets to the brim
with colored water and
floating lit candles, and
the decoration is simply
glorious. The instructions
are on page 137.

white gardenia wreath

As shown on page 80.

Materials

24-inch-diameter silk evergreen
wreath; white spray paint
2 yards of 2-inch-wide ivory
wire-edged ribbon
Hot-glue gun; hot glue
3 freeze-dried gardenia blossoms
9 freeze-dried white peony blossoms
12 freeze-dried white bridal roses
6 white pinecones
White 1-inch-diameter glass
ball ornaments
Queen-Anne's-lace; globe thistle
White yarrow; silver king artemisia
1-yard strand of small white pearls

Instructions

Spray the wreath lightly with
white paint; allow to dry
completely. Make a multi-loop
bow from the ribbon, leaving
streamers; glue to top.

Glue pinecones and sprigs of
globe thistle, yarrow, and
artemisia to wreath, alternating
materials for desired effect. Next,
glue three gardenias evenly
spaced around the wreath, and
add 11 roses, peonies, and sprigs
of Queen-Anne's-lace.

To finish, glue the remaining
rose to the center of the bow; add
tiny sprigs of desired materials.
Loop the pearls and glue to the
back of the bow, allowing loops
to hang 6 or 8 inches.

elegant hardanger doily

As shown on page 81.

Materials

Fabric

12×12-inch piece of 20-count
ivory Jobelan fabric

Threads

#8 and #5 cream pearl cotton
1 spool of #8 braid in color listed
in key, opposite

Supplies

Needle
Embroidery hoop

Instructions

Tape or zigzag the edges of
Jobelan fabric. Find the top row
of satin stitches on the chart,
opposite, and the vertical center of
fabric. Measure 3¼ inches from
top of fabric and two threads to
left of vertical center; begin first
satin stitch there. For all stitches,

Buttonhole Stitch

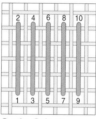

Satin Stitch

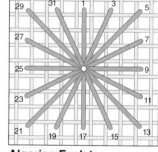

Algerian Eyelet

refer to the diagrams, *right*
and *opposite.*

Work satin-stitch Kloster
blocks and flowers first,
using one strand of #5 pearl
cotton. Next, use one strand
of #5 pearl cotton to work
lazy daisy stitches and
buttonhole stitch edging.

Use one strand of gold metallic
braid to work the cross-stitches
and eyelets; give each eyelet a
gentle tug to open up hole.

Cut and remove threads,
referring to the chart, *opposite.*
Thread needle with 30-inch length

Lazy Daisy

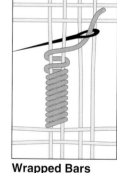

Wrapped Bars

of #8 pearl cotton. Wrap remaining
threads, making divided wrapped
bars with dove's eyes.

Trim fabric around outside
edge of doily, close to stitching.
Rinse doily in warm water; roll in
towel. While still damp, press
doily face down on terry towel.

106

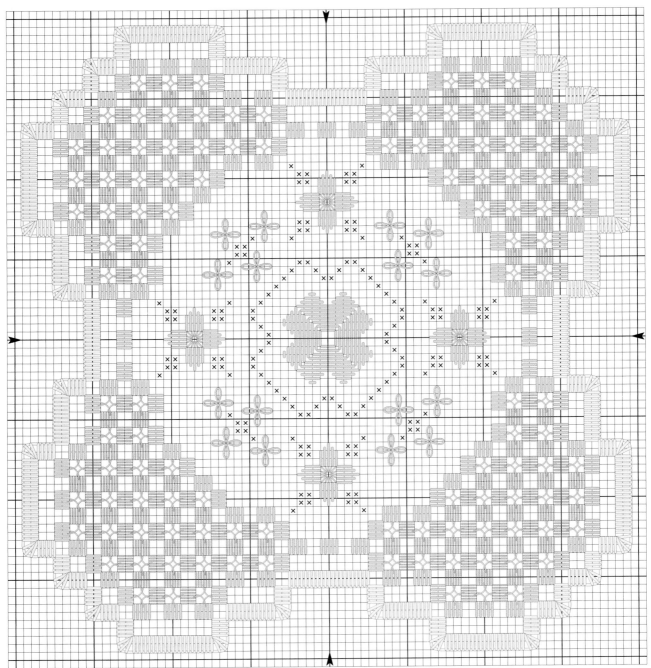

HARDANGER DOILY

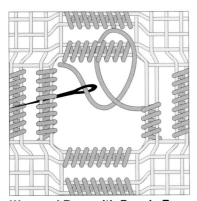

Wrapped Bars with Dove's Eye

HARDANGER DOILY

ANCHOR		DMC
	☒	102HL Kreinik gold #8 braid

SATIN STITCH

926	▯	712 Cream #5 pearl cotton

LAZY DAISY

926	▯	712 Cream #5 pearl cotton

BUTTONHOLE STITCH

926	▥	712 Cream #5 pearl cotton

ALGERIAN EYELET

	✳	102HL Kreinik gold #8 braid

ANCHOR		DMC

WRAPPED BARS WITH DOVE'S EYE

926	✳	712 Cream #5 pearl cotton

Stitch count: 78 high x 78 wide

Finished design sizes:
20-count fabric – 4⅞ x 4⅞ inches
28-count fabric – 5⅝ x 5⅝ inches
36-count fabric – 4⅜ x 4⅜ inches

frosty, no-sew snow family

As shown on page 82, snowman measures 10 inches tall, snow lady measures 8½ inches tall, and snow junior measures 7 inches tall.

Materials

Two 5-inch-diameter plastic-foam balls

Two 2- or 2½-inch-diameter jar lids

Hot-glue gun; hot glue

Two 4-inch-diameter plastic-foam balls (cut one of the balls in half)

1½-inch-diameter jar lid

18-gauge floral wire

Two 2½-inch-diameter plastic-foam balls (cut one of the balls in half)

Two 3-inch-diameter plastic-foam balls

Four 1½-inch-diameter plastic-foam balls

Eight 2-inch-diameter plastic-foam balls

Three jars of Duncan Snow Accents texturing material

Orange bakable modeling clay

Crafts knife; crafts glue

Six 5-millimeter black half-round beads; tracing paper

6×8-inch piece of dark blue polar fleece (snowman hat and snow lady mittens)

Three 1-inch-diameter light blue pom-poms (snowman hat and snow junior earmuff)

8×18-inch piece of teal polar fleece (snow lady hat, snowman mittens, and snow junior scarf)

10×19-inch piece of multicolor polar fleece (snow lady cape and snowman scarf)

4×4-inch piece of light blue polar fleece (snow junior mittens)

White string

2×19-inch piece of bright pink polar fleece (snow lady scarf)

Yellow terry cloth pipe cleaner (snow junior earmuff)

11 assorted plastic buttons

Small bits of Christmas greenery or miniature pinecones

Iridescent spray glitter

Instructions

Follow diagram, *opposite,* while assembling figures. Measurements on diagram are for snowman and snow lady; measurements in parentheses are for snow junior.

Wedge large jar lid into 5-inch plastic-foam ball for base of the snowman; glue in place. Repeat for base of snow lady. Assemble snow junior base in same manner, except use small jar lid and 4-inch ball.

Cut main body wire as noted in the diagram. Push wire through the ball from top of ball to jar lid base. Push appropriate half ball (upper body), cut side down, onto the wire; glue in place. Glue the head ball onto the wire.

Insert and center arm wire horizontally through upper body, pushing wire through area closer to back. Push one arm ball onto each end of the wire; slide up to body. Cut two small arm balls in half. Slide one half-ball onto each side as shown in the diagram. Shape the remaining half balls each by squeezing the opposite sides to make longer and more narrow for hands. Slide hands onto wires off-center, so they

appear to curve toward body front. Position arms as desired and hot-glue to secure in place. Smooth out the arms by pressing firmly with fingers. Press around torso to smooth waistline. Using fingers, apply Snow Accents over snow figures.

For carrot noses, knead orange clay until pliable. Roll three ⅜-inch-diameter balls. Shape the balls into a ⅞-inch-long carrot.

Rotating carrot, score carrot-like ridges using crafts knife. Bake in a 225° oven for 15 minutes; let cool. Push wide end of carrot into center of each face; glue in place.

Glue bead eyes to heads, placing eyes about ¼ inch above carrot nose.

For snowman hat, cut a 4×6-inch rectangle from the dark blue fleece. Fold rectangle in half, matching 4-inch-long edges. Glue one of the doubled 3-inch-long sides together for the back seam; turn to right side. Position hat on snowman's head and glue to secure. Fold front edge back

½ inch for brim; glue in place. Tuck and glue hat around neck. Glue pom-pom to tip.

For snow lady hat, cut a 5×6-inch rectangle from teal fleece. Glue center 3 inches on one 6-inch edge around lower head back. Pull each of two back corner points to center of back edge, shaping back of hat. Fold the front long edge back ½ inch for brim; glue around the face. Glue hat to head around bottom side edges.

For snow lady cape, trace pattern, *right*, onto tracing paper; cut out. Cut cape from multicolor fleece. Drape over shoulders and glue to secure.

For mittens, trace pattern, *right*, onto tracing paper and cut out. Cut six mittens, two for each snow figure, from fleece colors as noted in materials list. Knot end of 7-inch-long string through tiny hole in tip of each mitten. Cut a ¼×2-inch strip of contrasting color polar fleece for each mitten. Glue strip around top edge of mitten for trim, covering string knot; cut away excess. Tie end of mitten string around each hand.

For scarves, cut two 1¼×19-inch strips: one from bright pink fleece for snow lady; the other from multicolor fleece for snowman. Cut a 1¼×15-inch strip from teal fleece for snow junior. Fringe ends. Style scarves around necks; glue to secure.

For snow junior's earmuff, cut pipe cleaner to 9 inches. Fold in half and glue ends to head sides. Glue pom-poms over ends of pipe cleaner.

Glue one or two colored buttons to each scarf as shown in photograph, *page 82*. Glue one button to upper body of snow lady, two buttons down front of snow junior, and three buttons down front of snowman. Glue small bits of Christmas greenery, miniature pinecones, and/or small buttons to hat brims.

Spray figures with glitter. Wipe glitter from eyes before it dries.

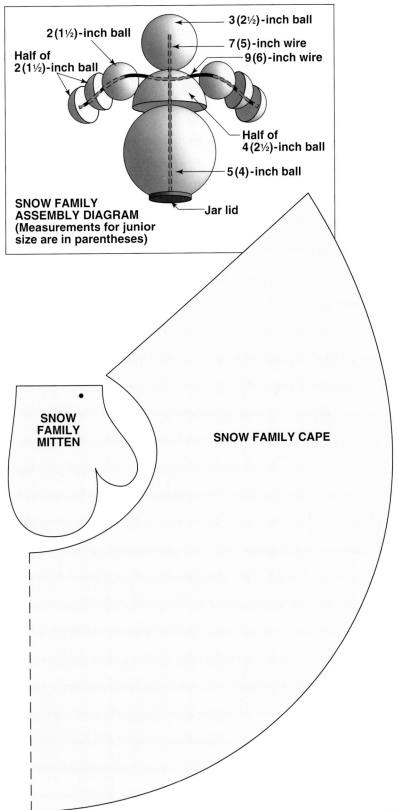

SNOW FAMILY ASSEMBLY DIAGRAM (Measurements for junior size are in parentheses)

3 (2½)-inch ball
2 (1½)-inch ball
7 (5)-inch wire
9 (6)-inch wire
Half of 2 (1½)-inch ball
Half of 4 (2½)-inch ball
5 (4)-inch ball
Jar lid

SNOW FAMILY MITTEN

SNOW FAMILY CAPE

snowman banner

As shown on page 83, banner measures 28½×22½ inches.

Materials

Tracing paper
Four 9×12-inch sky blue felt
  rectangles
Four 9×12-inch white felt rectangles
Two 9×12-inch lavender felt
  rectangles
One 9×12-inch fuchsia felt rectangle
One 9×12-inch teal felt rectangle
4×4-inch piece of orange felt
Cotton embroidery floss: pink,
  lavender, black, fuchsia, teal,
  orange, mint green, and white
Embroidery needle
55 assorted white buttons
14 colored buttons, in assorted
  sizes and shades of rose, blue,
  and teal
White quilting thread
Large-eyed hand sewing needle

Instructions

Enlarge and trace outlined shapes
from each snowman pattern,
page 113, onto tracing paper. Do
not trace shapes indicated only by
gray dotted lines. Trace hat, scarf,
and bow tie patterns, *opposite.* Cut
out all pattern pieces.

For snowman A, cut body pieces
and snow from white, nose from
orange, and hat pieces from fuchsia
felt. In addition, cut a 2×10½-inch
scarf from lavender felt.

For snowman B, cut the body
and snow pieces from white, and
nose from orange felt. In addition,
cut snowman B bow tie from fuchsia
and snowman B hat from teal felt.

For snowman C, cut body
piece and snow from white, hat
pieces from lavender, and nose

from orange felt. In addition, cut
a 1½×8-inch scarf from teal felt.

For snowman D, cut body and
snow pieces from white, vest and
hat pieces from fuchsia, and nose
from orange felt. In addition, cut
snowman D bow tie from teal felt.

For borders, sashing and tabs,
cut four 12×1½-inch strips from
teal, four 9×1½-inch and two
12×1½-inch strips from lavender
and two 9×1½-inch and two
4½×1½-inch strips from fuchsia
felt. Cut nine 1½×1½-inch
square blocks from white felt.

Use two plies of floss for all
stitching except decorative stitching
on hats and scarves, and where
otherwise specified. For decorative
stitching, use six plies of floss.

For snowman A, sew body
pieces to blue background
rectangle using white running
stitches around perimeters, about
¼ inch in from edge. Sew snow
to background along curved top
edge using light blue running
stitches. Sew hat pieces in place
using fuchsia running stitches.
Use small orange straight stitches
to affix nose. Make straight stitch
eyes and work arms using black
floss. Work French knot mouth
using six plies of black floss.
Decorate hat with pink straight
stitches around hat brim,
lavender French knots scattered
across brim, and lavender zigzags
and pink French knots on top
portion of hat. Make pom-pom as
for Snowman Doll instructions,
pages 112 and *114–115;* tack the

pom-pom to tip of hat. Knot the
scarf in middle; position on the
snowman according to the dotted
lines. Secure scarf with pink
French knots at dots. Use fuchsia
straight stitches in a V pattern for
fringe, tacked with pink near base
of V, as shown on pattern. Sew
button at X on snowman. Scatter
and stitch on approximately

11 white buttons across blue
background for the snowflakes.

For snowman B, sew body, snow,
and nose pieces in place as for
snowman A. Work straight stitch
eyes, mouth, and arms using black
floss. Fold hat piece from bottom
toward top along fold line and
position as shown on pattern. Sew
in place using fuchsia running
stitches. Work a fuchsia straight
stitch star at top. Decorate using
lazy daisies and French knots in
desired colors. Knot bow tie strip
in middle; position on snowman.
Secure bow tie with straight stitch
Vs in teal and mint green. Sew
buttons at Xs on snowman. Stitch
approximately 12 buttons across
blue background for snowflakes.

For snowman C, sew body pieces, snow, and nose pieces in place as for snowman A. Sew hat pieces in place using tiny lavender straight stitches. Make French knot eyes, running stitch mouth, and straight stitch arms using black floss. Decorate hat top with long teal straight stitches and brim with teal lazy daisies and French knots. Knot scarf in middle; position on snowman according to dotted lines. Secure scarf with lavender lazy daisy flowers with fuchsia French knot centers and scattered teal French knots. Sew buttons to hat and body at Xs. Scatter and stitch on approximately 16 buttons across blue background for the snowflakes.

For snowman D, sew body, snow, and nose pieces in place as for snowman A. Sew hat in place using lavender running stitches, tucking in ends of 1½×¼-inch strip at top as shown on pattern. Straight stitch black eyebrows and arms. Work French knot eyes and mouth using six plies of black floss. Sew vest pieces in place using fuchsia running stitches. Decorate vest with straight stitch stars using two plies of pink floss. Knot the bow tie in middle. Position the tie at base of neck and secure with fuchsia French knots at dots. Sew

buttons at Xs. Scatter and stitch on approximately 14 white buttons across blue background for snowflakes.

Arrange snowman blocks with A and B in top row and C and D in bottom row. Sew all assembly seams using white quilting thread. Whipstitch seams, piercing felt approximately ⅛ inch from edges. When seams are sewn and opened out, stitches will show.

Sew long side of teal sashing strip to left side of snowman A. In same manner, working left to right, sew 12-inch-long lavender strip to right side of A, Snowman B to

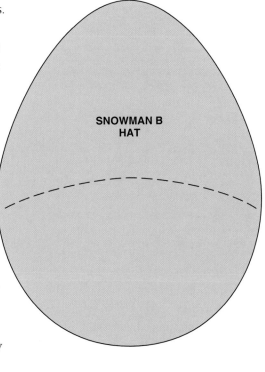

SNOWMAN B BOW TIE

SNOWMAN B HAT

SNOWMAN D BOW TIE

snowman banner — *continued*

right side of lavender strip, and teal strip to right side of snowman B. Repeat for bottom row, using snowmen C and D.

For top horizontal sashing, sew short end of 9-inch-long lavender strip to white block. In the same manner, working left to right, sew white block to remaining short end of lavender strip, another strip to white block, ending with another white block at far end. Repeat to make bottom horizontal sashing. Make middle sashing in same manner using white blocks and 9-inch-long fuchsia strips.

Sew middle sashing between rows of snowman blocks, matching seam lines. Sew top and bottom sashing to blocks in same manner.

Trim one short end of each tab strip to a point. For each tab, whipstitch straight end of tab to each white top corner block. Fold each pointed end to front as shown in photograph, *page 83*, and secure each with a white button.

snowman doll

As shown on page 83, snowman stands 12½ inches tall.

Purple sewing thread
Soft sculpture needle
Fabric paint pens: bright pink, bright yellow, and green
1½×5-inch strip of cardboard
Nine white buttons in assorted sizes

Instructions

Trace patterns, *pages 114–115*, onto tracing paper; cut out. From white polar fleece, cut eight lower body pieces using large body piece pattern, eight upper body pieces using small body piece pattern, and six head pieces. Cut hat brim from blue fleece and hat from purple fleece. Patterns include ¼-inch seam allowances.

Sew four lower body pieces together, sewing from A to B as shown on the pattern. Repeat, making two sets of four pieces. Sew sets together; turn right side out. Fill lower body half full with pellet beads; stuff remainder with fiberfill. Sew opening closed using button thread.

Sew upper body and head in same manner; stuff each with fiberfill, and sew closed. Hand stitch upper body to lower body and then head to upper body to complete the snowman figure.

Glue orange felt circle to center of front of head. Thread needle with 12 plies of black embroidery floss; knot end. Push needle down through top of head and out at top of one eye as shown on face diagram, *page 115*. Stitch down ¼ inch to complete eye; bring needle out at top of other eye and repeat to complete eye. Push needle out through head top. Glue black beads to head to make mouth as shown on the face diagram.

Cut a small hole on each side of the upper body to hold the twig arms. Glue the base of twig to each hole.

Tie teal scarf piece around neck. Using six plies of yellow floss, stitch one bottom edge of

Materials

Tracing paper
28×8-inch piece of white polar fleece
8×8-inch piece of purple polar fleece
3×5-inch piece of light blue polar fleece
2½×20-inch piece of teal polar fleece
½-inch-diameter circle of orange felt
White sewing thread
White button thread
Plastic polyfill pellet beads
Polyester fiberfill
Thick white crafts glue
Cotton embroidery floss: black, yellow, white, light pink, dark pink, and dark lavender
7 size 4-millimeter round black beads; two 5-inch-long twigs

SNOWMAN BANNER – SNOWMAN A

SNOWMAN BANNER – SNOWMAN B

SNOWMAN BANNER – SNOWMAN C

SNOWMAN BANNER – SNOWMAN D

1 Square = 1 Inch

113

snowman doll — *continued*

scarf to lower body, making floss stitches look like 1-inch-long fringe. On remaining end of scarf, knot floss in four separate places along edge, leaving 1-inch-long tails for fringe. Flip free end over one twig arm; glue to secure.

Sew hat back seam; turn right side out and stuff top. Glue hat to head. Work blanket stitch around hat brim using six plies of yellow floss. Glue brim to bottom of front of hat.

Using paint pens, dot scarf and hat with pink. Dot hat brim and tops of fringe stitches with green. Make two rows of yellow zigzags across front of hat as shown in photograph, *page 83*.

To make pom-pom, use one strand each of light pink, dark pink, and dark lavender floss. Holding three colors together, wrap floss strand 50 times around 1½-inch-wide strip of cardboard. Slide wraps carefully off the cardboard

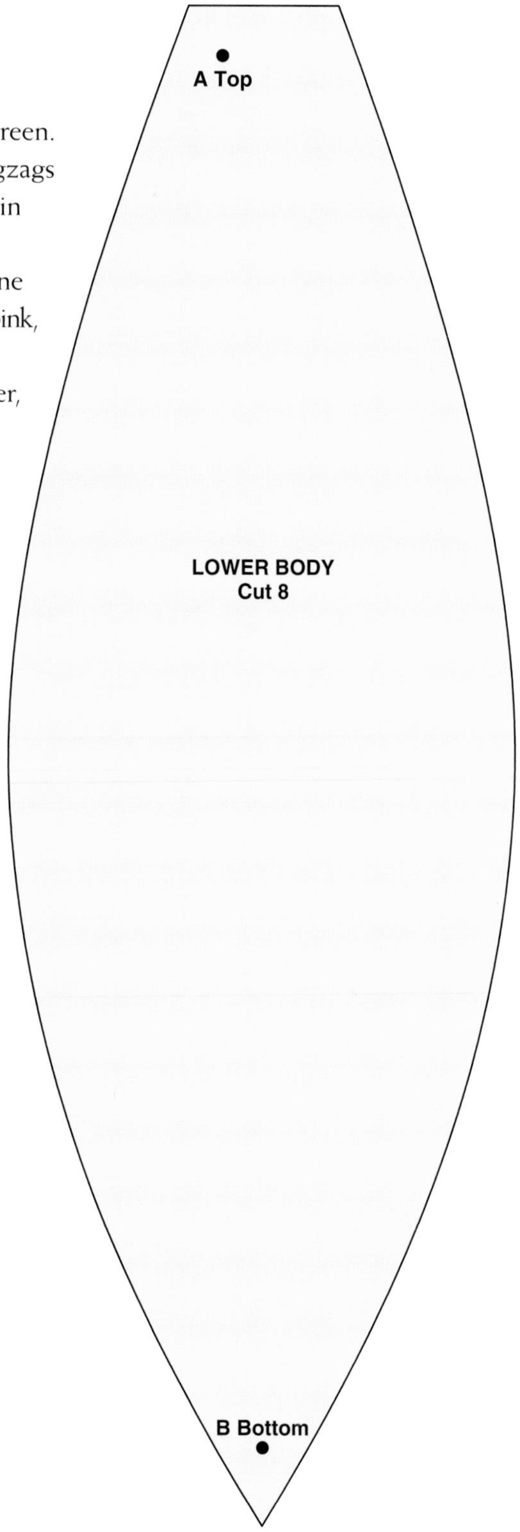

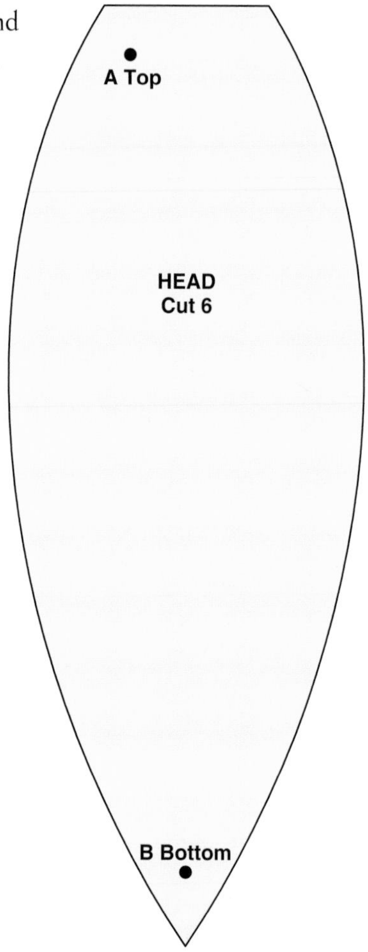

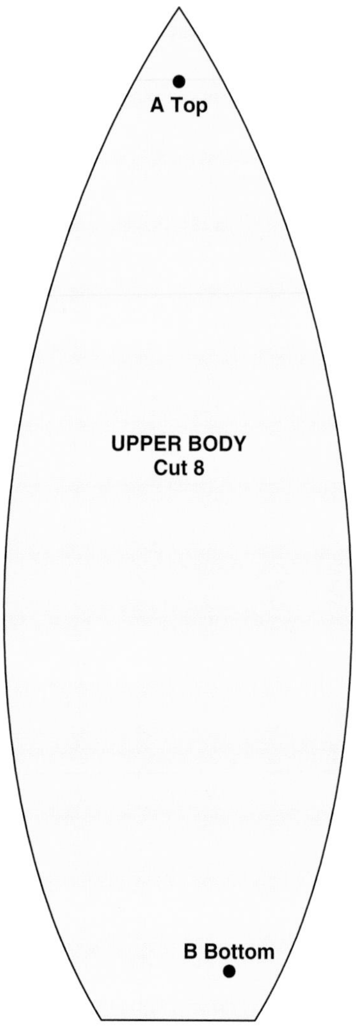

A Top

LOWER BODY
Cut 8

A Top

HEAD
Cut 6

A Top

UPPER BODY
Cut 8

B Bottom

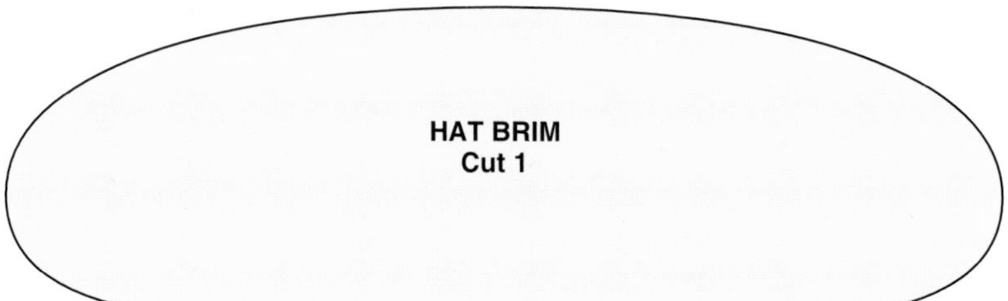

B Bottom

B Bottom

SNOWMAN DOLL

HAT BRIM
Cut 1

and tie tightly around the middle.
Cut loops and fluff strands into a
pom-pom, trimming if necessary.
Tack pom-pom to hat top.

Glue one button to each side
of head to resemble earmuffs.
Glue one button to right front
side of lower body.

Cut two 8-inch-long strands of
white floss. Thread and then knot
three buttons on each strand.
Tie one strand to each twig
arm, allowing buttons
to dangle.

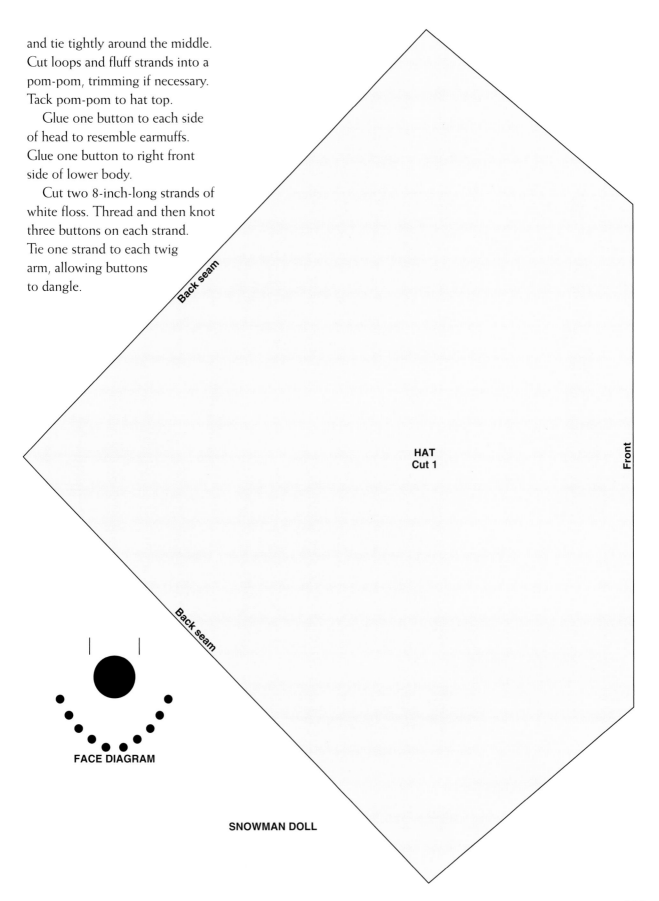

HAT
Cut 1

Back seam

Back seam

Front

FACE DIAGRAM

SNOWMAN DOLL

yo-yo stocking

As shown on page 86, stocking measures 16½ inches long.

Materials

Fabrics

⅔ yard of 45-inch-wide deep-red velveteen fabric

15×20-inch piece of fleece

½ yard of 45-inch-wide deep-red moiré taffeta

½ yard of 45-inch-wide red lining fabric

Small pieces of assorted shades of red, burgundy, violet, green, and pink

Supplies

Graph paper

Tracing paper

Fabric marking pen

2 yards of narrow cording

Threads to match fabrics

¾ yard of ½-inch-wide flat antique gold trim

50 fancy shank buttons, measuring ⅜- to ¾-inch in diameter

¾ yard of 3-inch-wide scalloped antique gold trim

Two yards of ³⁄₁₆-inch-diameter metallic gold cord

Instructions

Sew all pieces with right sides of fabric facing and clip curves. Patterns and measurements include ¼-inch seam allowances.

For stocking front, cut a 15×20-inch piece of velveteen. Baste fleece to back side of velveteen and machine-quilt using a 1-inch diagonal grid diamond pattern.

Enlarge stocking pattern, *opposite*, onto graph paper and trace yo-yo circles, *opposite*, onto tracing paper. Cut out pattern pieces.

Cut stocking front from quilted fabric. Transfer the heel and toe lines. From unquilted velveteen, cut a 5½×16-inch cuff, a 2×5½-inch hanging loop, and enough 1-inch-wide bias strips to make 2 yards. Cut the stocking back from the taffeta. Cut two lining pieces and a 5½×16-inch cuff lining from the lining fabric. From the assorted pieces of taffeta, cut 25 large circles and 25 small circles.

For yo-yos, turn under a scant ¼ inch around perimeter of each yo-yo circle and finger-press. Gather outside folded edge of each circle using a running stitch. Pull the gathers tight, knot the thread, and flatten into a circle with gathers in center.

Stitch ½-inch-wide gold trim to the toe and heel lines on stocking front.

For piping, sew bias velveteen strips end to end. Center cording lengthwise on the wrong side of the velveteen strip. Fold fabric around cording, raw edges together. Use a zipper foot to sew through both layers close to cord. Trim the seam allowance to ¼ inch. Baste piping around the stocking front along the side and bottom edges. Sew stocking front to back, leaving top open. Turn right side out.

Sew 11 yo-yos, gathered side up, to toe, securing center of each with a button and positioning yo-yos close together with overlapping edges. Sew 12 yo-yos to heel in the same manner.

Join short ends of velveteen cuff strip. Repeat for cuff lining. Stitch velveteen cuff to cuff lining around one long edge (bottom). Turn cuff right side out and stitch 3-inch-wide trim to bottom. Baste cuff to stocking top, matching raw edges.

Turn under ½ inch along long sides of hanging loop strip. Fold strip in half lengthwise and stitch close to folded edges. Fold the strip in half crosswise to form a loop; matching the short ends to raw edge, stitch loop to cuff at back seam.

Sew lining front to back, leaving top open and an opening at the bottom for turning. Slip stocking into lining with right sides facing, matching seams. Stitch around top edge. Turn right side out through bottom opening in lining and slip-stitch opening closed. Tuck lining into stocking and tack at seams.

Sew 27 yo-yos to cuff front as for heel and toe. Cut gold cord length in half and knot ends. Tie cords in a double bow and stitch to cuff below hanging loop.

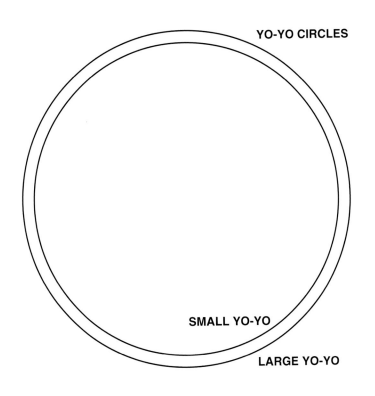

YO-YO CIRCLES

SMALL YO-YO

LARGE YO-YO

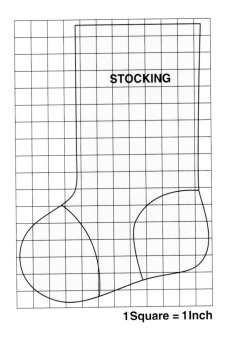

STOCKING

1 Square = 1 Inch

vintage hankie tree

As shown on page 87, framed tree measures 36×24 inches.

Materials

36×24-inch framed cork
   bulletin board
Gold metallic spray paint
40×28-inch piece of green
   cotton fabric
Staple gun
10 handkerchiefs
Pins; white facial tissues
16 assorted 1-inch-diameter
   brass buttons
6 assorted colored buttons
2-inch-diameter gold plastic star
Hot-glue gun; hot glue

Instructions

Remove frame from corkboard.
Spray paint frame gold and allow
it to dry.

Stretch the green cotton fabric
over the front of the corkboard;
staple the edges down in back.
Replace the covered corkboard
in frame.

To pin each handkerchief in
place, pinch center between
fingers, shake handkerchief, and
then pin center to the bulletin
board. Beginning 12 inches above
the bottom edge of the green
fabric, center four handkerchiefs
with pins approximately 3 inches
apart. For next row, center three
handkerchiefs about 6½ inches
above the first, using the same
spacing. In the same manner,
center two handkerchiefs above
the row of three, with the final
handkerchief at the top.

Insert a facial tissue under each
handkerchief to add dimension
if desired.

Hot-glue brass buttons in a
square pattern, four across and
four down, to fabric under tree to
resemble a Christmas tree trunk.
Hot-glue colored buttons to
handkerchiefs at random. Glue
the star to the top of the tree.

117

painted santa doorstop

As shown on page 88, doorstop stands 10¼ inches tall.

Materials

Tracing paper

8×12-inch piece of muslin

¼ yard of navy blue fabric with
    gold snowflake print, or similar
    blue holiday print

8×12-inch piece of freezer paper

Gesso

1-inch paint brush

Fine grit sandpaper

Tack cloth

Carbon paper

Ballpoint pen

Delta Ceramcoat acrylic paints:
    grape, metallic gold, navy blue,
    leaf green, wild rose, desert sun,
    medium flesh, black, denim
    blue, lichen gray, hammered
    iron, sandstone, magnolia white,
    yellow, blue jay, and mocha

Artists' brushes

Exterior varnish

Navy blue sewing thread

Polyester fiberfill

Polyfill pellet beads

Small funnel

32 inches of ⅛-inch-diameter
    metallic gold cord

Hot-glue gun; hot glue

Instructions

Trace the base pattern and doorstop outline, *opposite,* onto tracing paper and cut out. Cut base and back piece from blue and gold print. Lay muslin rectangle atop shiny side of freezer paper. Using medium heat, iron fabric to paper. After the paper has cooled, apply thin coat of gesso to fabric. Allow gesso to dry. Sand over gesso lightly in one direction; wipe with tack cloth.

Apply second thin coat of gesso, sand, and wipe with tack cloth. Place carbon paper between pattern and doorstop front; transfer front piece outline and Santa, excluding face detail, by tracing over lines with ballpoint pen. Do not cut out doorstop front until all the painting is completed.

Paint background grape. Add snowflakes and dots at random using metallic gold. Next, paint Santa's face medium flesh; allow to dry. Using pattern and carbon paper, transfer face detail. Shade nose and eyelids with desert sun. Blend wild rose into cheeks and tip of nose. Paint irises denim blue with black pupils. Dot the inner corner of each eye with wild rose. Outline eyes and nose in black.

Paint the coat and hat denim blue with navy blue shading. Paint the mittens blue jay; shade with denim blue. When the mittens are dry, dot with gold.

Paint pants, coat buttons, hat cuff, sleeve cuffs, collar, star buttons, and star on hat yellow. Add navy blue checks to cuffs and collar, following pattern. Shade pants with mocha and add thin navy blue stripes when dry. Paint star button thread lines using black.

Paint boots black; highlight with lichen gray.

Paint beard, mustache, and eyebrows lichen gray; shade with hammered iron. First using sandstone and then magnolia white, paint thin lines to detail all hair.

Paint holly leaves green and berries wild rose.

Using liner brush, outline clothing detail and holly leaves in black. Highlight the eyes, tip of nose, all stars, boots, and holly berries with magnolia white. Allow all paint to dry thoroughly.

Apply coat of varnish to painted doorstop front; allow to dry. Cut out the front along cutting line.

Sew the doorstop front to the back, using a ⅛-inch seam allowance. Leave an opening for turning. Sew the base to the bottom and clip the curves. Turn the doorstop right side out and stuff the top ¾ of figure firmly with polyester fiberfill.

Pour the polyfill pellet beads into the bottom, using a funnel if necessary. Whipstitch the opening closed. Hot-glue the gold cord over the seamed edges.

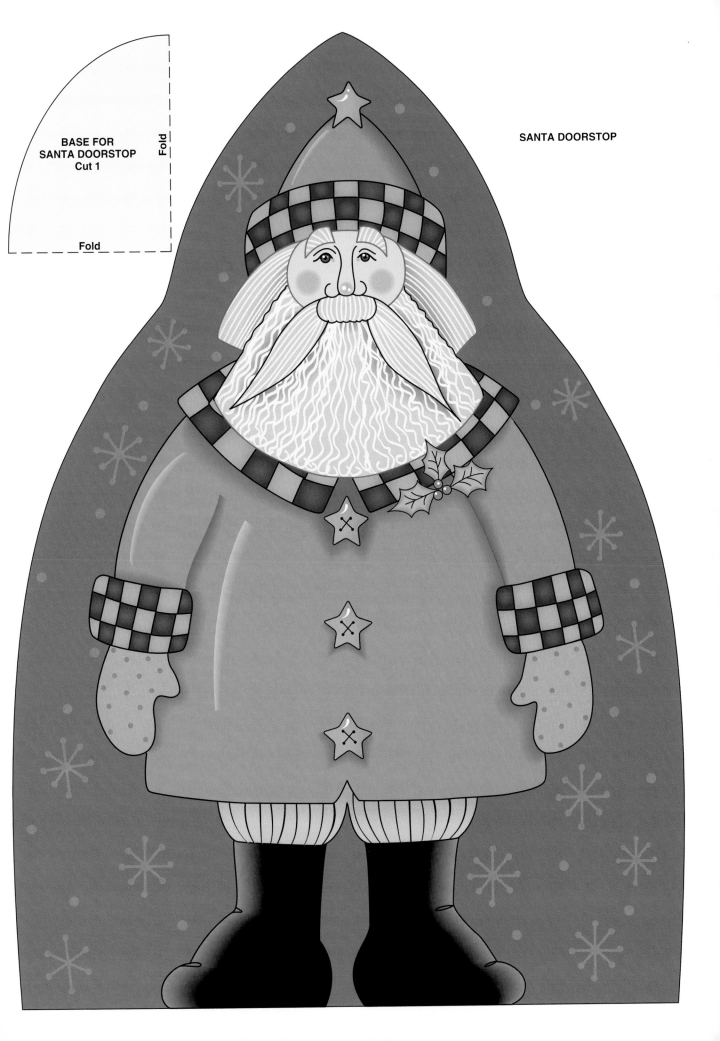

BASE FOR
SANTA DOORSTOP
Cut 1

Fold

Fold

SANTA DOORSTOP

chenille snowflake afghan

As shown on page 89, afghan measures 46×55 inches.
Crochet abbreviations are on page 320.

Materials

Lion Chenille Sensations "100%
Monsanto acrylic" worsted-
weight yarn (1.4-oz./87-yd. skein):
19 skeins of antique white
(80761.01) for MC Berella "4"
"Monsanto Acrylic with Bounce-
Back Fibers" worsted-weight yarn
(3.5-oz./100-gm. skein): 6 skeins
of winter white (8941) for CC
Size 5/F (3.75 mm) and 6/G
(4.25 mm) aluminum
crochet hooks
GAUGE: With CC and larger hook,
Rnd 1 = 2-inch-diameter; one
finished block = 9-inches-square.

Instructions

FIRST BLOCK: Beginning at
center using larger hook and CC,
ch 8; join with sl st to form ring.

Rnd 1: Ch 3 (counts as dc),
work 23 more dc in ring; join with
sl st in 3rd ch of beg ch-3.

Rnd 2: (Ch 3 (counts as dc), dc
in same dc as join = beginning cl
made), ch 3, (dc 2 tog in same dc
as join = cl made); * ch 3, sk 2 dc,
in next dc (cl, ch 3, cl); rep from *
around, ending ch 3, join with sl
st in top of first cl = 8 double cl.

Rnd 3: Sl st in first ch-3 sp, in
same sp (beginning cl, ch 3, cl); *
ch 3, sk next ch-3 sp, (cl, ch 3, cl)
in next ch-3 sp; rep from * around,
ending ch 3, sl st in top of first cl.

Rnd 4: Sl st in first ch-3 sp, in
same sp (beginning cl, ch 3, cl); *
ch 2, sc over ch-3 lps from rnds 2
and 3, ch 2 **, (cl, ch 3, cl) in next
ch-3 sp; rep from * around, ending

last rep at **; join with sl st in top
of first cl. Fasten off CC.

Rnd 5: With RS facing and
smaller hook, join MC with sl st in
any ch-3 sp. In same sp as join (beg
cl, ch 3, cl); * 5 trc in next sc, in next
ch-3 sp (cl, ch 3, cl), 3 trc in next sc
**, in next ch-3 sp (cl, ch 3, cl); rep
from * around, ending last rep at
**; join with sl st in top of beg cl.

Rnd 6: Ch 3 (counts as dc); * 3
dc in ch-3 sp, dc in top of next cl,
dc in each of next 2 trc, 5 dc in next
trc, dc in each of next 2 trc, dc in
top of next cl, 3 dc in ch-3 sp, dc in
top of next cl, dc in each of next 3
trc **, dc in top of next cl; rep from
* around, ending last rep at **; join
with sl st in third ch of beg ch-3 =
17 dc along each side, excluding
corner 5-dc groups. Fasten off MC.

Rnd 7: With RS facing and
larger hook, join CC with sl st in
third dc of any 5-dc corner. Ch 1,
3 sc in same dc as join; * sc in each
of next 21 dc **, 3 sc in next dc;
rep from * around, ending last
rep at **; join with sl st in first sc.

Rnd 8: Ch 1, sc in same sc as
join; * 3 sc in next sc **, sc in each
of next 23 sc; rep from * around,
ending last rep at **, sc in each of
last 22 sc; join and fasten off.

Rnd 9: With the RS facing
and smaller hook, join MC with sl
st in second sc of any corner 3-sc
group. Ch 1, 3 sc in same sc as
join, sc in next sc, [(working over
the center dc post from Rnd 6,
make a dc = fpdc made)], * sk the
sc behind the fpdc, sc in next sc,
sk next dc, fpdc over post of next

dc from Rnd 6 **; rep from * for
10 times more, 3 sc in next sc, sc
in next sc, fpdc over same post as
last fpdc; rep from * around,
ending last rep at **, rep from *
for 9 times, fpdc over same post as
first fpdc, sc in next sc; join = 12
fpdc along each side.

Rnd 10: Ch 3 (counts as dc); *
3 dc in next sc, dc in each of next
2 sc, (fpdc over fpdc, dc in next sc)
12 times, dc in next dc; rep from *
around; join with sl st in third ch
of beginning ch-3.

Rnd 11: Ch 1, sc in join; * sc in
next dc, 3 sc in next dc, sc in each
of next 3 dc, (fpsc over fpdc, sc in
next dc) 12 times, sc in next sc; rep
from * around; join and fasten off.
Make 29 blocks as for First Block.
Sc blocks tog on WS using CC
and in 6 rows, each with 5 blocks.

BORDER: With the RS facing
and larger hook, join CC with sl
st in second sc of any 3-sc-corner
group; ch 1, 3 sc in same sc, * sc in
each sc to joining, [[yo and draw
up a lp in corner of each of next 2
blocks, yo and draw through all 5
lps on hook = puff st made)]; rep
from * around, working 3 sc in
each corner; at end, join with sl
st in first sc.

Rnd 2: Ch 1, sc in first sc, in
next sc (sc, ch 3, sl st in sc just made
= picot made) for first corner, sc in
each sc to fourth sc before puff st,
(picot in sc, sc in next sc) twice,
picot in puff st, (sc in next sc, picot
in next sc) twice; cont as est around,
working next corners as for first.

Rnd 3: Sl st in each sc around,
sl stitching beneath each picot; at
end, sl st in first sl st; fasten off.

whimsical painted chair

As shown on page 94.

Materials

Adult's wood chair; sandpaper
Tack cloth; acrylic wood primer (for
 painted base)
Wood stain (for stained base)
Acrylic paints in desired colors
Small natural cosmetic sponge
Paintbrushes; drafting tape; pencil
Wood beads or motifs, twine,
 2 small screw eyes, and thick
 white crafts glue (optional)
Clear acrylic spray varnish

Instructions

Sand surfaces to prepare wood for
painting; wipe with a tack cloth. For
new wood to be painted, apply
coat of primer; allow to dry. Apply
desired base color to each section.
Apply second coat if necessary;
allow to dry. For wood to be stained,
apply according to manufacturer's
instructions; allow to dry.

   Refer to photograph, *page 94*,
and patterns, *right*, for design
ideas. For spokes and legs, paint a
variety of geometric or freehand
designs, using several colors. Use
tape as a mask and guide as
necessary to create blocks of
color. Add stripes of contrasting
color; make polka dots using eraser
end of pencil dipped in paint.

   If desired, paint wood motifs and
glue onto chair, using photograph
for ideas. For a hanging strand as
shown in photograph, thread
painted beads and motifs onto
twine. Knot each twine end onto
screw eye, which has been
attached to chair.

   After all paint is dry, spray
entire chair with acrylic varnish.

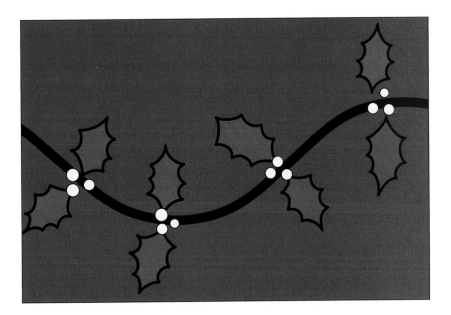

121

buttons the bear

As shown on page 95, bear stands 12 inches tall.

Materials

Fabric

¼ yard of Alfonso red mohair (red pile on a cream backing) with ⅜-inch-long pile

Threads

Cream sewing thread
Red sewing thread
Red carpet thread
#3 black pearl cotton

Supplies

Tissue paper
Thin cardboard
Fabric marking pen
Scissors
Large-eyed embroidery or leather needle
Beeswax
One 1×¼-inch bolt
Two 1-inch-diameter fiberboard disks with ¼-inch-diameter holes
T-pins; awl
Soft-sculpture needle
Two 8-millimeter antique shoe eye buttons
One ¼-inch lock washer
One ¼-inch nut
Needle-nose pliers
Polyester fiberfill
⅓ yard of 1½-inch-wide ecru cotton lace
Fifteen assorted antique pearl buttons
Leather thimble
Chopstick or small dowel

Instructions

Trace pattern, *pages 123–124,* onto tissue paper and cut out. Draw around pieces on cardboard and cut out to make templates. All patterns include ¼-inch seam allowances. Sew all seams with right sides facing, unless otherwise noted.

Place pattern templates on wrong side of a single thickness of mohair, positioning each piece so arrow runs in direction of nap. Trace around templates, reversing pieces where indicated. Using fabric marking pen, transfer pattern markings. Cut out fabric pieces using tip of scissors to snip through fabric backing and being careful not to cut pile on right side.

For head, join head side pieces along chin seam from neck front to nose. Hand-baste gusset between head pieces, matching dot to top of chin seam. Machine-stitch gusset in place. Remove basting threads, clip curves, and turn head right side out. Stuff head firmly. Thread large-eyed needle with a double strand of carpet thread. Knot thread ends and rub strands with beeswax. Work a running stitch around neck, allowing needle and thread to hang from last stitch. Insert bolt through hole in one disk. Push disk into neck opening with bottom of bolt extending below opening. Pull carpet thread to gather neck around bolt. Knot thread securely.

Sew ears together in pairs leaving bottoms open. Turn ears right side out. Turn under ¼ inch along ear bottom edges; slip-stitch closed. With upper edge of each ear on head gusset seamline, pin ears to head using T-pins. When ears are positioned, stitch them in place using red carpet thread.

For eyes, use awl to punch a hole at each eye position. Thread soft-sculpture needle with four strands of carpet thread and knot ends around wire loop of one eye button. Push needle into one eye hole, exiting behind ear on opposite side of head. Pull thread tight to sink eye in hole and knot thread. Repeat for remaining eye.

Trim away as much pile as possible on nose where it will be embroidered. Trim a scant ⅛ inch from pile on remainder of muzzle. Straight-stitch nose and claws, as shown on pattern, *pages 123–124,* using large-eyed needle and a single strand of pearl cotton. To make mouth, use a single strand of pearl cotton knotted at end. Hide knot behind embroidered nose and push needle out through point A on left side. Leaving stitch loose, push needle into face at point A on right side and out at point B. Bring the needle under the loose stitch and pull to tighten, creating an inverted V for mouth. Push needle back into the face at the base of the nose and knot thread.

For arms and legs, sew pieces together in pairs leaving marked openings unstitched. Sew a foot pad to each foot bottom, matching toe and heel Xs to front and back seams. Turn limbs right side out.

For body, sew the sides together, leaving marked

openings unstitched. Turn the body right side out. Make a hole at the dot on body top using awl. Push bolt end that extends from the head into body through hole. Entering from the body back

opening, slide the remaining disk and lock washer onto the bolt; secure both with nut. Tighten the nut using pliers until the head just barely turns.

Stuff arms, legs, and body firmly. Sew opening closed with a double strand of carpet thread coated with beeswax. Next, thread soft-sculpture needle with a double strand of carpet thread and knot ends. Sew arms to body by pushing needle through one arm at Xs, through body at Xs, and then through remaining arm at Xs. Pull thread tight and sew back through in opposite direction, exiting near starting point. Slide a button onto thread and push needle back through to outside of other arm.

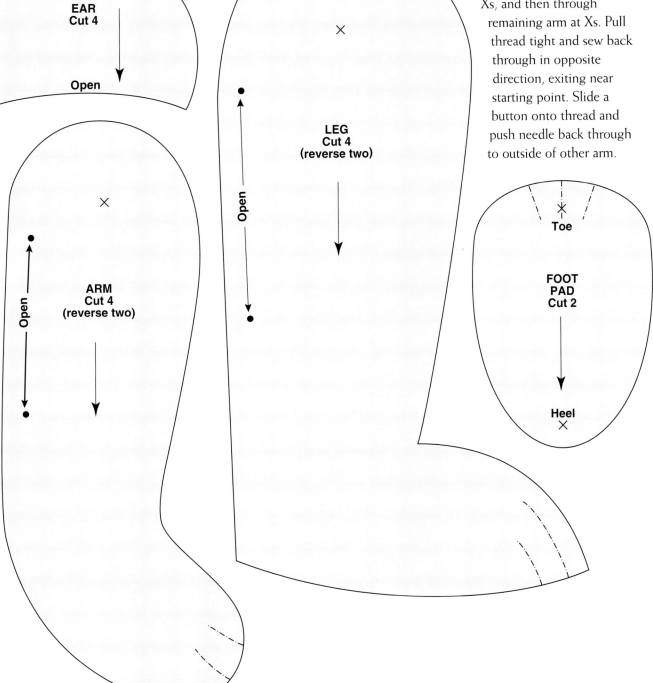

EAR
Cut 4

Open

ARM
Cut 4
(reverse two)

Open

LEG
Cut 4
(reverse two)

Open

FOOT PAD
Cut 2

Toe

Heel

buttons the bear — *continued*

Slide another button onto the thread and sew through again, exiting through one of holes in the button. Continue sewing back and forth in the same manner four more times, securing the buttons while stitching. Knot the thread on the inside of one arm. Sew legs to body in the same manner.

Tie lace in a bow around neck and trim ends. Using assorted pearl buttons, sew smallest button in right ear, a large button to middle of bow, a small button at dot on tummy, a small button to outside of each wrist to resemble cuff buttons, and three buttons up the side of each leg to resemble spat buttons. Smooth the pile away from the eyes using a finger dipped in water or styling mousse.

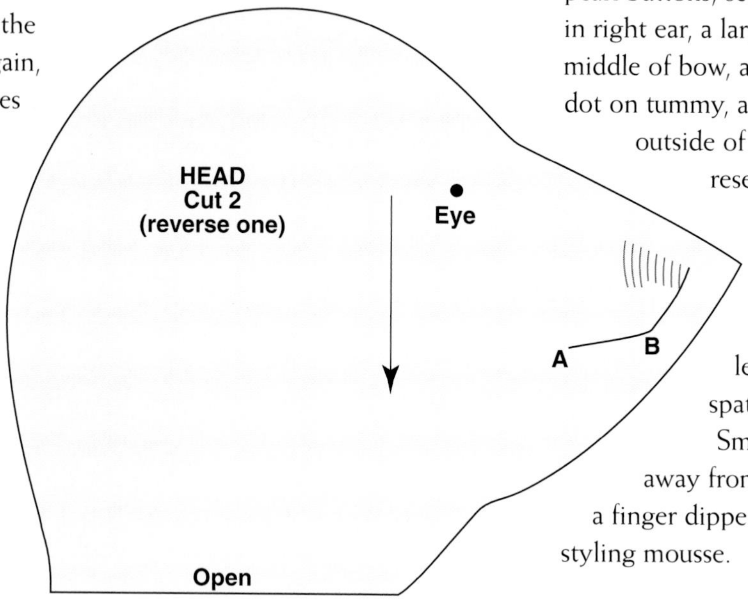

HEAD
Cut 2
(reverse one)

Eye

A   B

Open

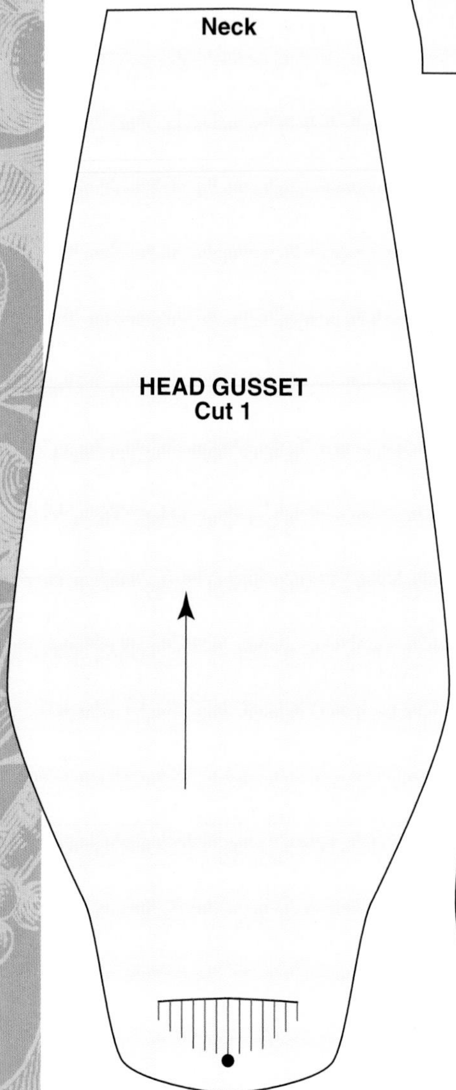

Neck

HEAD GUSSET
Cut 1

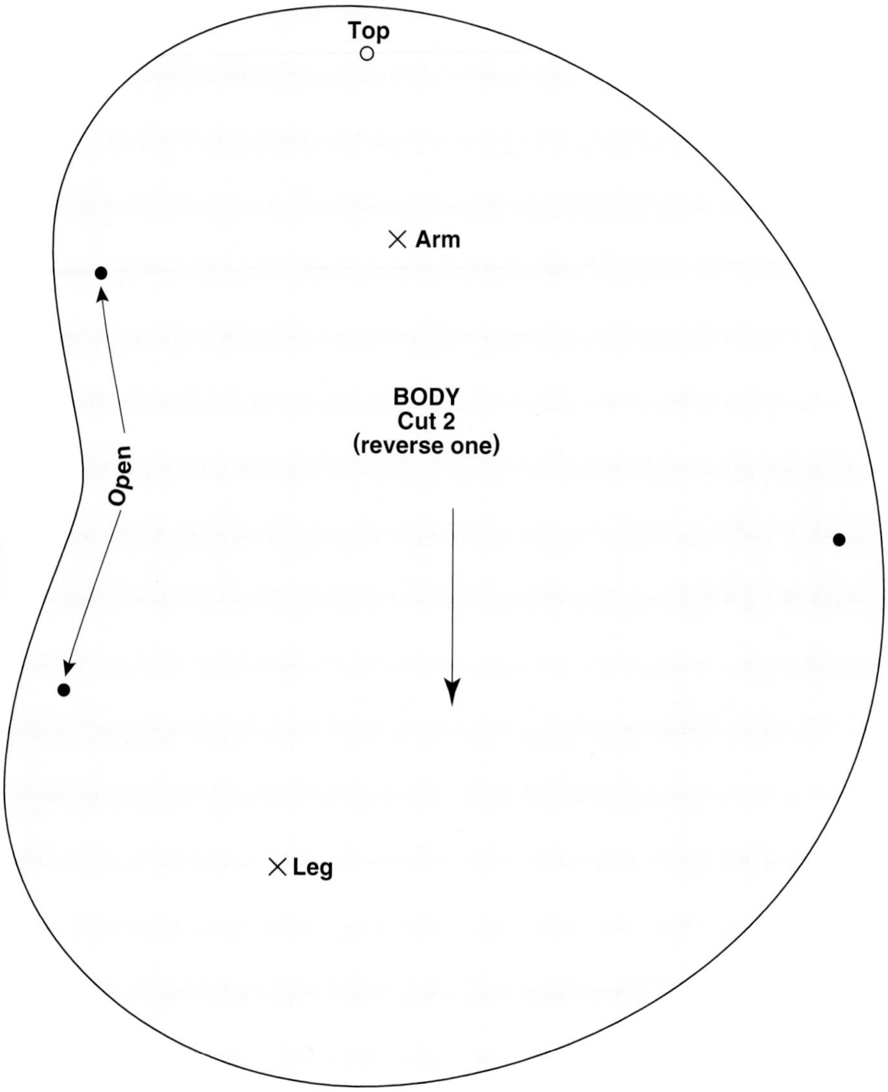

Top

✕ **Arm**

BODY
Cut 2
(reverse one)

Open

✕ **Leg**

splendid hardanger stocking

As shown on page 96, stocking measures 18½×11¾ inches.

Materials

Fabrics
25×18-inch piece of 20-count white Jobelan fabric

8×14-inch piece of 20-count white Jobelan fabric

½ yard of 45-inch-wide lightweight white twill fabric

½ yard of fusible knit interfacing

¼ yard of 45-inch-wide forest green cotton fabric

⅛ yard of red polyester or rayon jacquard

Threads
#5 and #8 white pearl cotton

003 Kreinik red #4 braid

009 Kreinik green #4 braid

Sewing threads: white and red

Supplies
Needle; embroidery hoop

5 yards of ⅛-inch-wide green satin ribbon

9 red seed beads; tracing paper

Water-soluble fabric marking pen

Tailors' chalk pencil

Instructions

Tape or zigzag edges of Jobelan to prevent fraying. To begin stocking front, measure 6½ inches from top and 3 inches in from left edge of 25×18-inch piece of fabric. Using #5 pearl cotton, begin first vertical row of four-sided backstitches there. For stitches, refer to diagrams, *pages 127 and 128.*

Work all vertical and horizontal rows of four-sided backstitches. Referring to chart, *pages 126–127,* work basic Hardanger candy canes, wreaths, stars, trees, flowers, and gingerbread men using satin stitches and #5 pearl cotton. When satin stitch designs are completed, add red backstitch stripes to candy canes, green lazy daisies and red straight stitch star "flowers" to wreaths, green eyelets to stars, green and red straight stitch star "ornaments" and red treetop star to trees, red cross-stitches to flowers, green cross-stitch eyes, red backstitch mouth, and green backstitch "icing" trim to gingerbread men. Work red and green lazy daisy leaves and straight stitch star "flowers" in partial squares along curved edges. Sew three red beads down front of gingerbread men for buttons.

Cut nine 2×2-inch squares of red fabric. Press under ⅛ inch along all edges. Using an appliqué stitch, hand-sew one red square to each unstitched square on stocking front.

Thread needle with green ribbon. Thread ribbon under horizontal and vertical rows of four-sided backstitches. Weave ribbon top to bottom and left to right, alternating horizontal and vertical rows. Leave 1-inch-long tails extending beyond each row.

Trace stocking outline, *pages 126–127,* onto tracing paper; cut out. Position tracing paper pattern atop stitchery, leaving approximately ⅝ inch between stitches and pattern along left and right edges. Trace around pattern using fabric marking pen. Stitch around stocking perimeter just inside marked outline. Cut out along outline; set stocking front aside.

For stitched cuff front, use 8×14-inch piece of Jobelan fabric and refer to chart. Measure 2½ inches in from 14-inch-long top edge and 2½ inches in from 8-inch-long left edge; begin stitching kloster blocks there. Use one ply of #5 pearl cotton to complete all kloster blocks and buttonhole edge around bottom of design. Work eyelets alternating green and red braid; give each a gentle tug to open hole.

Zigzag both edges of cuff as indicated on chart. Cut and remove threads between kloster blocks. Thread needle with one ply of #8 pearl cotton; wrap remaining threads, making divided wrapped bars with dove's eyes. Trim fabric along bottom, close to stitching.

Prewash white twill and green cotton fabrics. Soak interfacing in warm water for 10 minutes to relax fabric and remove excess fusing adhesive. Lay stocking front right side up atop adhesive side of interfacing and doubled thickness of twill fabric. Cut out interfacing and twill fabric to match stocking front. Fuse interfacing to wrong side of stocking front, following manufacturer's instructions.

Layer stocking front between right sides of twill pieces. Using zipper foot and shortened stitch length, join the pieces using an approximate ½-inch seam allowance. Sew alongside stitching on straight side edges. Turn stocking right side out and check seamline; adjust if necessary. Turn

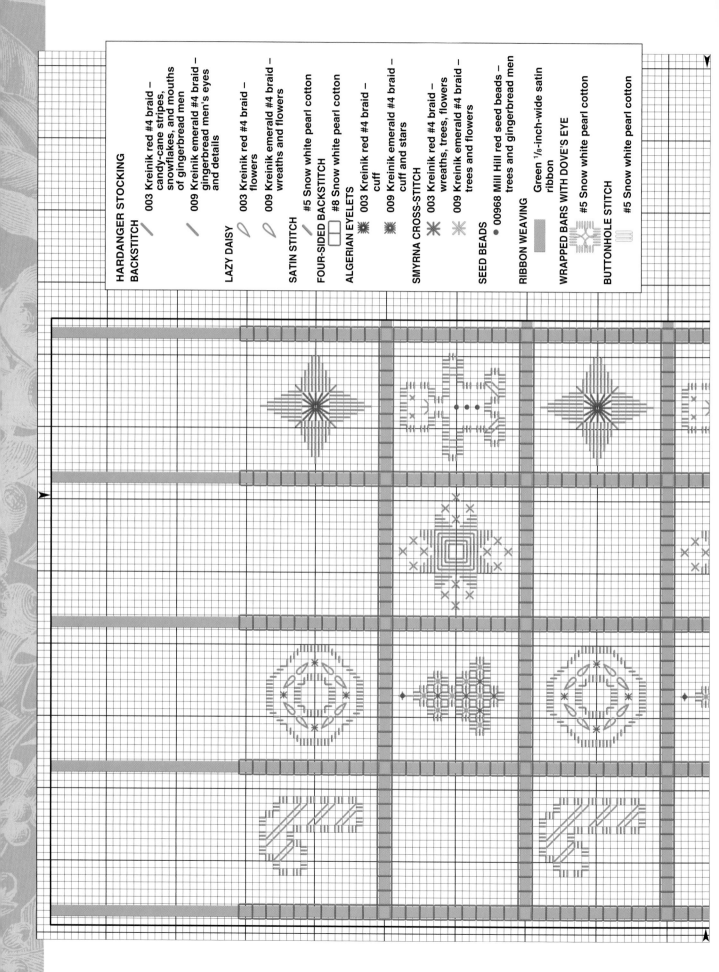

HARDANGER STOCKING

BACKSTITCH

003 Kreinik red #4 braid – candy-cane stripes, snowflakes, and mouths of gingerbread men

009 Kreinik emerald #4 braid – gingerbread men's eyes and details

LAZY DAISY

003 Kreinik red #4 braid – flowers

009 Kreinik emerald #4 braid – wreaths and flowers

SATIN STITCH

#5 Snow white pearl cotton

FOUR-SIDED BACKSTITCH

#8 Snow white pearl cotton

ALGERIAN EYELETS

003 Kreinik red #4 braid – cuff

009 Kreinik emerald #4 braid – cuff and stars

SMYRNA CROSS-STITCH

003 Kreinik red #4 braid – wreaths, trees, flowers

009 Kreinik emerald #4 braid – trees and flowers

SEED BEADS

• 00968 Mill Hill red seed beads – trees and gingerbread men

RIBBON WEAVING

Green 1/8-inch-wide satin ribbon

WRAPPED BARS WITH DOVE'S EYE

#5 Snow white pearl cotton

BUTTONHOLE STITCH

#5 Snow white pearl cotton

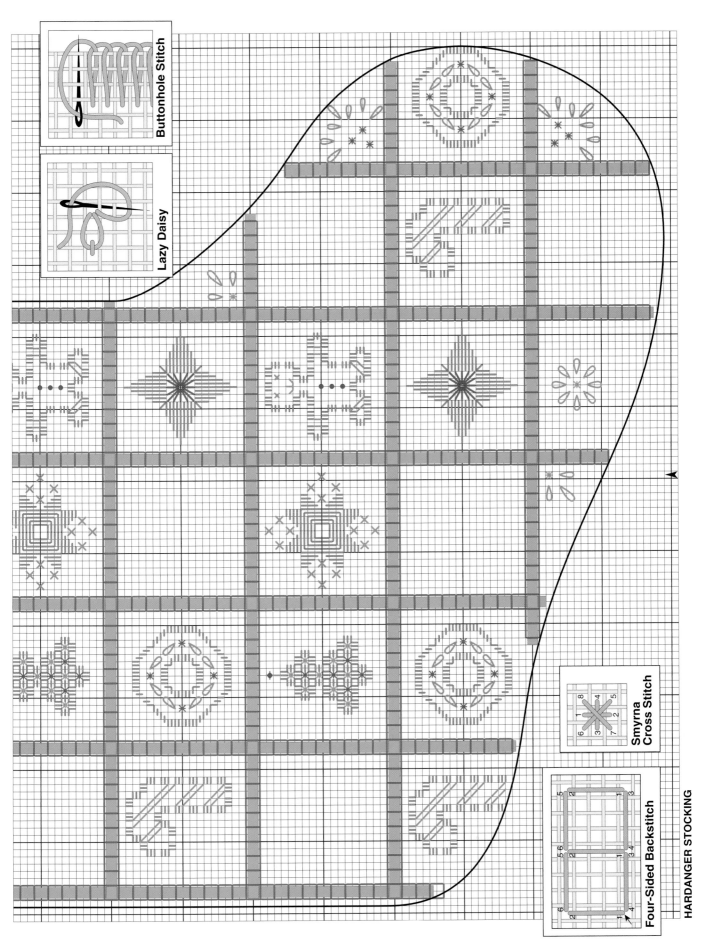

Buttonhole Stitch

Lazy Daisy

Smyrna
Cross Stitch

Four-Sided Backstitch

HARDANGER STOCKING

127

splendid hardanger stocking — *continued*

stocking wrong side out once again; trim seams to ¼ inch. Serge or zigzag seams to reduce bulk.

For cuff front lining, cut two pieces of green fabric slightly larger than Hardanger cuff piece. Layer green fabric with right sides facing. Pin Hardanger, wrong side up, atop green fabric. On green fabric, mark Hardanger cuff bottom outline using chalk pencil. Using tiny machine stitches, sew along outline. Trim seam allowance to ⅛ inch; trim and clip corners. Turn right side out; press. Pin Hardanger cuff, right side up, atop green cuff lining; trim top and sides of lining to match.

For cuff back, cut 7×9¼-inch piece of white twill. Fold in half to measure 3½×9¼ inches; press. Pin lined cuff front to cuff back, right sides facing and raw edges matching. Sew side seams; zigzag.

Place cuff inside stocking, matching fronts and backs, with right side of cuff facing wrong side of stocking. Sew cuff to stocking; finish seam. Turn cuff out and press.

For hanging loop, cut a 1×8-inch-long strip of green fabric. Sew long sides together using a ¼-inch seam allowance; trim seam and turn right side out. Match ends and tack to inside of stocking along seam, allowing loop to extend 1½ inches beyond top of stocking.

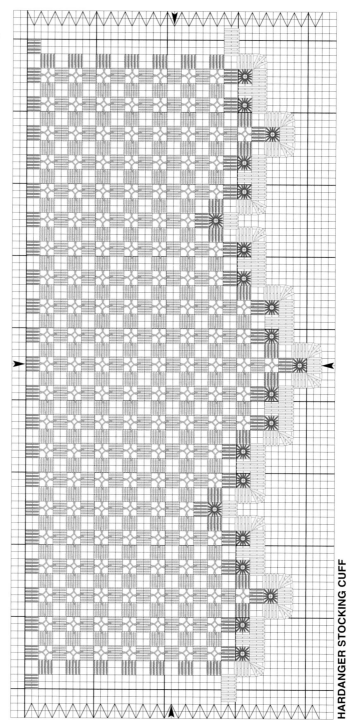

HARDANGER STOCKING CUFF

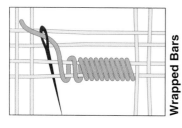

Wrapped Bars

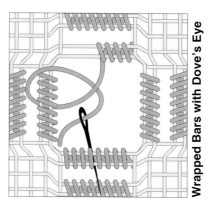

Wrapped Bars with Dove's Eye

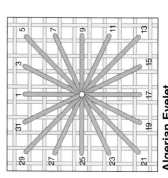

Algerian Eyelet

bear-paw quilt

As shown on page 97, quilt measures 70½×84½ inches.

Materials

2¾ yards of 45-inch-wide red
  cotton fabric
5¾ yards of 45-inch-wide
  white fabric
5½ yards of 45-inch-wide
  muslin backing
81×96-inch piece of quilt batting
9 yards of white bias binding
Cardboard or plastic for templates
Graph paper
Sewing and quilting thread

Instructions

The quilt consists of thirty
10-inch pieced blocks and
20 setting blocks set together
on point. Pieced blocks are
arranged in five rows of six
blocks each. The top piecing
includes 18 side triangles and four
corner triangles.

CUTTING SETTING BLOCKS:
Make a template for a 10-inch
square. (Templates for setting
blocks and setting triangles are
finished size.) Add ¼-inch seam
allowances to all sides when cutting.
Cut 20 white cotton squares.

For side and corner triangles,
cut square template in half
diagonally; label one triangle
"side." Cut other piece in half
again; label one triangle "corner."
Cut 18 side triangles and four
corner triangles. *Note:* Cut side

triangles with long side on straight
of grain and corner triangles with
short side on straight of grain.

CUTTING PIECED BLOCKS:
Using full-size pattern diagram,
below, make templates for A–C
pieces from cardboard or plastic,
adding ¼-inch seam allowances
all around; cut out. To use
templates, draw around them with
pencil on wrong side of fabric.
Note: Cutting instructions are for
one block. Amounts in ()s are for
cutting 30 pieced blocks. From
white fabric cut 24 (720) A, four
(120) B, and four (120) C pieces.
From red fabric, cut 24 (720) A
and four (120) B pieces.

PIECED BLOCK ASSEMBLY: Sew
white B triangle to red B triangle
to form square. Join six white A
triangles to six red A pieces

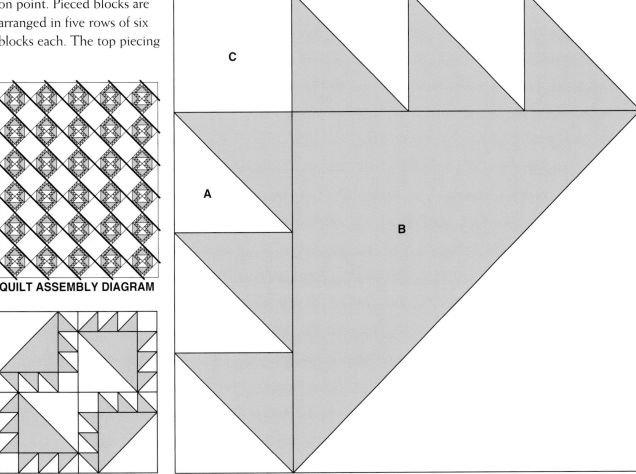

QUILT ASSEMBLY DIAGRAM

PIECED BLOCK DIAGRAM   **BEAR-PAW QUILT–FULL-SIZE PATTERNS**

bear-paw quilt — *continued*

similarly to form six small squares. Sew the squares together into two strips of three squares each. Sew one strip to one red side of the large square, red edges together. Add white C piece to the red end of the second strip and sew to other red side of square. Make

three more squares. Sew four squares together to make pieced block. Make 30 pieced blocks.

QUILT ASSEMBLY: Lay out blocks according to quilt assembly diagram shown on *page 129*. Stitch quilt together in diagonal rows, then stitch rows together.

FINISHING: Cut muslin yardage in half across width; sew the long edges together using ½-inch seam allowances. Piece the batting to fit and sandwich between the backing and the quilt top. Baste the layers together in several directions across the quilt to hold; quilt as desired. Bind the raw edges with bias binding.

nature lover's candles and leaves

As shown on pages 98–99.

Materials
Candle wax
Hammer; chisel or screwdriver
Small pail; old tin can
Hot plate or stove
Old saucepan
For Candles
Candle wicking
1-inch dowel or broomstick for
    hanging
For Leaves
Natural leaves; waxed paper

Instructions
Break wax into small pieces using hammer and chisel. Place wax into old tin can and place can in water in saucepan. Water should be at least ⅓ the depth of the pan. Place pan over low to medium heat. Water will bubble and melt wax in can. NEVER put wax directly on the burner.

After the wax is melted, remove the can and the saucepan from

the stove and place it on a covered surface.

Fill pail at least ¾ full with very cold water.

Cut a piece of candle wicking twice the length of desired candle plus 6 inches. Holding wicking in middle, dip wick into hot wax then into cold water. (At first, little wax seems to stay on wicking, but after dipping a few times, candles will start to form.) By holding wick in

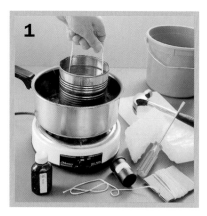

Dip candle wicking into melted wax by holding the wicking in the center.

Repeat, dipping back and forth between candle wax and cold water until desired thickness of candle is obtained.

Hang candles over a suspended dowel or broomstick until completely dry.

the middle, you create two candles. Be sure to keep candles separated while dipping. Repeat, dipping candles back and forth from wax to water until the

desired thickness is obtained. Hang candles over a suspended dowel or broomstick until dry.

To make Hand-Dipped Leaves, choose leaves that are complete

and in good shape. They need not be dry. Holding leaf by stem, dip leaf into hot wax. Suspend in the air for about 30 seconds. Lay on waxed paper to dry.

tinsel and hydrangea topiary

As shown on page 100, topiary stands 14 inches tall.

Materials

Terra-cotta pot in desired size
Old pail
Water
Oil-based silver spray paint
4 large hydrangea flower
    blossoms on long stems, dried
Florist's foam block to fit inside pot
1 yard of ¾-inch-wide silver ribbon
Florist's wire
Spanish and sphagnum moss

Instructions

For marbleized pot, fill pail half full with cold water. Spray silver paint on top of the water. Submerge clay pot in the water and pull back up through paint. Allow the pot to dry thoroughly. Repeat if necessary to achieve the desired effect.

For hydrangea arrangement, spray paint hydrangea blossoms silver; allow to dry. Set aside.

Fit the foam block into the silver-painted pot. Group the

blossoms together with one slightly higher than the others; wire stems together below the blossoms. Push stems into foam block until bottom of blossoms are approximately 4 inches above top edge of pot.

Make a bow from ribbon and wire to stems at base of blossoms. Fill the pot with Spanish moss. Arrange sphagnum moss on top.

bird napkin ring

As shown on page 100, napkin ring measures approximately 3×4½ inches, excluding ring to hold napkin.

Materials

Small reproduction bird print, cut
    to approximately 3×4 inches
3×4-inch piece of heavyweight art
    paper, in color to blend with
    background of bird print
Crafts glue
24 inches of silver tinsel garland
Hot-glue gun
Hot glue

Instructions

Trim the bird print carefully around bird and leaf detail as desired, making sure the print still measures at least 2×3 inches.

Glue the print to the art paper using crafts glue. Trim the art paper around the print, leaving the borders as desired around the edges of the print.

Trim the fringe on the garland to ½ inch. Glue the garland around the back of the print, allowing the fringe to show from the front.

Using the remainder of the garland, form a 1½-inch-diameter loop on the back of the print to hold the napkin; hot-glue the ends securely in place.

country patchwork stocking

As shown on page 101, finished stocking measures 16½ inches long.

Materials

Tracing paper

Template plastic or cardboard

Water-soluble marking pen

9×9-inch piece of 18-count beige-gray Davosa evenweave fabric

6×18-inch piece of dark burgundy fabric

¼ yard of assorted burgundy print cotton fabrics

⅛ yard of assorted dark green print cotton fabrics

¼ yard of assorted ecru cotton fabrics or select areas from embroidered garments, handkerchiefs, and doilies

18×24-inch piece of muslin

12×18-inch piece of cotton quilt batting

12×18-inch piece of desired backing fabric

Threads to match fabrics

Embroidery hoop

Embroidery and crewel needles

Deep garnet (DMC 902) cotton embroidery floss

#3 Beige-gray (DMC 640) pearl cotton

⅔ yard of piping cord; 16 assorted ½-inch-diameter buttons

Instructions

Trace pattern pieces, *pages 134–135,* enlarging stocking shape; cut out. Cut prairie point and triangle patterns from template material. Trace around cuff and toe patterns onto evenweave fabric using marking pen, keeping pattern pieces on straight of grain. Mark seam lines; do not cut out.

Cut 11 prairie point squares from a dark burgundy print fabric. From another burgundy print, cut two hanging loops and one 1×24-inch strip for piping.

For each triangle-pieced block, you will need two matching colored triangles and two matching ecru triangles. From burgundy and dark green fabrics, cut a total of 72 triangles, 36 of each color, in pairs of matching fabrics. From assorted ecru fabrics, cut a total of 72 triangles.

For striped blocks, cut 1×20-inch strips as follows: three from assorted burgundy fabrics, three from assorted dark green fabrics, and six from assorted ecru fabrics.

Cut two stocking shapes from muslin for lining and one stocking shape each from cotton batting and backing fabric.

Sew pieces together with right sides facing, using ¼-inch seam allowances unless otherwise indicated. Press all seams open.

To piece triangle block, sew a colored triangle and an ecru triangle together along one short edge to form a larger triangle (see diagram, *opposite);* make two, matching fabrics. Sew larger triangles together along the long edge to complete the block. Make 36 blocks.

To piece the striped blocks, join three 1×20-inch strips together along the long edges as follows: sew one dark green strip to each side of an ecru strip, one burgundy strip to each side of an

ecru strip, one ecru strip to each side of a dark green strip, and one ecru strip to each side of a burgundy strip. Cut the striped pieces into ten 2-inch-wide blocks.

Arrange blocks in nine rows of eight blocks each, alternating striped and triangle-pieced blocks and referring to diagram, *opposite,* for placement. Four striped blocks will be leftover. Sew blocks into rows, then sew rows together to complete pieced fabric.

Trace a second stocking pattern onto tracing paper, omitting the cuff and toe and adding ¼-inch seams to edges. This is the

patchwork front pattern.

Position patchwork front pattern even with the top edge of the pieced fabric. Trace around the shape and cut out.

Cross-stitch name or initials on cuff if desired, using the alphabet, *opposite,* and three plies of deep garnet floss. Work beige-gray running stitches in grid pattern over cuff and toe as shown on the chart, *opposite.* Cut out both shapes. Zigzag stitch the edges to prevent them from raveling.

To assemble stocking front, press one prairie-point square in half on diagonal, then press in half again, matching folded edges. Make a total of 11 prairie points. Referring to photograph, *page 101*, position four prairie points along top edge of pieced stocking front and three along toe edge, slightly overlapping them and placing points facing toward center of stocking. Baste in place.

Center cording lengthwise on wrong side of piping strip. Fold fabric around cording, raw edges even. Use zipper foot to sew through both fabric layers close to cording. Cut self-covered piping into two 9-inch-long pieces and one 6-inch-long piece. Sew one long piece to top edge of pieced stocking front and short piece to toe edge. Trim excess piping. Sew remaining piece of piping to top edge of cuff; press seam allowances to inside. Referring to photograph, pin remaining prairie points to wrong side of cuff along top edge. Topstitch in place on seam line between piping and cuff. Sew toe and cuff to pieced stocking front.

To assemble stocking, baste batting to the wrong side of stocking front. Sew button to center of each striped block; tie center of each triangle-pieced block using pearl cotton thread. With right sides facing, sew stocking front to backing (⅝-inch

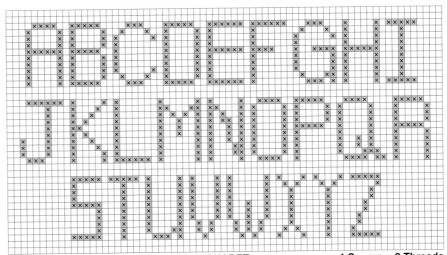

COUNTRY PATCHWORK STOCKING ALPHABET　　　　**1 Square = 3 Threads**

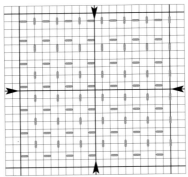

COUNTRY PATCHWORK STOCKING CUFF AND TOE
1 Square = 3 Threads

seam), leaving top edge open. Clip curves, turn stocking right side out; press.

Sew lining shapes together along curved edge, using a ⅝-inch seam allowance. Trim seam; press under ¼ inch along top edge. Slip lining inside stocking; pin to stocking along top edges.

For hanging loop, join long edges of strips. Turn right side out; fold in half widthwise. Run gathering stitches ½ inch from raw edges; pull to gather loop end. Slip end between lining and stocking at back seam. Slip-stitch lining to stocking top edge, securing loop.

COUNTRY PATCHWORK
ASSEMBLY DIAGRAM

PATCHWORK STOCKING		
ANCHOR	**DMC**	
897	☒	902 Garnet
RUNNING STITCH		
903	╱	640 Beige-gray #3 pearl cotton – background

TRIANGLE
BLOCK

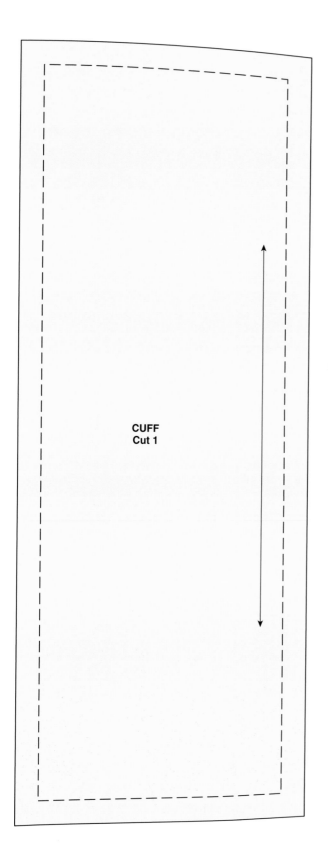

CUFF
Cut 1

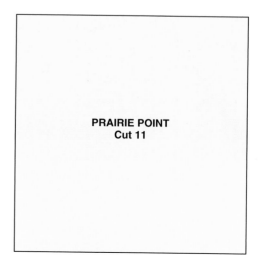

PRAIRIE POINT
Cut 11

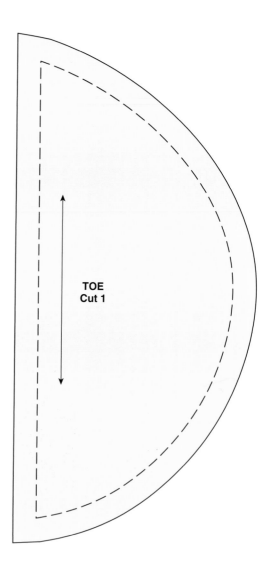

TOE
Cut 1

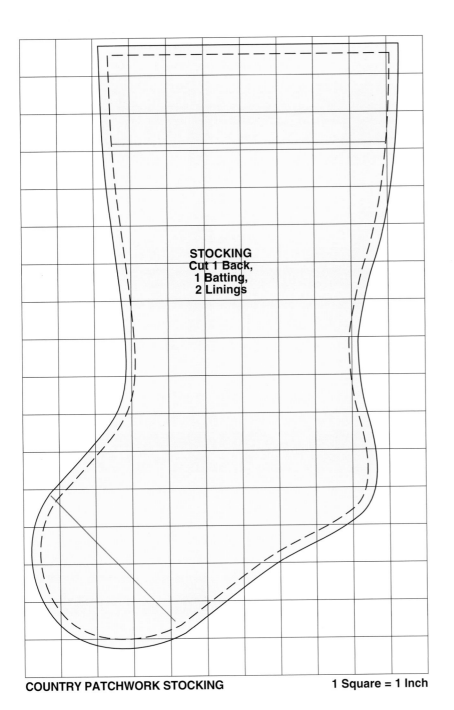

STOCKING
Cut 1 Back,
1 Batting,
2 Linings

COUNTRY PATCHWORK STOCKING

1 Square = 1 Inch

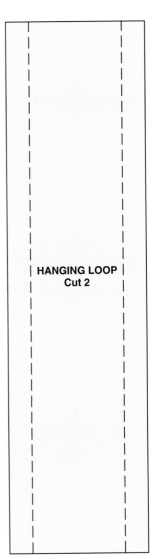

HANGING LOOP
Cut 2

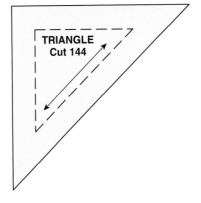

TRIANGLE
Cut 144

vintage music cases

As shown on page 102.

Materials

Old suitcase with metal hardware
   and leather trim
Black acrylic paint
Gold metallic spray paint
Artists' paintbrushes: 1- and
   ½-inch flat
Paintbrushes: 2- and 3-inches-wide
Old sheet music printed on
   medium to thick paper stock
Scissors or crafts knife
Mod Podge decoupage medium

Instructions

Spray all hardware gold. Allow some overspray onto body of suitcase or trim if necessary to get maximum coverage; let dry.

Paint leather trim black, working carefully around the hardware. In addition, paint any visible inside edges. Allow paint to dry.

Plan general placement of music, creating a random pattern by positioning music at different angles. Begin next to black trim. Using scissors or knife, cut angled pieces to fit. If suitcase surface is textured, it may help to brush medium onto suitcase before applying sheet music. Apply a thin coat of decoupage medium to the back of the first piece. Smooth piece onto suitcase, butting cut edge against black trim. Smooth out wrinkles. When working around the odd-shaped trim or hardware, lap music over hardware, press firmly along edges, allow to dry, and trim away overlap with knife. Continue applying pieces of sheet music, layering as desired and working toward center.

When music is dry, spread two coats of decoupage medium over the entire suitcase, avoiding the hardware and letting it dry between coats.

christmas rose chair

As shown on page 103.

Materials

Old or antique chair; sandpaper
Acrylic wood primer; soft rag
Acrylic paints; paintbrushes
Small natural cosmetic sponge
Stiff ½-inch flat paintbrush
Crafts knife; acrylic clear varnish
Gold Rub n buff highlighting
   medium

Instructions

Prepare surfaces, if needed, by lightly sanding and priming wood. Choose smooth surfaces to be painted deep red, such as front and back surfaces of legs and front and back surfaces of vertical chair back pieces. These surfaces will be painted last.

When creating multi-colored relief sponge painting, reserve darkest colors for deepest crevices, layering colors from darkest to lightest, and using less paint for each layer. End with lightest color on most raised surface.

To paint relief areas on chair, use a sponging technique. Use a palette of deep red, purple, pink, and yellow ochre, or an area like this rose. Use the very deep red for overall base color. Paint carved relief areas according to Step 1, *opposite*. To blend and highlight colors, see Steps 2 and 3, *opposite*. Do not overwork. Allow the paint to dry.

To paint an area like the leaves, see Step 4, *opposite*.

For remaining surfaces, paint deep blue and sponge with thinned turquoise, using techniques as for relief areas; allow to dry. Next, paint the previously reserved areas deep red. Allow paint to dry thoroughly.

Follow Step 5, *below*, to spatter speckles on desired areas.

Seal the chair with varnish. Using finger, very lightly apply a small amount of Gold Rub n buff to the most raised areas. Rub off with a soft rag. Seal the chair a second time.

Use deep and vibrant purples to paint the deep crevices. Apply these two colors quickly without allowing them to dry. The colors will somewhat blend together.

Before totally dry, but still tacky, use a clean water-dampened sponge and very lightly blend the purple and red together just enough to eliminate harsh brush strokes.

To highlight raised areas, use a sponge and thinned pink paint to gently dab on soft highlights. Repeat with a light ochre color. Do not overpaint.

Paint leaf areas with dark green, using dark blue for deep crevices; blend using a sponge. After dry, apply a light layer of turquoise and a light layer of lime green for highlights.

To splatter-paint surfaces, use a stiff, coarse paintbrush and deep red and metallic gold paints. Dip brush into one paint at a time. Use a crafts knife to scrape across the bristles.

glittering goblets

As shown on pages 104–105.

Materials
Clear crystal goblets
White crafts glue
Small bowl or dish
Golden glitter
Food coloring
Floating candles

Instructions
Wash and dry goblets. Carefully cover rim of each goblet with white crafts glue. Fill a small bowl or dish with glitter. Press goblet rims into glitter. Let dry.

Carefully fill goblets with colored water and float a candle in each.

the stately evergreen

*S*urely the focal
point of holiday
decorating, the grand
Christmas tree takes
center stage in this
project-packed chapter.
Whether you cherish
romantic trims or are
drawn to a natural
look, you'll find
dozens of projects to
make, love, and share.

country holiday ornaments

Leftover buttons from Grandma's button box along with scraps of wood and fabric make the irresistible decorations on this charming country Christmas tree. Button Candy Canes and Faux Wooden Candles hang amid painted Wooden Heart and Star Ornaments. A calico fabric Hearts-and-Stars Garland, accented with buttons, is draped among the branches while simple Envelope Ornaments hold sweet surprises. A Button Star Topper crowns our holiday tree. The instructions and patterns for all of these decorations begin on page 142.

hearts-and-stars garland

As shown on pages 140–141, finished garland measures approximately 2⅔ yards long.

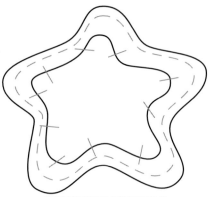

STITCHING EXAMPLE

Materials

8×10-inch piece of template plastic
⅛ yard each of three 45-inch-wide red calicos
⅛ yard each of three 45-inch-wide gold calicos
⅛ yard each of three 45-inch-wide blue calicos
⅛ yard of 45-inch-wide green calico
Erasable fabric marker
⅛ yard of fleece; fabric glue
Red, blue, green, and gold cotton embroidery floss
5½ yards of ecru carpet thread
Assorted buttons
Tapestry and sewing needles

Instructions

For ornaments, trace pattern outlines, *right,* onto template plastic. Draw a freehand line around perimeter of each, adding ⅜ to ⅝ inch all around. Cut out shapes along second outlines. Draw around templates onto fabrics, making six pairs of each of the four shapes on a variety of fabrics; cut out. From fleece, cut six of each shape.

Trim templates to original outlines and trace around these smaller templates on paper side of iron-on adhesive, making twelve of each shape. Fuse two of each shape to each of six fabrics. Cut out. From remaining fabric, tear fourteen ¾×4-inch strips.

Following manufacturer's instructions, fuse smaller hearts onto larger hearts; smaller stars onto larger stars of same shape. Make two of each color and print

combination, so when sewn together, fronts and backs match.

Use one ply of floss in desired color to work straight stitches around edge of smaller shapes as shown on diagram, *above right.*

Layer appropriate fleece shape between each matching pair of fabric shapes. Use one ply of floss to work a running stitch around perimeter ⅛ inch from edge. Glue button to center of each side.

For garland, tie a small loop in one end of carpet thread. Thread other end into tapestry needle. Thread a button onto needle, push it to the loop, and secure

with a half knot. Thread on three more buttons and half knot each in place 1 to 1½ inches apart. Thread an ornament, pushing needle through center ¼ inch from top. Secure with a half knot 1½ inches from last button. Continue threading four buttons and an ornament onto thread until all have been used.

Tie a fabric strip around thread between second and third buttons between each shape.

wooden heart and star ornaments

As shown on pages 140–141.

Materials for one of each

Drawing paper; pencil
10×14-inch piece of ¼-inch plywood
12×16-inch piece of ½-inch pine
Red, gold, and blue acrylic paint
½- and 1-inch-wide flat paintbrushes
Assorted buttons
24×½-inch torn strips of red and blue plaid fabrics
Hot-glue gun; hot glue
Medium grit sandpaper
Drill and ⅛-inch drill bit; bandsaw

Instructions

Use patterns, *opposite*, as a guide to draw a 2¾×2⅞-inch small star, 4⅜×3¾-inch large star, 4⅜×2¾-inch narrow heart, and 6¾×4¼-inch wide heart pattern. Or, use a commercial copier to enlarge patterns to approximate sizes; cut out. Draw around each pattern onto ½-inch pine.

Cut the patterns freehand, trimming ¼ to 1 inch from each; trace on ¼-inch plywood. Cut out all pieces using the bandsaw. Sand edges lightly.

Paint shapes, using contrasting colors on pieces with same shape. When paint is dry, sand all edges once more for a worn look.

Glue plywood shapes atop pine. Hot-glue a button to center front of each ornament. Drill a ⅛-inch hole through each ornament near top. Thread a fabric strip through hole; tie ends to make a hanging loop.

button star topper

As shown on page 141.

Materials

Drawing paper; pencil
12×18-inch piece of ¼-inch plywood
Red and gold acrylic paint; small flat paintbrush; 140–150 buttons
36 inches of 18-gauge wire
Hot-glue gun; hot glue
Medium-grit sandpaper
Drill and ⅛-inch drill bit; bandsaw

Instructions

Use large star pattern, *opposite*, as a guide to draw a 10½×9-inch star pattern. Or, use a commercial copier to enlarge the pattern to approximate size; cut out. Draw around pattern on plywood. Cutting pattern freehand, trim 1 to 1¼ inches from edges and draw around pattern on plywood again. Cut out stars using bandsaw. Sand all edges lightly.

Paint large star red and small star gold. Sand edges for a worn look. Glue small star atop large star.

Drill two holes, ½ inch apart, about 4½ inches from top point of star. Cut wire length in half and thread both pieces through holes with ends extending out back (for securing ornament to tree).

Glue buttons to front of small star in an overlapping pattern.

faux wooden candles

As shown on pages 140–141, candles measure 4 inches tall.

Materials for each candle

4-inch-long piece of
⁵⁄₁₆-inch-diameter dowel
Pencil sharpener; drill and ³⁄₃₂-inch drill bit; ½-inch flat paintbrush
Acrylic paint in desired color
Medium grit sandpaper; thick white crafts glue
1-inch-long piece of string
Tree clip-on candleholder

Instructions

Sharpen one end of dowel with a pencil sharpener, leaving a ⅛-inch-diameter flat surface at tip. (Or, leave top flat to give appearance of a candle that has been burned.)

Drill a ³⁄₃₂-inch hole in top of dowel. Paint; allow to dry. Sand lightly. Glue end of string into hole. Place candle in candleholder.

clever envelope ornaments

As shown in a variety of sizes on page 141.

Materials

Small manilla clasp envelopes
Paper punch; thin twine
Assorted buttons; colorful gift wrap
Shredded ribbon; candy

Instructions

Cut the flap off the envelope, if desired. On the side of the envelope that is (or would be) under the flap, punch a small hole near each corner, ¼ inch from the top edge. Cut three pieces of twine, each about the length of the envelope. Tie one end of one piece of twine through each hole. Tie two buttons onto each strand of twine, spacing the buttons at random. Tie the ends of the twine strands together in a knot.

Punch two more holes, close together, in the back of the envelope near the top center and thread remaining piece of twine through hole. Knot ends together to make a hanging loop. Fill bag as desired.

button candy canes

As shown on pages 140–141, candy cane measures 5 inches long.

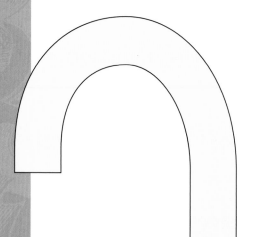

Materials for each ornament

4×6½-inch piece of ¼-inch
    plywood
Red acrylic paint; small paintbrush
Seven ⅝-inch red buttons
Seven ⅝-inch cream buttons
10-inch-long piece of monofilament
Hot-glue gun; hot glue; medium-grit
    sandpaper; tracing paper
Drill and ⅛-inch drill bit; bandsaw

Instructions

Trace pattern, *left,* onto tracing paper and cut out. Draw around pattern on plywood and cut out using bandsaw. Drill a hole through the top.

Sand cutout lightly; paint red. Sand edges once more for a worn look. Thread monofilament through hole and knot ends to make a hanging loop. Glue buttons to candy cane front, alternating colors and overlapping edges.

music ensemble evergreen

Wrap your tree in pleasing notes and golden instruments for a most harmonious feel. For a closer look at the trims, see the next page.

golden musical instruments

Harps, trumpets, horns, violins, and saxophones make beautiful music and elegant ornaments for your tree. Painted metallic gold, the trims have details made from tiny dowels. The Wooden Melody Garland has a staff of golden cord. The instructions are on pages 148–150.

Sheet music, photocopied, cut, and folded, is transformed into simple yet stunning tree ornaments. String the stars into a garland or let them hang alone for a striking effect. Instructions and patterns are on pages 150–151.

singing star ornaments

golden musical instruments

As shown on pages 145–146, instruments vary from 2½×6½ to 4½×8 inches.

Materials for one set of five

Tracing paper
12×18-inch piece of ¼-inch
  plywood
Bandsaw; drill; ⅛-inch drill bit
Sandpaper
1/16-inch-diameter dowel (for harp
  and violin)
⅛-inch-diameter dowel (for French
  horn, trumpet, and saxophone)
Utility scissors
Thick white crafts glue or hot-glue
  gun and hot glue

Gold spray paint
Five 8-inch-long pieces of gold
  metallic rattail cord

Instructions

Trace the instrument patterns,
below and opposite, onto tracing
paper; cut out. Draw around the
patterns on plywood; transfer

circles. Cut out using a bandsaw.
Drill ⅛-inch holes at circles.
Sand pieces lightly.

Cut dowels into pieces using
dowel lines marked on patterns as
guides. Glue the dowel pieces
onto the instruments as shown on
the patterns.

Spray all pieces gold; allow to
dry. Tie gold cord through the
holes into hanging loops.

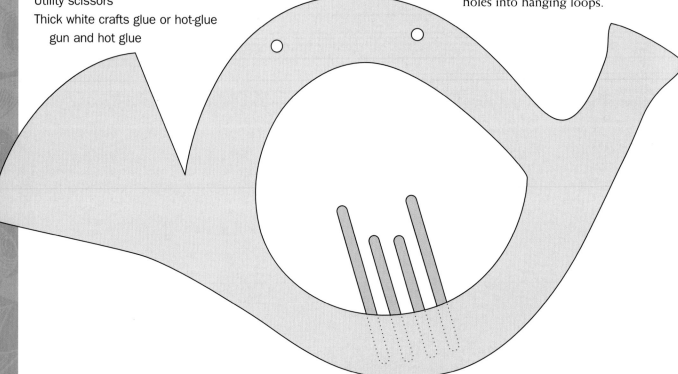

wooden melody garland

As shown on pages 145–146, finished garland measures approximately 8 feet long.

Materials

Tracing paper
1×2-foot sheet of ¼-inch plywood
Bandsaw
Sandpaper

Drill; ⅛-inch drill bit
Black acrylic spray paint
Gold metallic acrylic paint
½-inch paintbrush
45 feet of gold metallic rattail cord

Instructions

Trace musical note pattern, *page 150,*
onto tracing paper; cut out. Draw
around pattern on plywood seven
times; transfer circles for holes.

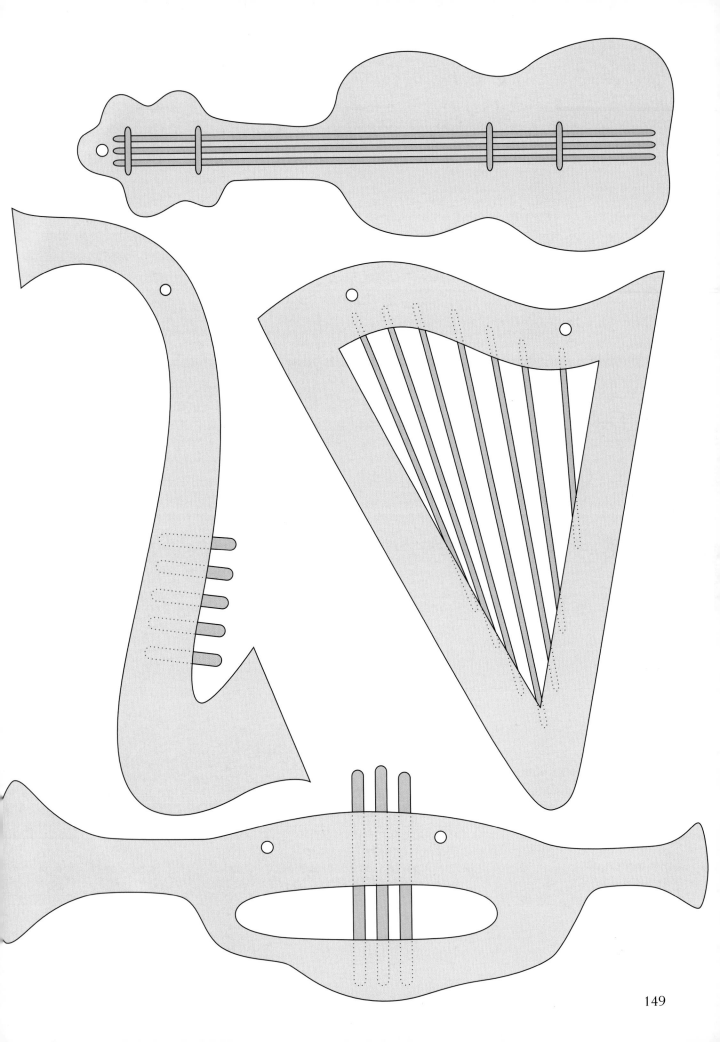

Cut out notes using a bandsaw; sand lightly. Drill ⅛-inch holes at the circles.

Spray notes black. When dry, brush edges lightly with gold and allow to dry.

Cut cord into 9-foot-long pieces. Beginning with first musical note right side up, thread cord piece in and out of the top sets of horizontal holes. Thread a second cord piece through the second set of holes in the same manner. Repeat with the remaining three cord pieces. Next, turn a second note upside down so the round part is at the top and thread it onto the cord pieces in the same manner, sliding on the second note until it is 10 inches from first. Continue threading notes onto cords in the same manner, alternating positions. After all ten notes are threaded and spaced 10 inches apart, knot cord ends together and trim.

singing star ornaments

As shown on page 147, stars vary from 5½×5½ to 9×9 inches.

Materials for one star

Page of sheet music; tracing paper
Lightweight cardboard; ruler
Large sewing needle; knitting
   needle or other scoring stylus

For ornaments

Fine gold cord
6-millimeter gold beads

For garland

⅛-inch hole punch
Red crochet thread; small gold bells

Instructions

Trace star patterns, *opposite,* onto tracing paper; cut out. *Note:* There are three sizes given. Draw around patterns on cardboard, making a template for each star; cut out. Trace around templates onto sheet music, tracing number of stars desired; cut out stars.

Poke a small hole in the center of the star using a needle.

singing star ornaments — *continued*

Referring to pattern, *below,* use the scoring stylus and ruler to score solid lines on the right side of each star. Turn star over; score broken lines.

Fold each point on line scored on front. Turn each star over and fold on the lines scored on back.

For ornaments, thread needle with fine gold cord; pull through tip of one point. Remove the needle and thread ends of cord through one or two gold beads. Knot the ends together to make a hanging loop.

To make a garland, randomly arrange a row of stars in various sizes, overlapping points. Cut off overlapping tips (points). Punch holes in trimmed tips. Using 8-inch-long pieces of crochet thread, tie star tips together through holes, slipping a bell onto one of the thread ends before tying. Pull points together until they touch, and knot the thread.

SINGING STAR ORNAMENTS—PATTERN IN THREE SIZES

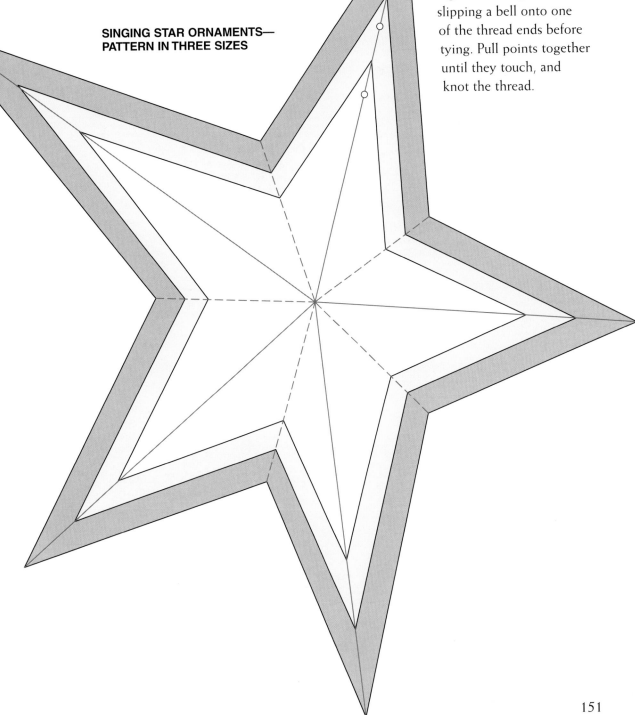

victorian elegance

A charming Christmas of long ago is re-created with our collection of ornaments inspired by exquisite antique trims. Sparkling tinsel, subtle colors, and unlimited embellishments so typical of Victorian times fill our naturally shaped evergreen tree. See the following pages to make this beautiful vision of days gone by.

beaded star ornament

As shown on pages 152–153 and right, ornament measures 3½ inches in diameter. Note: Wired beads are available in a bendable wire strand. They are packaged on spools and sold by the yard at crafts stores.

Antique Ornament

Materials

16 inches of silver wired
    bead strand
12 inches of gold wired
    bead strand
Fine-gauge crafts wire
Assorted small gold beads
Six colored bugle beads
One 5-millimeter-diameter red bead

Instructions

Bend the silver bead strand into a star shape following the star outline pattern, *below*. Cut away the excess bead strand and wire the ends together at the top.

Bend the gold bead strand to form a circle around the star with points of star touching the inside of the circle. Wire the top star point to the circle. Wire each bottom point to the circle, leaving 4-inch-long wire tails.

String two bugle beads and then seven to 10 small gold beads in the desired pattern onto each wire. Bring the wires together and thread a red bead over both wires.

Separate the wires once again; string the remaining gold and colored beads in the established pattern on each wire until only ½ inch of unbeaded wire remains. Bend wire ends up and poke them back through the second bead from bottom to secure in place.

Reproduction Ornament

Attach thread or wire at the top for a hanging loop.

BEADED STAR ORNAMENT

scalloped oval with sunburst

As shown on pages 152–153 and opposite, ornament measures 5¾×7 inches.

Materials

Tracing paper
10×16-inch piece of lightweight posterboard
Scissors with scalloped blades
Spray adhesive
Spray paint: white, hot pink, gold

Non-tarnishing glitter
Thick white crafts glue
Angel card measuring approximately 4½×4½ inches
1×1-inch square of foamcore board
8 inches of gold metallic thread
Bright blue dimensional fabric paint

Instructions

Trace patterns, *right,* onto tracing paper and cut out. Draw around patterns onto posterboard to make two ovals, two sunbursts, and one small star. Cut out posterboard pieces. Cut around edge of each oval using the scallop blade scissors. Glue ovals back to back using spray adhesive. Glue sunbursts back to back in the same manner.

Spray center of oval and upper part of sunburst white. Spray bottom third of oval, points of sunburst, and small star hot pink. Lightly spray top third of oval, center of sunburst, and small star with gold paint. While paint is wet, sprinkle pieces generously with non-tarnishing glitter. Allow to dry.

Glue angel to oval with most of the angel showing above the dotted line indicating top edge of sunburst. Glue foamcore to X on oval. Glue sunburst atop the foamcore piece, matching the top edge to the dotted line on oval. Glue small star to X on sunburst. Add blue paint dots to star.

Pierce hole in the top of the ornament and tie with gold thread for a hanging loop.

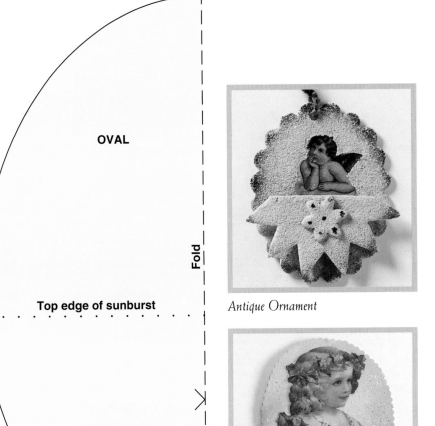

OVAL

Fold

Top edge of sunburst

Antique Ornament

Reproduction Ornament

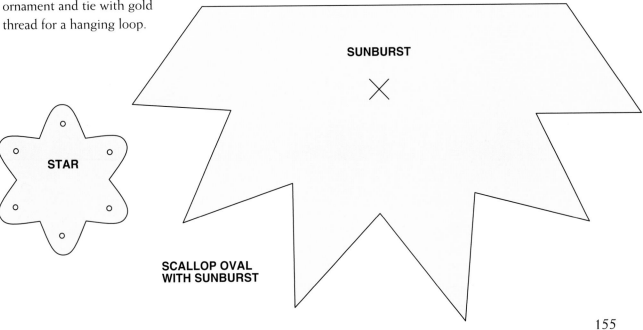

SUNBURST

STAR

**SCALLOP OVAL
WITH SUNBURST**

155

heavenly angel ornament

As shown on pages 152–153 and right, *ornament measures about 4×4½ inches.*

Antique Ornament

Materials

Two 4-inch-diameter lightweight
    posterboard circles
Spray adhesive
3 yards of red crepe paper
    streamer
Clear acrylic spray varnish
Tape
Gold spray paint
12 inches of gold tinsel garland
Brown liquid shoe polish
24-gauge craft wire
Victorian scrap angel or
    reproduction angel card
    measuring about 3½×4 inches
12 inches of gold metallic thread

Instructions

Glue posterboard circles back to back using spray adhesive. Cut crepe paper streamer in half lengthwise. Tape one end of one crepe paper strip to one side of circle at center. Wrap streamer around circle, lapping edges in spiral fashion until the posterboard circle is covered. While wrapping, stretch crepe paper so it is snug but does not bend the circle. Tape end of crepe paper at center when finished.

Spray entire circle with varnish; allow to dry. Next, spray lightly with gold paint.

Trim fringe on tinsel garland to measure ½ inch. Rub brown shoe polish over garland for an antique look; let dry. Cut garland length in half. Poke two tiny holes in center of circle. Hold garland lengths together in the center; wire center to circle front.

Reproduction Ornament

Arrange garland lengths; glue angel card to circle atop the garland.

Poke a small hole in the top of the ornament. Tie gold metallic thread through the hole for a hanging loop.

tinsel heart

As shown on pages 152–153 and opposite, *heart measures 6×7 inches.*

Materials

Tracing paper; pen
8×10-inch piece of corrugated
    cardboard
Straight pins
Narrow-looped silver tinsel garland
Craft wire
One 1-inch-diameter gold
    Christmas ball ornament
Three 1-inch-diameter green
    Christmas ball ornaments
Silver tinsel; gold spray paint
8 inches of silver metallic thread

Instructions

To create heart pattern refer to diagram, *opposite*. Trace pattern onto tracing paper. Lay tracing atop cardboard. Trace firmly over pattern lines using pen, leaving the imprint of pattern in cardboard. Push pins into cardboard every inch along imprint and at the turning or crossing points.

Wind wire tightly around silver tinsel garland in a spiral fashion so garland will hold its shape when it is bent. Following arrows shown on pattern, *right,* begin at A and bend wired garland around pins to B then back to A over and down to B, forming heart shape. Secure ends by twisting them around wired-garland of heart shape.

In same manner, use wired garland for heart center starting at C to D and then attaching to sides for shape as needed.

Secure center at top X with wire. Then wire a gold ball to heart at red X at top of center diamond. Wire a green ball to each remaining red X.

Tie strands of tinsel to bottom point of heart. Spray ornament with gold paint to give it the look of an antique. Tie metallic thread through top of ornament for a hanging loop.

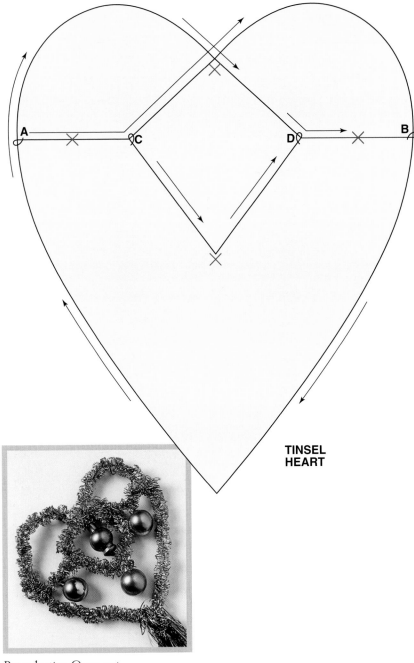

TINSEL HEART

Antique Ornament

Reproduction Ornament

victorian star tree topper

As shown on pages 152 and 158, star measures 11 inches across.

Materials
Graph paper
Two 10½×14-inch pieces of clear 10-count plastic canvas

Eight 12-inch-long silver tinsel stems
Fine-gauge craft wire
15 feet of silver tinsel garland

6×6-inch piece of posterboard
6×12-inch piece of gold floral foil
Red spray paint

victorian star tree topper — *continued*

Instructions

Enlarge star pattern, *below,* onto graph paper and cut out.

Using the star pattern, cut two stars from the 10-count clear plastic canvas. Whipstitch the stars together around the outer edge using the 12-inch-long silver tinsel stems and leaving the star open between the bottom two points.

Using pieces of wire, attach tinsel garland to star front and back, reserving 24 inches of tinsel garland for center star. First wire garland around perimeter of the star, then fill in center. Set the star aside.

Cut a 5-inch-diameter scalloped circle from the posterboard, cutting each scallop to span approximately 1½ inches. Clip 1 inch toward the center of the circle between each scallop.

Cover the front and back of the scalloped posterboard piece with gold foil, cutting slits to match those on the posterboard shape. Using fingers, bend and curve gold foil scallops toward the front of the shape. Spray both sides of shape with red paint; allow to dry.

Trim fringe on 24-inch-long piece of tinsel garland to ½ inch. Loop tinsel into a five-point star; wire together at center to hold shape. Punch two small holes in center of scalloped circle and wire small tinsel star to the

Antique Ornament

Reproduction Ornament

center. Wire scalloped circle to center front of large star. Trim tinsel at star points. Lightly spray star with gold paint.

VICTORIAN STAR TREE TOPPER   **1 Square = 1 Inch**

trumpeting cherub

As shown on pages 152–153 and **opposite,** *ornament measures 5 inches in diameter.*

Materials

Two 4-inch-diameter posterboard circles
Spray adhesive; crafts glue
Silver tinsel garland
White spray paint
1×1-inch square of foamcore
Victorian scrap angel or reproduction angel card, measuring approximately 3½ inches wide
12 inches of silver metallic thread

Instructions

Glue two posterboard circles back to back using spray adhesive. Next, glue silver tinsel garland around front of posterboard circle, overlapping edge of circle approximately ½ inch. Lightly spray tinsel with white paint.

Glue square of foamcore to center front of circle; glue scrap angel to foamcore.

Poke hole in top of ornament. Tie a silver cord through hole for a hanging loop.

Antique Ornament

Reproduction Ornament

diamond tinsel ornament

As shown on pages 152—153 and **below,** *ornament measures about 5½×5½ inches.*

Antique Ornament

Reproduction Ornament

DIAMOND TINSEL ORNAMENT

Materials

Four 12-inch-long
    silver tinsel pipe
    cleaner stems
2 feet of silver tinsel garland
24-gauge craft wire
Four 1-inch-diameter silver
    Christmas ball ornaments
Gold spray paint
Red spray paint
6 inches of silver metallic thread

Instructions

Bend silver tinsel pipe cleaner stems, referring to the pattern, *above right,* into a 4×4-inch square. Add individual cross pieces next, twisting stems around each other, as necessary, to secure in place.

Trim tinsel fringe on garland to measure ½- to ¾-inch long. Wrap garland around tinsel frame. Secure with wire.

Use wire to attach a silver ball to the red Xs at top and center of pattern, referring to photograph, *left,* for placement. Then lightly spray the entire ornament with gold paint to give it the look of an antique.

To "antique" the red balls, dip the remaining silver balls into water then spray them with red paint. Allow to dry. Wire balls to the ornament at red Xs at sides.

Tie a silver thread to the top for a hanging loop.

naturally white-on-white holiday tree

Winter's frosty sparkle is captured on this lovely evergreen dressed in ornaments and garlands of white. Paper candles, beaded crocheted snowflakes, nature's own leaves dipped in shiny white wax are only a few of the elegant ornaments on this already beautiful tree from the forest. For a closer look at each of the ornaments and garlands, and for instructions for each project, turn to pages 162–167.

candle and heart garland

As shown on pages 160–161, each motif measures $4\frac{5}{8} \times 4\frac{3}{8}$ inches.

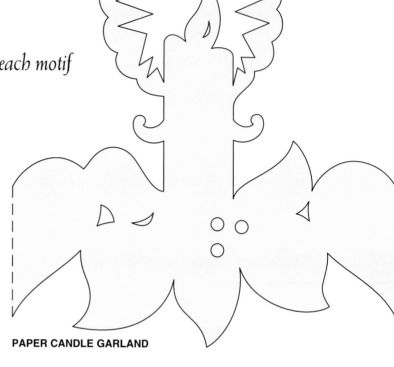

PAPER CANDLE GARLAND

Materials

Tracing paper
#2 pencil
5-inch-wide strip of white butcher
  paper, cut to desired length
Teaspoon
Scherenschnitte scissors or crafts
  knife and cutting mat or old
  magazine
Cellophane tape

Instructions

Trace pattern, *above,* onto tracing paper, using pencil. Place the pencil-sketched side of tracing paper facing white paper strip, centering design between top and bottom edges and aligning one side edge. Using rim of teaspoon, stroke firmly along pencil lines until complete image is transferred.

Accordion fold butcher paper strip at each end of design, using dotted lines on pattern as a guide and keeping top and bottom edges even.

To cut design, use scherenschnitte scissors to cut around outside lines of design. (Be sure not to cut along fold

lines.) Or, tape edges of paper to cutting mat and use crafts knife. Unfold garland and retrace inside cut lines on every repeat. Cut out carefully with scherenschnitte scissors or crafts knife.

To finish, press on the pencil-traced (wrong) side with a warm iron.

162

crocheted snowflakes

Shown on pages 160–161, round ornament has a 5-inch diameter, the six-pointed star measures 5 inches across widest points, and the 12-pointed star measures 6 inches across widest points.
Crochet abbreviations are on page 320.

Materials

Coats Big Ball cotton crochet
   thread, size 30: one ball of white
   will make several ornaments
Size 14 steel crochet hook
Beading needle
Stiffy Fabric Stiffener
Waxed paper; cardboard
Straight pins; paintbrush
One 12-inch length of white satin
   ribbon for each ornament

For 12-Pointed Star Ornament

114 size 3-millimeter pearls
54 size 4-millimeter pearls
54 size 5-millimeter pearls
12 size 6-millimeter pearls
402 silver-lined rochailles beads

For Six-Pointed Star Ornament

90 size 3-millimeter pearls
6 size 4-millimeter pearls
18 size 5-millimeter pearls
582 silver-lined rochailles beads

For Round Ornament

384 size 3-millimeter pearls
512 silver-lined rochailles beads

Instructions

TECHNIQUES: Beaded Chain
Stitch (bch): Bring up a bead, yo
behind the bead and draw
through lp on hook.
   Pearled Chain Stitch (pch):
Bring up a pearl, yo behind the
pearl and draw through lp on hook.
   Beaded Single Crochet (bsc):
Insert hook into stitch, bring up a
bead, yo behind the bead, yo and

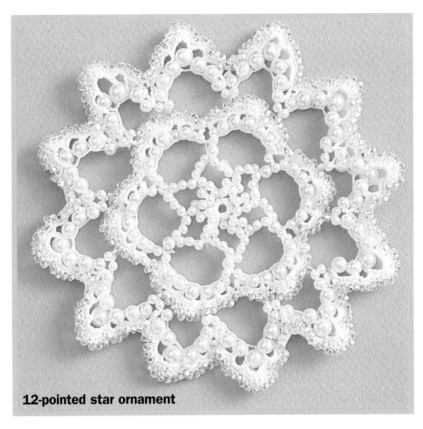

12-pointed star ornament

draw through both lps on hook.
   Pearled Single Crochet (psc):
Work as for bsc using a pearl.
   Right Thread (RT): Thread
running through pearl or bead on
right-hand side.
   Left Thread (LT): Thread
running through pearl or bead on
left-hand side.

FOR ALL TECHNIQUES: To
string beads or pearls, cut a 1-yard
length of cotton, and thread into
needle. Follow directions for
numbers and sequence of beads
or pearls to string.

FOR FINISHING: To block an
ornament, pin it face down onto
cardboard which has been
covered with waxed paper.
Following the manufacturer's
instructions, paint fabric stiffener
onto thread portions of ornaments
and leave to dry. Repeat the paint
process once more. After
completely dry, remove pins and
peel the ornament away from the
waxed paper.

12-POINTED STAR
ORNAMENT: String 30 (3 mm)
pearls. Ch 6; join with sl st to
form ring.

crocheted snowflakes — *continued*

Rnd 1 (RS): Ch 1, 12 sc in ring; join with sl st in first sc; turn.

Rnd 2: (5 pch, sk 1 sc, sl st in next sc) 6 times. Fasten off.

Rnd 3: String [3 (3 mm) pearls, 1 (4 mm) pearl, 3 (3 mm) pearls] 6 times. With the WS facing, join thread with a sl st in RT of the third pearl in any 5-pch group, ch 1, (7 pch, sl st in RT of third pearl of next 5-pch group) 6 times. Fasten off.

Rnd 4: String [3 (3 mm) pearls, 2 (4 mm) pearls, 1 (5 mm) pearl, 2 (4 mm) pearls, and 1 (3 mm) pearl] 6 times. With the WS facing, join thread in RT of any 4-mm-pearl with sl st. Ch 1, (9 pch, sl st RT in next 4 mm-pearl) 6 times. Fasten off.

Rnd 5: String 126 beads. With the RS facing, join thread with sl st in RT of second 3 mm-pearl of any 9-pch-group. * Ch 2, sc RT next pearl, (ch 3, sc RT next pearl) twice, ch 5, sc RT next pearl, (ch 3, sc RT next pearl) twice, ch 4, sk last 3 mm-pearl of this group and first 3 mm-pearl of next group, sc RT next pearl; rep from * around for 5 times more.

Rnd 6: * 3 sc in ch-2 sp, 4 sc in each of next 2 ch-3 sps, in ch-5 sp (sc, hdc, 2 dc, trc, 2 dc, hdc, sc), 4 sc in each of next 2 ch-3 sps, sk ch-4 sp; rep from * for 5 times more; turn.

Rnd 7: * (bsc in each of next 3 sc, sk 1 sc) twice, sk 1 sc, bsc in each of next 7 sts, (sk 1 sc, bsc in each of next 3 sc) twice, sk next sc, bsc in each of next 2 sc; rep from * around for 5 times more, ending with sl st in skipped sc at beginning of rnd. Fasten off.

Rnd 8: String [1 (3 mm) pearl, 1 (4 mm) pearl, 2 (5 mm) pearls, 1 (6 mm) pearl, 2 (5 mm) pearls, 1 (4 mm) pearl, and 1 (3 mm) pearl] 12 times. With WS facing, join thread in RT of seventh bead from Rnd 7 join. * 9 pch, sk 9 beads, sl st RT next bead, 9 pch, sk 10 beads, sl st RT next bead; rep from * 5 times more. Fasten off.

Rnd 9: String 276 beads. With the RS facing, join thread with sl st in RT of first 4-mm-pearl of any 9-pch-group. * Ch 3, sc RT next pearl, (ch 4, sc RT next pearl) twice, ch 6, sc RT next pearl, (ch 4, sc RT next pearl) twice, ch 3, sk 2 (3 mm) pearls, sc RT next 4-mm-pearl; rep from * around for 11 times more.

Rnd 10: Ch 2, sl st in next ch-3 lp, * 5 sc in each of next 2 ch-4 lps, in ch-6 lp (sc, hdc, 2 dc, trc, 2 dc, hdc, sc), 5 sc in each of next 2 ch-4 lps, sk next 2 ch-3 lps; rep from * for 11 times more, ending with sl st in first sc; turn.

Rnd 11: * (Sk 1 sc, bsc in each of next 4 sc) twice, sk 1 st, bsc in each of next 7 sts, sk 1 st, (bsc in each of next 4 sc, sk 1 sc) twice; rep from * for 11 times more, ending with sl st in first sc. Fasten off.

Block ornament. Slip a 12-inch length of ribbon through one scallop for hanging loop.

SIX-POINTED STAR ORNAMENT: String 42 beads. Ch 6; join with sl st to form ring.

Rnd 1: Ch 1, 12 sc in ring; join with sl st in first sc; turn.

Rnd 2: (7 bch, sk 1 sc, sl st in next sc) 6 times. Fasten off.

Rnd 3: String [4 beads, 1 (4 mm) pearl, and 4 beads] 6 times. With the WS facing, join thread with sl st in RT of second bead of any 7-bead group. * (Ch 2, sc RT next bead) twice, ch 4, sc RT next bead, ch 2, sc RT next bead,

Six-pointed star ornament

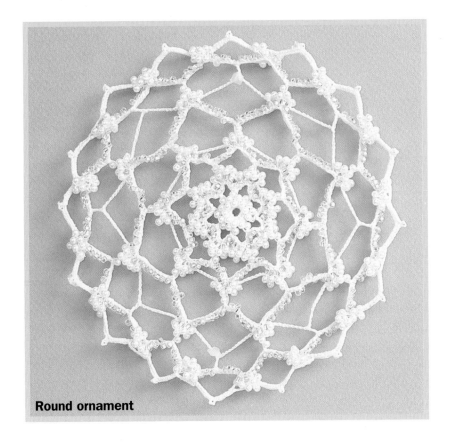

Round ornament

ch 2, sk 2 beads, sc RT next bead; rep from * for 5 times more, ending with sl st in join; turn.

Rnd 4: * 2 sc in each of next 2 ch-2 sps, in ch-4 lp (sc, ch 3, sc), 2 sc in each of next 2 ch-2 sps; rep from * for 5 times more; turn.

Rnd 5: * Bsc in each of next 4 sc, ch 2, sk next sc, psc in ch-3 lp, ch 2, sk next sc, bsc in each of next 4 sc; rep from * for 5 times more, ending with sl st in beg bsc. Fasten off.

Rnd 6: String [5 (3 mm) pearls, 7 beads, 1 (5 mm) pearl, and 7 beads] 6 times. With the WS facing, join thread with sl st in ch-2 sp before any pearl; * sc RT next pearl, 5 pch, sc LT in same pearl, sc next ch-2 sp, 7 bch, pch, 7 bch, sc next ch-2 sp; rep from * for 5 times more, ending with sl st in first sc. Fasten off.

Rnd 7: String [5 (3 mm) pearls, 10 beads, 1 (5 mm) pearl, 10 beads] 6 times. With the WS facing, join thread with sl st in

RT of bead just before any 5 mm-pearl. Ch 1, sc in join; * ch 2, sc RT next pearl, 5 pch, sc LT same pearl, ch 2, sc LT next bead, 10 bch, 1 pch, 10 bch, sk (6 beads, 5 pearls, and 6 beads), sc RT next bead; rep from * for 5 times more, ending with sl st in first sc. Fasten off.

Rnd 8: String [12 beads, 1 (5 mm) pearl, 12 beads] 6 times. With the RS facing, join thread with sl st in RT of center pearl of any 5-pearl group. * (Ch 2, sc RT next pearl) twice, (ch 2, sc RT next bead) 10 times, ch 2, sc RT next pearl, ch 5, sc RT of third pearl of next 5-pearl group; rep from * for 5 times more.

Rnd 9: * 3 sc in each of next 13 ch-2 sps, ch 1, sk ch-5 lp; rep from * for 5 times more, ending with sl st in first sc; turn.

Rnd 10: (Sc in next ch, 12 bch, pch, 12 bch, sk 39 sc) 6 times, ending with sl st in first sc; turn.

Rnd 11: Ch 1, sl st RT next

bead, ch 3 (counts as first dc); * (ch 1, dc RT next bead) 11 times, ch 1, dc RT pearl, ch 3, dc LT same pearl, (ch 1, dc LT next bead) 12 times, dc RT next bead; rep from * for 5 times more, omitting final dc in last rep and ending with sl st in third ch of beg ch-3; turn.

Rnd 12: String [12 beads, 5 (3 mm) pearls, 12 beads] 6 times. (Bsc in each of next 12 ch-1 sps, 5 psc in ch-3 sp, bsc in each of next 12 ch-1 sps) 6 times; at end, sl st in first sc and fasten off.

Block ornament. Slip a 12-inch length of ribbon through one point for a hanging loop.

ROUND ORNAMENT: String 24 (3 mm) pearls. Ch 8; join with sl st to form ring.

Rnd 1: Ch 1, 16 sc in ring; join with sl st in first sc; turn.

Rnd 2: (3 pch, sk 1 sc, sl st in next sc) 8 times; turn.

Rnd 3: Ch 3, sk 1 pearl, sl st RT of next pearl, (ch 8, sk 2 pearls, sl st RT of next pearl) 8 times; turn.

Rnd 4: String 48 beads. (Sc in next ch, bsc in each of next 6 ch, sc in next ch, sc into same thread of Rnd 2 pearl as before) 8 times, ending with sl st in first sc. Fasten off.

Rnd 5: String 72 (3 mm) pearls. With the WS facing, join thread with sl st in LT of second bead of any 6-bead group; * 3 pch, sl st LT next bead, (3 pch, sl st RT next bead) twice, ch 3, sl st LT second bead of next 6-bead group; rep from * 7 times more. Fasten off.

Rnd 6: String 96 beads. With the WS facing, join thread with sl st in RT of fifth pearl of any 9-pearl group. (Ch 14, sl st RT corresponding pearl of next

crocheted snowflakes — *continued*

9-pearl group) 8 times.

Rnd 7: (Sc next ch, bsc in each of next 12 ch, sc in next ch, sc around Rnd 6 and into RT of same Rnd 5 pearl as before) 8 times, ending with sl st in first sc. Fasten off.

Rnd 8: String 72 (3 mm) pearls. With WS facing, join thread with sl st in LT of fifth bead of any 12-bead group. * 3 pch, sl st LT of next bead, (3 pch, sl st RT of next bead) twice, ch 8, sl st LT of fifth bead of next 12-bead group; rep from * 7 times more. Fasten off.

Rnd 9: String 160 beads. With WS facing, join thread in RT of fifth pearl of any 9-pearl group. (Ch 22, sl st RT fifth pearl of next 9-pearl group) 8 times.

Rnd 10: * Sc next ch, bsc in each of next 20 ch, sc in next ch,

sc around Rnd 9 into RT of same Rnd 8 pearl as before; rep from * for 7 times more, ending with sl st in first sc. Fasten off.

Rnd 11: String 72 (3 mm) pearls. With WS facing, join thread with sl st in LT of ninth bead of any 20-bead group. * (3 pch, sl st LT next bead), (3 pch, sl st RT next bead) twice, ch 20, sl st LT of ninth bead in next 20-bead group; rep from * for 7 times more. Fasten off.

Rnd 12: String 208 beads. With RS facing, join thread in RT of fifth pearl of any 9-pearl group, (ch 15, trc in next ch-20 lp, ch 15, sl st RT of fifth pearl of next 9-pearl group) 8 times; turn.

Rnd 13: * (Sc in next ch, bsc in each of next 13 ch, sc in next ch), sc in trc, rep bet ( ) again, sc around Rnd 12 into RT of same

Rnd 11 pearl as before; rep from * for 7 times more. Fasten off.

Rnd 14: String 144 (3 mm) pearls. With WS facing join thread with sl st in LT of sixth bead of any 13-bead group. * 3 pch, sl st RT of next bead, 3 pch, sl st LT of same bead, 3 pch, sl st RT of next bead, ch 12, sl st LT of sixth bead of next 13-bead group; rep from * for 7 times more; turn.

Rnd 15: * In ch-12 lp [8 sc, (ch 3, sl st in st prior to ch-3 just made = picot made), 8 sc], ch 6, pass the ch-6 lp behind the pearl cluster; rep from * for 15 times more; at end, join with sl st in first sc. Fasten off.

Block the ornament. Cut a 12-inch length of ribbon and slip through one point for a hanging loop.

silver pinecone garland

As shown on pages 160–161 and below, garland measures approximately 5 feet long.

Materials

25 pinecones; 10 to 15 nuts
6 large seed pods or similar dried natural material
Drill; ⅛-inch-diameter drill bit
6-foot-long piece of strong fishing line
Large-eyed needle
Silver spray paint

Instructions

Drill ⅛-inch-diameter hole through each nut, pinecone, and seed pod. Thread needle with one end of fishing line. Thread

first pinecone onto line, push to end leaving 6-inch tail. Knot tail around pinecone to secure end of garland. Randomly thread materials onto line. Secure end of line around last piece.

Spray paint entire garland silver; allow to dry.

CROCHETED SNOWFLAKE
AND EUCALYPTUS
TREE TOPPER

1 Square = 1 Inch

eucalyptus tree topper

As shown on page 160, star measures 10×11 inches.

Materials

Tracing paper
Carbon paper; ballpoint pen
12×12-inch piece of ¼-inch plywood
Scroll saw; drill with ⅛-inch bit
12 inches of medium gauge wire
Fine grit sandpaper
White acrylic paint
Silver glitter brush-on paint
5 to 7 stems of eucalyptus
Hot-glue gun; hot glue; silver spray
    paint; Crocheted Snowflake
    (*pages 163–166*); 1⅓ yards of
    3-inch-wide silver mesh ribbon

Instructions

Enlarge the star pattern, *above left*, and trace onto tracing paper. Place carbon paper between the pattern and wood; transfer outline, tracing over lines with ballpoint pen.

Cut out star with scroll saw. Drill two holes through the center, approximately 1¼ inches apart. Sand the edges smooth.

Paint the entire star white; allow to dry. Brush silver glitter paint over the front.

Thread ends of wire through holes from front to back; twist wires together at back to secure.

Spray paint the eucalyptus silver; allow to dry. Bend the stems of the eucalyptus as necessary to form star shape and hot-glue to star, covering the wood. Carefully secure the crocheted snowflake to the front of the star atop the eucalyptus, using dabs of hot glue.

Wire the ribbon to the back of the star, leaving long tails. Use the wire ends to secure the star to the treetop.

white-as-snow cookies

As shown on pages 160–161 and right.

Materials

1 recipe Rolled Sugar
    Cookie Dough
8 ounces vanilla-flavored candy
    coating, cut up
3 tablespoons shortening
Edible glitter, optional

Instructions

On a lightly floured surface, roll a portion of chilled cookie dough ⅛ inch thick. With a 3- or 3½-inch star or snowflake cookie cutter or a 5-inch tree cookie cutter, cut out cookies. Reroll scraps. With a smaller star or flower cutter (about ¾ inch in diameter), cut out a shape in the center of each cookie, if desired. Use ¼-inch assorted-shaped cutters or a sharp knife to cut smaller designs. Use a straw to cut a hole in top for hanging. Place on ungreased cookie sheets.

Bake in a 375° oven for 7 to 8 minutes or till edges are firm and bottoms are very lightly browned. Transfer to wire racks; cool.

Heat and stir 8 ounces candy coating and shortening over very low heat till mixture begins to melt. Remove from heat; stir till smooth. Dip cooled cookies, face down, into melted mixture, shaking cookies gently to smooth any ripples in coating. Transfer to wire racks. Sprinkle with edible glitter. Makes 24 cookies.

Rolled Sugar Cookie Dough: In a large mixing bowl beat ⅓ cup butter and ⅓ cup shortening with electric mixer on medium speed for 30 seconds. Add 1 cup all-purpose flour, ¾ cup sugar, 1 egg, 1 tablespoon milk, 1 teaspoon baking powder, 1 teaspoon vanilla, and dash salt. Beat till combined. Beat in 1 cup all-purpose flour. Divide in half. Cover and chill 3 hours or till easy to handle.

beribboned
evergreen

Beautifully wrapped from the very top of its branches to the glorious gifts below, our ribbon tree is trimmed with rolls of silk and satin ribbons that lovingly intertwine around the evergreen. Tucked in among the branches are ornaments—all created with ribbons, jewels, and lace. Ribbon Cocarde Ornaments, Mirrored Star Ornaments, Flower Ribbon Prisms, Lace-Framed Father Christmas Ornaments, and ribbon-embroidered Sachet Pillowettes grace this breathtaking display. Instructions and close-up views of all the ornaments start on page 170.

sachet pillowettes

As shown on pages 168–169 and below, *ornaments measure 4½×4½ inches.*

Materials

12×18-inch piece of Zweigart eggshell Puzzle Damask
Tracing paper
Three 6×6-inch squares of netting
Fine-point black permanent marker
Water-soluble fabric marking pen
Medium pistachio (DMC 367) cotton embroidery floss
7-millimeter-wide embroidery ribbon: wine and teal
4-millimeter-wide embroidery ribbon: hunter green and light mauve
Embroidery needle
Size 18 chenille needle
Hand-sewing needle
Seven 3×4-millimeter translucent green pebble beads
24 inches of ⅛-inch-wide ivory satin ribbon
Ivory sewing thread; polyester fiberfill
1½ yards of ¼-inch-diameter ivory satin cord; potpourri

Instructions

Cut the fabric into three 6×6-inch squares and three 4½×4½-inch squares.

Trace designs, *opposite*, onto tracing paper. For each design, position netting over tracing paper and trace using fine-point marker. Next, position netting square atop larger fabric square and trace over design using fabric marker.

Work stem stitches on each ornament using three plies green embroidery floss. Complete the design using ribbon. For straight stitches and lazy daisies, keep ribbon as smooth and flat as possible while working.

For Ornament 1, work straight stitches and light green shaded French knots using teal, lazy daisy flowers using wine, and lazy daisy leaves using hunter green. Work pink shaded French knots using light mauve.

For Ornament 2, work the straight stitch flowers using wine. Add five straight stitch spokes atop the wine stitches using light mauve. Stitch three large light green lazy daisy flower petals using teal ribbon, and dark green

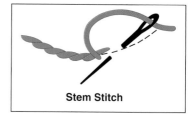

SACHET PILLOWETTES
STEM STITCH
Seafoam green – stems
STRAIGHT STITCH
Wine 7mm silk ribbon – flowers on Ornament 2
Mauve 4mm silk ribbon – flowers on Ornament 2
Teal 7mm silk ribbon – leaves on Ornament 1
LAZY DAISY
Mauve 4mm silk ribbon – flowers on Ornament 3
Teal 7mm silk ribbon – leaves on Ornaments 2 and 3
Wine 7mm silk ribbon – flowers on Ornaments 1 and 3
Hunter green 4mm silk ribbon – leaves on all Ornaments
FRENCH KNOT
Mauve 7mm silk ribbon – flowers on Ornaments 1 and 3
Teal 4mm silk ribbon – flowers on Ornament 1
BEADS
Green pebble beads – flower centers on all ornaments

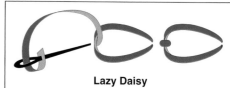

Stem Stitch

Lazy Daisy

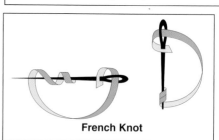

French Knot

ORNAMENT 1

ORNAMENT 2

ORNAMENT 3

lazy daisy leaves using hunter green ribbon.

For Ornament 3, work lazy daisy flowers using wine ribbon and light green flower petals using teal. Work pink lazy daisy petals and colonial knots using light mauve, and dark green lazy daisy leaves using hunter green.

Sew beads to ornaments as on patterns, *above.*

For each ornament, trim stitched square to 4½×4½ inches. Cut an 8-inch length of ivory ribbon. Fold ribbon in half, stack ends, and pin to the center top of stitched square with edges even.

Sew ornament front to back using ¼-inch seam allowance and

leaving opening for turning. Turn, press, and stuff. Hand stitch ivory cord around perimeter, tucking ends into opening. Sew opening closed.

flower ribbon prisms

As shown on pages 168—169 and right, *ornaments measure 4 inches across.*

Materials

42 inches of ¼-inch-wide wire-edged ribbon in desired color

10 inches of 24-gauge copper wire

Crystal drop ornament

Instructions

Working from center, loop ribbon back and forth for bow, leaving 8-inch-long streamers. Twist wire around center to secure. Use remaining wire to secure top of prism to bow center and make a hanging loop. Separate and shape ribbon loops as shown in photograph, *right*. Wrap streamers around a pencil to form spirals.

mirrored star ornaments

As shown on pages 168–169 and right, *ornaments measure 4×4 inches.*

Materials

Tracing paper
5×5-inch piece of matboard
Tapestry needle
Gold metallic spray paint
Clear acrylic spray sealer
Six 40×22.5-millimeter
diamond-shaped mirrors
in desired color; 6-millimeter
gold bead
18 inches of gold
metallic thread
23×15-millimeter pink
acrylic cushion bead
½-inch-diameter clear
2-hole button

Instructions

Trace the star pattern, *left,* onto tracing paper and cut out. Trace around the pattern onto matboard; cut out. Poke a hole through the top point and center of star with needle.

Spray both sides of star gold. When dry, spray both with acrylic sealer.

Glue mirror to each star point, ⅛ inch in from edges. Slide bead to center of gold thread. Next, thread both gold thread tails onto needle and slide on pink bead until it stops next to gold bead. Push needle through center hole in star from front to back, bringing pink bead up against star front. On back side, thread one tail through each hole in button and knot. Thread needle once again with tails and push through hole in top point of star, from back to front. Knot ends to complete hanging loop.

ribbon cocarde ornament

As shown on pages 168–169 and right, *cocarde measures 5 inches in diameter.*

Materials

3-inch-diameter circle of matboard
Straight pin
Gold metallic spray paint
Tapestry needle
1¼ yards of 1½-inch-wide
wire-edged woven metallic
ribbon in pink or blue

½ yard of ⅜-inch-wide
wire-edged fabric ribbon in
pink or blue
Thick crafts glue; jewel glue
40-millimeter-diameter gold
jewelry "doughnut," or similar
jewelry finding
34×26-millimeter blue or pink
plastic cameo or similar jewel

Instructions

Spray back of matboard circle gold; allow to dry. Pierce hole in center with tapestry needle. Cut 1½-inch-wide ribbon into fourteen 3-inch-long pieces.

Referring to Diagram A, *right,* position each ribbon piece with the long edges at the top and bottom. Fold top corners down to center. Next, fold left bottom point of triangle to right bottom point to make smaller triangle. Make 14 cocarde points in the same manner.

Tie bow in the center of ⅜-inch-wide ribbon, leaving long streamers. Spread thick crafts glue over front of circle. Glue streamer ends to circle, approximately 1 inch apart for hanger. Referring to Diagram B, *below,* position cocarde points around circle using center hole as a placement guide, with fold toward outer edge. Tuck each cocarde point slightly inside fold of previous point.

Use jewel glue to glue gold "doughnut" jewelry piece to center, with cameo on top.

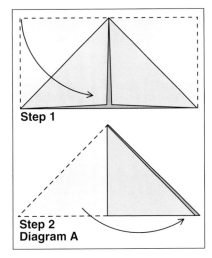

Step 1

Step 2
Diagram A

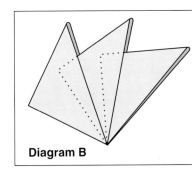

Diagram B

lace-framed ornaments

As shown on pages 168–169 and **left,** *each ornament measures 5×7 inches.*

Materials

5×7-inch piece of matboard
Gold metallic spray paint
5×7-inch piece of gold gift wrap
Spray adhesive
Tapestry needle
5×7-inch Victorian cotton lace frame, with oval opening
1 yard of 7-millimeter-wide green or rose silk ribbon
Three ½-inch-diameter gold jingle bells; jewel glue
Santa cutout or Victorian scrap to fit 5¼×3¼-inch oval opening in lace frame
18 inches of gold metallic thread

Instructions

Spray back of matboard gold; allow to dry. Affix gold paper to matboard front with spray adhesive. With matboard positioned lengthwise, pierce hole in each top corner using needle.

Thread silk ribbon in and out through holes around perimeter of lace frame. Begin and end at center top, leaving tails of equal length. Thread jingle bells onto tails and tie in a bow.

Glue lace to covered matboard front using jewel glue. Center Santa cutout within the frame, tucking bottom edge under lace. Thread the gold metallic thread end through each hole from the front to the back. Knot ends at back to complete hanging loop.

christmas cookies

Lovingly decorated or spoon-dropped quickly—it just wouldn't be Christmas without cookies to tempt and please! So warm up the oven and get ready to try dozens of new recipes sure to become favorites for generations to come.

a chocolate lover's christmas

Open a jar of peanut butter and stir up (from top) rich Peanut Butter Cup Chocolate Cookies, Peanut Butter Sandwich Cookies, chocolate-drizzled Peanut Butter Oatmeal Rounds, and layered Peanut Butter Chocolate Shortbread. The recipes are on pages 178–179.

Savor the surprise of spice in (from top) Cinnamon-Chocolate Crisscrosses, Chocolate Snickerdoodles, frosted Chocolate-Spice Cutouts, and Gingerbread Brownies. The brownies are trimmed with a lacy design made by sprinkling powdered sugar through a paper doily. The recipes are on pages 180–181.

chocolate plus spice

peanut butter sandwich cookies

If you don't have a scalloped round cookie cutter, use a plain round cutter. As shown on page 176.

Ingredients

- ½ cup shortening
- ½ cup peanut butter
- ½ cup granulated sugar
- ½ cup packed brown sugar
- ¾ teaspoon baking soda
- 1 egg
- 2 tablespoons milk
- 1¾ cups all-purpose flour
- Fudge Filling

Method

Beat shortening and peanut butter in a mixing bowl with an electric mixer on medium speed for 30 seconds. Add granulated sugar, brown sugar, and baking soda; beat till combined. Add egg and milk; beat till well combined. Beat in as much flour as you can with the mixer. Stir in remaining flour with a wooden spoon. Divide dough in half. Cover and chill 1 to 2 hours or until easy to handle.

Roll one portion of dough ⅛-inch thick on a lightly floured surface. Cut out using a 2-inch scalloped round cutter. Place cutouts 1 inch apart on an ungreased cookie sheet. Bake in a 375° oven about 8 minutes or until lightly browned. Cool on a wire rack. Repeat with remaining dough.

Spread bottom surface of half of the cookies with a tablespoon of Fudge Filling. Top each with another cookie right-side up. Makes 25 sandwiched cookies.

Fudge Filling: Melt 12 ounces semi-sweet chocolate over low heat, stirring constantly. Remove from heat. Stir in 1½ cups dairy sour cream and ¾ cup finely chopped peanuts. (Mixture will stiffen as it cools.)

peanut butter oatmeal rounds

This delicious recipe makes over five dozen cookies. As shown on page 176.

- 2 eggs
- 1 teaspoon vanilla
- 1¼ cups all-purpose flour
- 2 cups rolled oats
- 1 cup semisweet chocolate pieces (6 ounces)
- Melted semisweet chocolate

Method

Beat butter or margarine and peanut butter in a large bowl with an electric mixer on medium speed for 30 seconds. Add granulated sugar, brown sugar, baking powder, and baking soda; beat until combined. Add eggs and vanilla; beat until combined. Beat in flour with mixer. Stir in rolled oats and chocolate pieces with a wooden spoon. Drop dough from a rounded teaspoon 2 inches apart onto an ungreased cookie sheet.

Bake in a 375° oven 10 minutes or till edges are lightly browned. Cool on a wire rack. Drizzle with melted chocolate. Makes about 60.

Ingredients

- ¾ cup butter or margarine
- ½ cup peanut butter
- 1 cup granulated sugar
- ½ cup packed brown sugar
- 1 teaspoon baking powder
- ½ teaspoon baking soda

peanut butter cup chocolate cookies

Sink your teeth into chunks of gooey, chocolate-covered peanut butter cups. Yum!
As shown on page 176.

Ingredients

½ cup shortening
½ cup butter or margarine
¾ cup granulated sugar
¾ cup packed brown sugar
1 teaspoon baking soda
2 eggs
2 ounces unsweetened chocolate, melted and cooled
1 teaspoon vanilla
2¼ cups all-purpose flour
2 cups coarsely chopped chocolate-covered peanut butter cups

Method

Beat shortening and butter or margarine in mixing bowl with electric mixer on medium to high speed for 30 seconds.

Add granulated sugar, brown sugar, and baking soda; beat until combined. Add eggs, chocolate, and vanilla; beat until combined. Beat in as much flour as you can with mixer. Stir in remaining flour. Stir in chopped peanut butter cups.

Drop dough from a rounded tablespoon 2½ inches apart onto ungreased cookie sheet. Bake in a 375° oven for 10–12 minutes. Cool on cookie sheet. Remove and cool on a wire rack. Makes 32.

peanut butter chocolate shortbread

This shortbread is divinely rich, so cut thin wedges.
As shown on page 176.

Ingredients

1½ cups butter or margarine
1½ cups sifted powdered sugar
1½ teaspoons vanilla
2 cups all-purpose flour
⅔ cup unsweetened cocoa powder
2 tablespoons cornstarch
¼ teaspoon salt
1 cup finely chopped unsalted peanuts
1 cup creamy peanut butter
1 cup sifted powdered sugar
¼ cup semisweet chocolate pieces
16 milk chocolate kisses
16 whole unsalted peanuts

Method

Beat butter or margarine in a large mixing bowl for 30 seconds. Add 1½ cups powdered sugar and vanilla. Add flour, cocoa powder, cornstarch, and salt; beat until smooth. Stir in chopped peanuts. Reserve 1⅓ cups of cocoa mixture. Press remaining cocoa mixture in the bottom and up the sides of an ungreased 10-inch tart pan with a removable bottom, or in the bottom and 1 inch up the sides of a 10-inch springform pan.

Stir together peanut butter and 1 cup powdered sugar in a bowl; stir in chocolate pieces. Pat mixture into a 9-inch circle on a piece of waxed paper. Invert into chocolate shortbread crust. Carefully remove waxed paper. Spoon remaining cocoa mixture over peanut butter mixture, carefully pressing to cover. Using the tines of a fork, score shortbread into 16 wedges.

Bake in a 325° oven about 50 minutes or until surface looks slightly dry. Cool slightly. While warm, place a chocolate kiss on each wedge. When kiss softens (about 10 minutes), top with a peanut. Score wedges again. Cool completely. Remove sides of pan; cut into wedges. Makes 16.

cinnamon-chocolate crisscrosses

Press in design with the tines of a fork, just as you would for peanut butter crisscross cookies. As shown on page 177.

Ingredients

- ½ cup butter or margarine
- 1 cup sugar
- 2 teaspoons baking powder
- 1 teaspoon ground cinnamon
- 4 ounces semisweet chocolate, melted and cooled
- 2 eggs
- 1 teaspoon vanilla
- 2½ cups all-purpose flour
- Granulated sugar

Method

Beat butter or margarine in a large mixing bowl with an electric mixer on medium to high speed for 30 seconds. Add the 1 cup sugar, baking powder, and cinnamon; beat until combined. Add melted chocolate, eggs, and vanilla; beat until well combined. Beat in as much of the flour as you can with the mixer. Stir in any remaining flour with a wooden spoon. Cover and chill the dough for 1 to 2 hours or until easy to handle.

Shape dough into 1-inch balls. Place 2 inches apart on ungreased cookie sheet. Using the tines of a fork dipped in additional sugar, flatten balls to about ½-inch thickness by pressing the fork in two directions to form crisscross marks. Bake in a 375° oven for 7 to 8 minutes or until edges are set.

Cool on cookie sheet for 1 minute. Remove cookies and cool on a wire rack. Place in an airtight container and store at room temperature up to 3 days. Makes about 64.

chocolate snickerdoodles

No one knows how these crinkle-top sweets got their name, but kids love to say it almost as much as they love to eat the cookies. As shown on page 177.

Ingredients

- ½ cup butter or margarine
- 1 cup sugar
- ¼ teaspoon baking soda
- ¼ teaspoon cream of tartar
- 1 egg
- ½ teaspoon vanilla
- ⅓ cup unsweetened cocoa powder
- 1 cup all-purpose flour
- 2 tablespoons sugar
- 1 teaspoon ground cinnamon

Method

Beat the butter or margarine in a mixing bowl with an electric mixer on medium to high speed for about 30 seconds. Add the 1 cup sugar, baking soda, and cream of tartar; beat until combined. Add the egg and vanilla; beat until well combined. Stir together the cocoa powder and the flour. Beat in as much of the flour mixture as you can with the mixer. Stir in any remaining flour mixture.

Drop by slightly rounded teaspoons 2 inches apart onto an ungreased cookie sheet. Stir together the remaining sugar and cinnamon. Sprinkle the dough with the sugar-cinnamon mixture. Bake in a 375° oven for 9 to 11 minutes or until the edges are firm. Cool on a wire rack. Makes about 30.

chocolate-spice cutouts

We cut mitten, bell, and tree cookies and decorated them with white, red, and green icing. As shown on page 177.

Ingredients

- ½ cup shortening
- ½ cup sugar
- 1 teaspoon baking soda
- ¾ teaspoon ground ginger
- ½ teaspoon baking powder
- ½ teaspoon ground cinnamon
- ¼ teaspoon ground cloves
- 1 egg
- ½ cup dark corn syrup
- ¼ cup milk
- 3 cups all-purpose flour
- ½ cup unsweetened cocoa powder
  Decorating Icing

Method

Beat shortening in a mixing bowl with an electric mixer on medium to high speed for 30 seconds. Add sugar, baking soda, ginger, baking powder, cinnamon, and cloves; beat until combined. Add egg, corn syrup, and milk; beat until combined. Stir together flour and cocoa powder. Beat in as much of the flour mixture as you can. Stir in remaining flour mixture. Divide dough in half. Cover and chill about 1 hour or until easy to handle.

Roll each portion of dough on a lightly floured surface to ⅛-inch thickness. Cut with desired 2- or 3-inch cookie cutters. Place cutouts 1 inch apart on a greased cookie sheet.

Bake in a 375° oven for 5 to 7 minutes or until slightly puffed and set. Cool on cookie sheet for 1 minute. Remove and cool on wire rack. Pipe on Decorating Icing with a decorating bag and writing tip. Makes about 36.

Decorating Icing: Combine 3 cups sifted powdered sugar and enough milk (about 3 to 5 tablespoons) to make of piping consistency. If desired, stir in a few drops of food coloring.

gingerbread brownies

Taste the subtle difference a dash of spice makes. As shown on page 177.

Ingredients

- 1½ cups all-purpose flour
- 1 cup sugar
- ¼ cup unsweetened cocoa powder
- 1 teaspoon ground ginger
- 1 teaspoon ground cinnamon
- ½ teaspoon baking soda
- ½ teaspoon ground cloves
- ¼ cup butter or margarine, melted
- ⅓ cup molasses
- 2 eggs
  Powdered sugar

Method

Combine flour, sugar, cocoa powder, ginger, cinnamon, baking soda, and cloves in a large mixing bowl. In a separate bowl, combine melted butter or margarine, molasses, and eggs. Add to flour mixture; stir until combined. Do not beat (the batter will be thick). Spread batter in a greased 13×9×2-inch baking pan. Bake in a 350° oven for 20 minutes. Do not overbake. Cool on wire rack. Dust with powdered sugar sprinkled through a paper doily. Cut into squares. Makes 24.

let heaven and nature sing

These heavenly cookies are almost too pretty to eat! In fact, before baking you can make a hole in the top of any of these cookies to turn them into lovely tree ornaments. The recipes for both the Heavenly Cutout Cookies and Divine Molded Almond Cookies are opposite.

heavenly cutout cookies

Heavenly symbols create divine cutouts. As shown opposite.

Ingredients

- ½ cup butter (no substitutes)
- 1 3-ounce package cream cheese
- 1½ cups sifted powdered sugar
- ½ teaspoon baking powder
- 1 egg
- ½ teaspoon vanilla
- 1¾ cups all-purpose flour
  Powdered Sugar Icing
  Powdered food coloring (optional)
  Colored decorating sugar (optional)
  Tiny decorating candies (optional)

Method

Beat butter and cream cheese in a medium mixing bowl with electric mixer on medium speed for 30 seconds. Add powdered sugar and baking powder; beat until combined. Beat in egg and vanilla. Beat in as much flour as you can. Stir in any remaining flour with a wooden spoon. Divide dough in half. Cover and chill 1 hour or until dough is easy to handle.

Roll dough, half at a time, to ⅛-inch thickness. Cut into desired shapes using cookie cutters. Arrange cutouts 1 inch apart on an ungreased cookie sheet.

Bake in a 375° oven for 7 to 8 minutes or until edges are set. Cool on a wire rack. If desired, glaze tops with Powdered Sugar Icing, or pipe icing on top using a decorating bag fitted with a fine writing tip. If desired, brush with powdered food coloring, or decorate with decorating sugar or candies. Makes about 42.

Powdered Sugar Icing: Stir together 1 cup sifted powdered sugar and ¼ teaspoon vanilla. Stir in milk, 1 teaspoon at a time, until icing is of piping or drizzling consistency. If desired, tint with a little liquid or paste food coloring.

Note: Make holes in cookies for decoration or hanging before baking. Place cutouts on a baking sheet. Holding a drinking straw vertically, make holes. Twist straw gently to remove dough.

divine molded almond cookies

Use an almond paste made without syrup or liquid glucose. As shown opposite.

Ingredients

- 1 cup butter, softened (no substitutes)
- 2 ounces almond paste, crumbled (¼ cup)
- ½ cup sugar
- 2½ cups all-purpose flour
  Powdered Sugar Icing (see recipe above); Egg Paint

Method

Beat butter and almond paste in a mixing bowl with electric mixer on medium speed until combined; beat in sugar. Stir in flour with wooden spoon. If necessary, knead in remaining flour with hands.

Angel Cookies: To make angel, shape dough into one 1¼-inch ball, one ¾-inch ball, two ¼-inch balls, and two 1-inch balls.

For body, flatten largest ball to ¼-inch-thick triangle on ungreased cookie sheet. For head, attach ¾-inch ball at top point of triangle; flatten to a 1¼-inch round. For feet, attach ¼-inch balls to base of triangle. For wings, attach 1-inch balls to opposite sides of triangle; shape into triangles. Paint with Egg Paint.

Bake in a 325° oven about 15 minutes or until edges are light brown. Cool on wire rack. Decorate, if desired, using Powdered Sugar Icing in a decorating bag with a fine writing tip. Makes about 20.

Stamped Cookies: Form dough into 1½-inch balls. Place on ungreased cookie sheet. Using 2-inch cookie stamps dipped into sugar, press firmly to flatten dough and make patterns on tops. Bake in a 350° oven for 8 to 10 minutes or until edges are light brown. Cool on wire rack. Makes about 40.

Egg Paint: Beat together 1 egg yolk and ¼ teaspoon water in a small mixing bowl. Divide mixture among three or four small bowls. Add 2 or 3 drops food coloring to each bowl; mix well. Paint desired colors of egg yolk mixture onto unbaked cookies, using a small, clean paintbrush. If paint thickens, stir in water a drop at a time.

cookie exchange

Invite cookie lovers of all ages into your kitchen to share a sampling of cookies most dear to their hearts. They'll arrive with old family favorites and leave smitten with cookie possibilities. Turn the page for all of these cookie recipes and to page 191 for several clever cookie container ideas.

white chocolate cherry twists

As shown on pages 184–185.

Ingredients

- ¾ cup butter, softened
- 1 cup sugar
- 1 teaspoon baking powder
- 1 egg
- 1 teaspoon vanilla
- 2½ cups all-purpose flour
- ⅓ cup finely chopped candied red cherries
  Few drops red food coloring
- 2 ounces white chocolate baking squares, finely chopped
- 2 ounces white chocolate baking squares, chopped, optional
- 2 teaspoons shortening, optional

Method

In a large mixing bowl beat the butter with an electric mixer on medium to high speed about 30 seconds or until softened. Add the sugar and baking powder; beat until combined. Beat in the egg and vanilla. Beat in as much of the flour as you can with the mixer. Using a wooden spoon, stir in any remaining flour. Divide dough.

To half of the dough stir in the chopped candied cherries and food coloring until combined. To the remaining half of the dough stir in 2 ounces finely chopped white chocolate. Wrap each portion of dough in clear plastic wrap or waxed paper and chill for 30 minutes or until dough is easy to handle.

For each cookie, on a lightly floured surface, shape a slightly rounded teaspoonful of red dough into a 6-inch rope. Repeat with a teaspoonful of white chocolate dough. Place ropes side by side and twist together. Pinch ends to seal. Form twisted ropes into canes, if desired. Place twists or canes 2 inches apart on an ungreased cookie sheet. Bake cookies in a 375° oven for 8 to 10 minutes or until edges are firm and lightly browned. Cool cookies on cookie sheet for 1 minute. Remove cookies from cookie sheet and cool on a wire rack.

If desired, in a heavy small saucepan melt the 2 ounces white chocolate baking squares and the 2 teaspoons shortening over very low heat until chocolate melts, stirring constantly. Drizzle mixture over cookies. Let stand until chocolate sets. Place cookies in a single layer in an airtight container and store at room temperature for up to 3 days. Makes 56 cookies.

sugar cookie dough

Used for Cashew Cookies and Frosted Sugar Cookie Cutouts recipes, opposite, and Chocolate Mint Pillows recipe, page 190.

Ingredients

- ¾ cup butter
- ¾ cup shortening
- 2 cups sugar
- 2 teaspoons baking powder
- ½ teaspoon salt
- 4 eggs
- 2 teaspoons vanilla
- 5 cups all-purpose flour

Method

In a large mixing bowl beat together the butter and shortening with an electric mixer on medium to high speed about 30 seconds or until combined. Add the sugar, baking powder, and salt. Beat until combined, scraping bowl. Beat in the eggs and vanilla. Beat in as much of the flour as you can with the mixer. Stir in any remaining flour.

Divide dough into 3 portions. If necessary, cover and chill dough for 3 hours or until easy to handle. Use dough to make Cashew Cookies, Frosted Sugar Cookie Cutouts, and Chocolate Mint Pillows.

cashew cookies

As shown on pages 184–185.

Ingredients

- ⅓ recipe Sugar Cookie Dough (see recipe opposite)
- ½ cup finely chopped cashews
- 1 slightly beaten egg white
- 1 cup finely chopped cashews
- 36 whole cashews

Method

In a medium mixing bowl combine the ⅓ recipe cookie dough and ½ cup finely chopped cashews. Using a wooden spoon, stir until combined. Wrap dough in clear plastic wrap or waxed paper and chill about 3 hours or until dough is easy to handle.

Lightly grease 2 cookie sheets. Shape dough into 1-inch balls. Roll in egg white, then in the 1 cup finely chopped cashews. Place balls 2 inches apart on the prepared cookie sheets. Using the bottom of a glass or your hand, slightly flatten each cookie. Carefully press a whole cashew onto the top of each cookie. Bake in a 350° oven for 8 to 10 minutes or until cookies are just lightly browned on bottom. Carefully remove cookies from cookie sheet and cool on a wire rack. Makes 36 cookies.

frosted sugar cookie cutouts

As shown on pages 184–185.

Ingredients

- ⅓ recipe Sugar Cookie Dough (see recipe opposite)
- 1 recipe Meringue Powder Glaze (see right) or other desired icing, optional

Method

On a well-floured surface, roll one half of dough (keep remaining dough chilled) to ¼-inch thickness. Using desired cookie cutters and dipping into flour between cuts, cut dough into shapes. Place cookies 1 inch apart on an ungreased cookie sheet. Bake in a 375° oven for 6 to 8 minutes. Cool cookies on cookie sheet for 1 minute. Carefully remove from cookie sheet and cool on a wire rack. Decorate cookies as desired. Makes about 36 cookies.

Meringue Powder Glaze:
In a medium mixing bowl beat together 2 tablespoons meringue powder, ¼ cup warm water, and 2 cups sifted powdered sugar with a fork until smooth. Gradually stir in about 1½ cups additional sifted powdered sugar to make a smooth glaze that is spreadable but not runny. (It should have a flowing consistency and be too thin to hold ridges when spread.) Using powdered or liquid food coloring, color glaze as desired.

To Make Ahead:
Bake the cookies as directed, except do not frost. Place cooled cookies in a freezer container and freeze for up to 1 month. Before serving, let the cookies thaw. Decorate as desired.

whimsical gingerbread cookies

As shown on pages 184–185.

Ingredients

- 1 cup butter
- ⅔ cup packed brown sugar
- ⅔ cup molasses
- 4 cups all-purpose flour
- 2 teaspoons finely shredded orange peel
- 1⅔ teaspoons ground cinnamon
- 1 teaspoon ground ginger
- ¾ teaspoon baking soda
- ¼ teaspoon ground cloves
- 1 egg
- 1⅓ teaspoons vanilla
- 1 recipe Butter Frosting

Method

In a medium saucepan combine butter, brown sugar, and molasses. Stir over medium heat just until butter melts and sugar dissolves. Pour into a large mixing bowl; cool for 5 minutes.

Meanwhile, in another bowl stir together flour, orange peel, cinnamon, ginger, baking soda, and cloves; set aside.

Add egg and vanilla to butter mixture; mix. Add flour mixture; beat at low speed until well combined. (If necessary, stir in last portion of flour mixture by hand.) Divide dough in half. Wrap each dough portion in clear plastic wrap or waxed paper; chill at least 2 hours or overnight.

Shape cookies as directed, right. Bake in a 350° oven for 8 to 10 minutes or until edges are firm. Cool on cookie sheet for 1 minute. Using a wide metal spatula, remove cookies from cookie sheets and cool on a wire rack.

Decorate as desired using Butter Frosting to pipe onto the cooled cookies, adding expressions and details such as eyes, mouths, etc., and color on the snowman's hat and the tree decorations. Makes 24 to 30 cookies (varies with the shape selected).

For each reindeer, shape dough into one 1¼-inch ball and three ½-inch balls. On ungreased cookie sheet flatten the 1¼-inch ball to ½ inch and form it into a diamond shape for head. Flatten one of the ½-inch balls to ½-inch to form nose; place it on top of head, slightly lower than center. Shape remaining ½-inch balls into long diamonds and attach to head for ears. Use broken pretzel twists for antlers, inserting into dough at top of head.

For each snowman, shape the dough into one 1-inch ball, one ¾-inch ball, two ½-inch balls, and one ¼-inch ball. On an ungreased cookie sheet flatten the 1-inch ball to ½-inch for body. Flatten the ¾-inch ball to ½ inch and attach to the body for the head. Shape one ½-inch ball into a triangle and attach to the head for a hat. Shape the other ½-inch ball into a log about 1-inch long; place it between the hat and head, atop the dough, curving to fit like a brim. Attach ¼-inch ball at tip of hat to form a tassel. If desired, shape another ¼-inch ball and place on head for nose. Insert broken pretzel twists for arms, if desired.

For each tree, shape dough into one 1-inch ball, one ¾-inch ball, one ½-inch ball, and one ¼-inch ball. On an ungreased cookie sheet flatten 1-inch ball to ½ inch and shape it into a triangle. Flatten ¾-inch ball to ½ inch; shape it into a triangle, and attach it to peak of large triangle. Shape ½-inch ball into a triangle and attach it to second triangle, slightly overlapping at point. Attach the ¼-inch ball to middle of bottom triangle for a trunk. If desired, shape another ¼-inch ball into a star and place atop tree.

Butter Frosting: In mixing bowl combine ⅓ cup melted butter, 3 cups sifted powdered sugar, and enough milk (about 2 to 3 tablespoons) to make of piping consistency. Tint frosting using liquid or paste food coloring.

To Make Ahead:

Bake cookies as directed, except do not decorate with frosting. Place the cooled cookies in a single layer in a freezer container and freeze for up to 1 month. Before serving, let thaw. Decorate as desired.

anise hazelnut tea cakes

As shown on pages 184–185.

Ingredients

- 1 cup butter
- 2¼ cups all-purpose flour
- ½ cup sifted powdered sugar
- 1 tablespoon water
- 1 teaspoon anise seed, crushed
- 1 teaspoon vanilla
- ¾ cup finely chopped hazelnuts (filberts), almonds, or pecans
- 1 cup sifted powdered sugar
- ½ teaspoon powdered food coloring (optional)

Method

In a large mixing bowl beat butter with an electric mixer on medium to high speed for 30 seconds. Add half of the flour; beat at low speed until combined. Add the ½ cup powdered sugar, water, anise seed, and vanilla. Beat just until combined. Beat or stir in remaining flour. Stir in nuts. Cover and chill dough about 1 hour or until easy to handle.

Shape dough into 1-inch balls. Place cookies 1 inch apart on an ungreased cookie sheet. Bake in a 325° oven for 18 to 20 minutes. Remove cookies from cookie sheet and cool on a wire rack.

In a self-sealing plastic bag place 1 cup powdered sugar and the powdered food coloring. Add a few cookies to bag at a time and shake gently to coat. Place cookies in an airtight container and store at room temperature up to 3 days. Makes about 4½ dozen cookies. (*Note:* If powdered food coloring is omitted, coat cookies again with additional powdered sugar just before serving.)

cranberry-apricot florentines

As shown on pages 184–185.

Ingredients

- ⅓ cup butter or margarine
- ⅓ cup milk
- ¼ cup sugar
- 1 cup finely chopped macadamia nuts or sliced almonds
- ½ cup snipped dried cranberries or dried tart red cherries
- ¼ cup snipped dried apricots
- ¼ cup all-purpose flour
- ¾ cup semisweet chocolate pieces
- 2 teaspoons shortening
- 2 ounces white chocolate baking squares, chopped
- 2 teaspoons shortening

Method

Grease and flour a cookie sheet. (Repeat greasing and flouring for each batch.) Set aside.

In a heavy medium-size saucepan combine butter or margarine, milk, and sugar. Bring to a full rolling boil, stirring occasionally. Remove from heat. Stir in the macadamia nuts or almonds, cranberries or cherries, and apricots. Stir in flour.

Drop the batter from a level tablespoon at least 3 inches apart onto prepared cookie sheet. Using back of a spoon, spread batter into 3-inch circles.

Bake in a 350° oven about 8 minutes or until edges are lightly browned. Cool on cookie sheet for 1 minute. Carefully remove cookies from cookie sheet and cool on waxed paper.

In a heavy small saucepan heat semisweet chocolate pieces and 2 teaspoons shortening over very low heat just until melted, stirring occasionally. In another heavy small saucepan heat the white chocolate and 2 teaspoons shortening over very low heat just until melted, stirring occasionally.

Spread bottom of each cookie with a scant teaspoon of the semisweet chocolate mixture. Drizzle the white chocolate mixture onto dark chocolate. To marble, draw the tines of a fork through white chocolate. Let cookies stand, chocolate side up, until the chocolate is set. Place cookies in a single layer in an airtight container and store in refrigerator for up to 3 days. Makes about 24.

lemon poppy seed shortbread

As shown on pages 184–185.

Ingredients

2 ⅓ cups all-purpose flour
⅓ cup sugar
1 tablespoon poppy seed
1 cup butter
2 teaspoons finely shredded lemon peel
1 recipe Lemon Glaze
Coarse pastel multi-colored sugar

Method

In a large mixing bowl stir together the flour, sugar, and poppy seed. Using a pastry blender, cut in the butter until mixture resembles fine crumbs and starts to cling. Stir in the lemon peel. Form the mixture into a ball and knead until smooth.

On a lightly floured surface, roll dough to slightly less than ½-inch thickness. Using 1½- to 2-inch cookie cutters, cut dough into shapes. Place the cookies 1 inch apart on an ungreased cookie sheet. Bake in a 325° oven for 20 to 25 minutes or until bottoms just start to turn brown. Remove cookies from cookie sheet and cool on wire rack.

Lightly spread cookies with Lemon Glaze. Sprinkle with multi-colored sugar. Let the cookies stand until the glaze is set. Place in an airtight container and store at room temperature up to 3 days. Makes about 16 to 20 cookies.

Lemon Glaze: In a small bowl stir together 1½ cups sifted powdered sugar, 2 teaspoons lemon juice, and enough milk (about 2 tablespoons) to make glaze easy to spread.

chocolate mint pillows

As shown on pages 184–185.

Ingredients

⅓ recipe Sugar Cookie Dough (see recipe page 186)
¼ teaspoon mint extract
Few drops green food coloring
4 1.55-ounce bars milk chocolate

Method

In a medium mixing bowl combine ⅓ recipe cookie dough, mint extract, and green food coloring. Using a wooden spoon, stir until combined and dough is a light to medium green. If necessary, add more coloring. Divide dough in half. Wrap each half in clear plastic wrap and chill about 3 hours or until dough is easy to handle.

On a lightly floured surface, roll one portion of dough (keep other portion chilled) into a 10×6-inch rectangle. Cut into fifteen 2-inch squares.

Break chocolate bars into rectangles along markings. Place one small rectangle of chocolate on one half of each of the squares of dough. Bring other half of dough up and over to cover chocolate and form a rectangle. Place squares 1 inch apart on a lightly greased cookie sheet. Using a fork, press edges together to seal. Repeat with other portion of dough.

Bake cookies in a 375° oven for 8 to 10 minutes or until edges are firm and bottoms are lightly browned. Remove cookies from cookie sheet; cool on a wire rack.

Place remaining pieces of chocolate in a heavy small saucepan and heat over very low heat until just melted, stirring almost constantly. Spoon the melted chocolate into a small self-sealing plastic bag. Seal the bag and snip a small corner from bag. Pipe a small scroll or other design onto tops of cooled cookies. Place cookies in refrigerator for a few minutes until chocolate is set. Place cookies in a single layer in an airtight container and store at room temperature for up to 3 days. Makes 30 cookies.

cookie containers

Razzle, dazzle containers are the fitting final step for your tasty treasures. Give guests packaging options that will bowl them over. Choose bright new pails lined with colorful cellophane, paper bags decorated with punch holes, jars of all kinds, or purchased lightweight acrylic containers just big enough for one very special cookie.

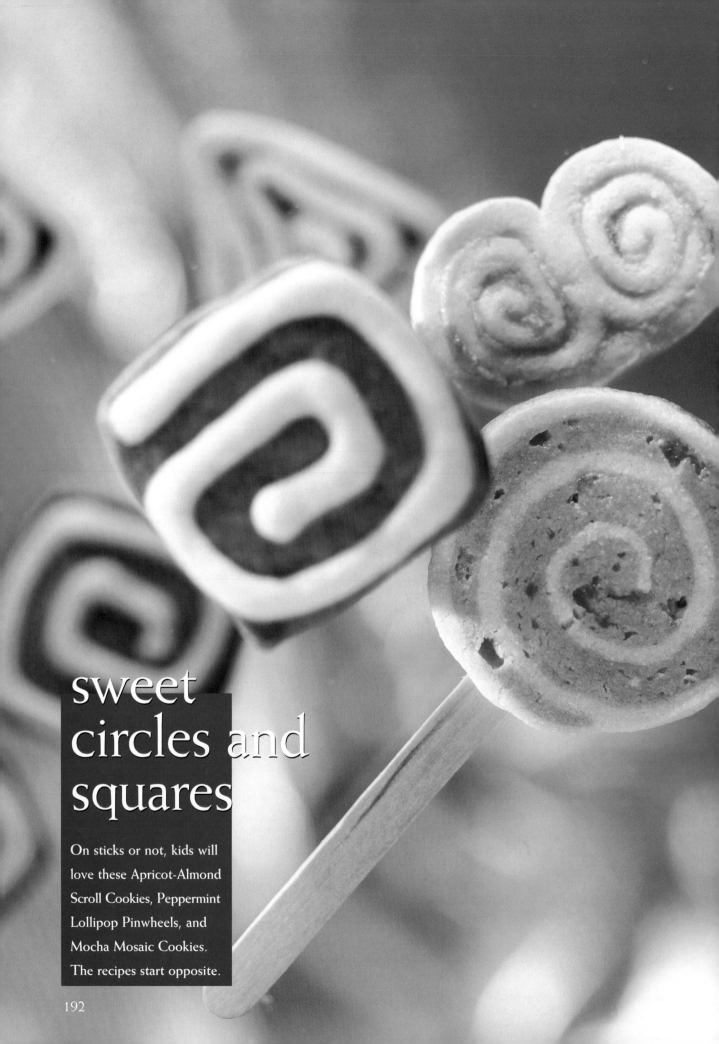

sweet circles and squares

On sticks or not, kids will love these Apricot-Almond Scroll Cookies, Peppermint Lollipop Pinwheels, and Mocha Mosaic Cookies. The recipes start opposite.

peppermint lollipop pinwheels

As shown opposite.

Ingredients

- 1 cup butter or margarine
- 1 cup sugar
- 1/3 teaspoon baking powder
- 1 egg
- Few drops peppermint extract
- 2 2/3 cups all-purpose flour
- Several drops red food coloring
- 1/4 cup finely crushed peppermint candies

Method

Beat butter or margarine in a large mixing bowl with an electric mixer on medium to high speed for 30 seconds. Add sugar and baking powder; beat till combined. Beat in egg and peppermint extract till thoroughly combined. Beat in as much of the flour as you can with the mixer. Stir in any remaining flour.

Divide dough in half. Add red food coloring and peppermint candies to one-half of dough; mix until thoroughly combined. Leave remaining dough plain. Cover both halves and chill about 1 hour or until easy to handle.

Roll each half of dough between two sheets of waxed paper into a 13×11-inch rectangle. Place peppermint dough on a baking sheet. Place in freezer for 15 to 20 minutes or until firm. Remove from freezer. Remove top sheets of waxed paper from plain dough and peppermint dough. Carefully invert peppermint dough over plain dough. Remove top sheet of waxed paper. Let stand 5 minutes or until dough is easy to roll.

Roll up, jelly-roll style, starting from one of the long sides, removing bottom sheet of waxed paper as you roll. Pinch to seal. Cut roll in half crosswise. Wrap each half in waxed paper or clear plastic wrap. Chill dough about 4 hours or until firm.

Arrange *wooden sticks* about 4 inches apart on lightly greased baking sheets. Remove one roll from the refrigerator. Unwrap and reshape slightly, if necessary. Cut dough into 3/8-inch-thick slices. Place slice of dough over one end of each stick, so that end of stick is about 1/2 inch from top edge of cookie slice (see tip *page 195*). Bake in a 375° oven for 10 to 12 minutes or until edges are firm. Cool on cookie sheet for 1 minute. Remove and cool completely on wire racks. Repeat with remaining dough. Makes about 34.

Peppermint Pinwheels: Omit wooden sticks. Cut dough into 1/4-inch-thick slices. Place 2 inches apart on a lightly greased cookie sheet. Bake as directed. Makes about 50.

apricot-almond scroll cookies

As shown opposite.

Ingredients

- 1/2 cup finely snipped dried apricots
- 1/2 cup almond paste (1/2 of 8-ounce can)
- 3/4 cup butter or margarine
- 3/4 cup sugar
- 1 teaspoon baking powder
- 1 egg
- 1 teaspoon vanilla
- 2 1/3 cups all-purpose flour

Method

For filling, combine dried apricots and enough *boiling water* to cover. Let stand 20 minutes or until softened. Drain, reserving liquid. Crumble almond paste into a bowl. Add drained apricots and enough of reserved apricot liquid (about 1 tablespoon) to make of spreading consistency. Set aside.

Beat butter or margarine in a large mixing bowl with an electric mixer on medium to high speed for 30 seconds. Add sugar

apricot-almond scroll cookies — *continued*

and baking powder; beat until combined. Beat in egg and vanilla until thoroughly combined. Beat in as much of the flour as you can with the electric mixer. Stir in any remaining flour. Divide the dough in half. Cover and chill the dough about 1 hour or until easy to handle.

Roll one half of dough between two sheets of waxed paper into a 14×9-inch rectangle. Remove top sheet of waxed paper. Spread half of the filling over dough to within ¼ inch of

edges. Roll up, jelly-roll style, starting from both short sides of the dough and rolling toward the center (see tip *opposite*), removing bottom sheet of waxed paper as you roll. Press lightly at the center to seal. Wrap in waxed paper or clear plastic wrap. Repeat with remaining dough and filling. Chill about 4 hours or until firm, up to 24 hours.

Remove one roll from the refrigerator. Unwrap and reshape slightly, if necessary. Cut into ¼-inch-thick slices. Place 2 inches apart on a greased cookie sheet.

Bake in a 375° oven for 10 to 12 minutes or until the edges are firm. Cool on the cookie sheet

tip *Wrap rolls of dough in clear plastic wrap; twist the ends tightly to seal. Place the wrapped rolls in tall drinking glasses before chilling so the rolls will not flatten from resting on the refrigerator shelf.*

for 1 minute. Remove cookies and cool completely on wire racks. Repeat with the remaining dough. Makes about 72.

mocha mosaic cookies

Use a small metal spatula to smooth and square off the sides of the dough log. As shown on page 192.

Ingredients

- 1 tablespoon coffee liqueur or milk
- 2 teaspoons instant espresso powder or instant coffee crystals
- ½ cup butter or margarine
- ¾ cup sugar
- ½ teaspoon baking powder
- 1 egg
- 1 ounce semisweet chocolate, melted and cooled
- 1¾ cups all-purpose flour
  Cream Dough

Method

Stir together coffee liqueur and espresso powder or coffee crystals in a small bowl or custard cup; set aside for a few minutes until coffee is dissolved.

Beat butter or margarine in a large mixing bowl with an electric mixer on medium to high speed for 30 seconds. Add sugar and baking powder; beat until combined. Beat in egg, chocolate, and liqueur mixture until thoroughly combined. Beat in as much of the flour as you can with

the mixer. Stir in any remaining flour with a wooden spoon.

Cover and chill dough about 1 hour or until easy to handle. Shape dough into a 1¾-inch square log 10 inches long. Wrap in waxed paper or clear plastic wrap. Chill about 4 hours or until firm, up to 24 hours. Shortly before baking, prepare Cream Dough. Place Cream Dough in a heavy clear plastic bag.

Cut dough into ¼-inch-thick slices. Place about 2 inches apart on an ungreased cookie sheet.

Snip a small corner of the Cream Dough bag with scissors. Carefully pipe the Cream Dough in a square coil pattern over the cookie slices (see tip *below*). Bake in a 375° oven for 9 to 11 minutes or until the edges are firm. Cool on cookie sheet for 1 minute. Remove cookies and cool on wire racks. Makes 40.

Cream Dough: Beat 2 tablespoons butter in a small bowl on medium speed for about 30 seconds. Add 2 tablespoons sugar, beat until combined. Add 3 tablespoons light cream or milk. Beat in ½ cup all-purpose flour until smooth.

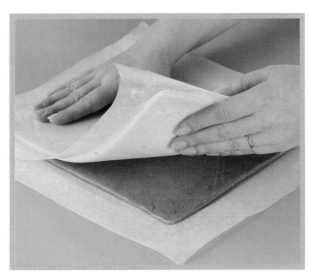

tip *Chill the top layer of dough in the freezer for 15 to 20 minutes or until firm—it will be like stiff cardboard. This will allow you to easily invert the top layer over the bottom layer of dough, lining up the edges. Let the two layers of dough rest until they are easy to roll, about 5 minutes.*

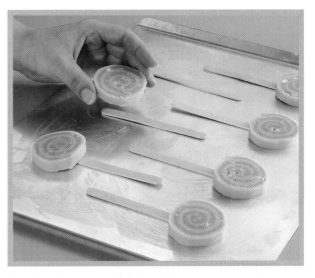

tip *For efficient spacing on the cookie sheet, alternate the direction of the wooden sticks. Place the dough slices over the sticks, leaving about ½ inch between the end of the stick and the top of the cookie. The dough will bake onto the stick.*

tip *Grasp the bag tightly with one hand. With the fingertips of other hand, gently apply pressure to the bag. Use the outside edges of the mocha cookie as your guide for piping the cream dough pattern. To help keep your hands steady, rest your elbows on the countertop.*

tip *Use the waxed paper to lift the roll of dough, gently nudging it forward with your thumbs and peeling away the excess paper as you roll. This method keeps the roll smooth and uniform. It keeps your hands cleaner, too.*

getting ready for santa

What could be more fun than making special treats for Santa. These Quilt Block Cookies are as much fun to make as they are to eat, and they leave plenty of room for colorful imagination. Recipes for the cookies and Santa's Cocoa Mix are opposite.

quilt block cookies

As shown opposite and at right.

Ingredients

⅓ cup margarine or butter
⅓ cup shortening
2 cups all-purpose flour
¾ cup sugar
1 egg
1 tablespoon milk
1 teaspoon baking powder

1 teaspoon vanilla
  Egg Paint (see recipe
  on page 183)

Method

Beat margarine and shortening with an electric mixer about 30 seconds or until softened. Add about half the flour, the sugar, egg, milk, baking powder, vanilla, and *dash salt*. Beat until combined. Beat or stir in remaining flour. Divide dough in half. Cover and

After scoring the dough with a wooden skewer, paint the cookies with Egg Paint. When the cookies are baked, the egg mixture becomes shiny and the score lines separate slightly, resembling the seams of a pieced quilt.

chill about 3 hours or until easy to handle.

Roll half of the dough on a lightly floured surface to a ¼-inch thickness. Cut into 4-inch squares. Use a skewer and ruler to score quilt patterns. Use Egg Paint to color in sections.

Bake in a 350° oven for 15 minutes or until done. Cool on cookie sheet 2 to 3 minutes. Remove cookies and cool on a wire rack. Makes about 24.

santa's cocoa mix

As shown opposite.

Ingredients

1 8-quart package (about 10 cups) nonfat dry milk powder
1 16-ounce package (about 4¾ cups) sifted powdered sugar
1¾ cups unsweetened cocoa powder
1½ cups instant malted milk powder

1 6-ounce jar (1¾ cups) powdered nondairy creamer
  Marshmallows or whipped cream (optional)

Method

Combine nonfat dry milk powder, powdered sugar, unsweetened cocoa powder, instant malted milk powder, and nondairy creamer in a large bowl. Stir until thoroughly combined. Store cocoa mixture in an airtight container. Makes about 16 cups or enough for 48 (8-ounce) servings.

For each individual serving, place ⅓ cup cocoa mixture in a mug; add ¾ cup boiling water. Stir to dissolve. Top with marshmallows or a dollop of whipped cream.

big batch baking

Fast Florentines take a fraction of the time that the traditional version requires and have the same rich fruit-and-nut flavor. Use a doily to stencil Simple Sandies with powdered sugar before cutting. The recipes are opposite.

fast florentines

Traditional Florentines have bottoms spread with chocolate. Spreading the tops of these bars is quicker. As shown opposite.

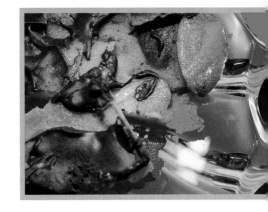

Ingredients

- ⅓ cup butter or margarine
- ⅓ cup milk
- ¼ cup sugar
- 2 tablespoons honey
- 1 cup sliced almonds
- ⅔ cup mixed candied fruits and peels, finely chopped
- ⅓ cup all-purpose flour
- ½ cup semisweet chocolate pieces

Method

Line a 15×10×1-inch baking pan with heavy foil and generously grease the foil.

Combine butter or margarine, milk, sugar, and honey in a medium saucepan. Bring to a full rolling boil, stirring occasionally. Remove from heat. Stir in almonds and candied fruits and peels. Stir in flour until combined. Spread evenly in prepared pan. Bake in a 350° oven for 20 to 25 minutes.

Remove from oven to a wire rack. Sprinkle with chocolate pieces. Cool 10 minutes to soften chocolate. Spread chocolate over baked bars (will not completely cover surface). Lift foil from pan to cutting board. Carefully cut warm cookies into 2×1-inch bars (do not separate). Cool completely. Separate into bars, cutting with knife again, if necessary. Store in refrigerator. Makes 54.

simple sandies

First, pat the rich dough onto the bottom of the pan using a small piece of waxed paper. Then spread with a small spatula or knife to level the dough. As shown opposite.

Ingredients

- 1 cup butter (no substitutes)
- ½ cup sugar
- ¼ teaspoon baking powder
- 1 tablespoon water
- 2 teaspoons vanilla
- 2 cups all-purpose flour
- 1 cup finely chopped pecans
  Powdered sugar

Method

Beat butter in a large mixing bowl for 30 seconds. Add sugar and baking powder; beat until combined. Add water and vanilla and beat until combined. Beat in as much flour as you can. Stir in any remaining flour and chopped

pecans. Spread dough in a greased 15×10×1-inch baking pan.

Bake in a 325° oven about 20 minutes or until golden around the edges of pan. Place doily on the surface; sift powdered sugar over doily, moving it as necessary to make design over entire surface. Cool on wire rack. Cut cookies into diamond shapes. Makes about 45.

gifts from the kitchen

*S*hare your love of
baking and crafting
this holiday season
with a little help from
this idea-filled chapter.
From sweet things to
bake to fun packaging
options to present your
goodies, your gifts
from the kitchen will
always be remembered.

jeweled tins and goodies

For fragile baked goods, nothing could be finer than to present them in a beautifully decorated covered tin, lined with a lovely cross-stitched bread cloth or towel. The tins are decorated with bows, bells, acrylic jewels, and sparkling cord in most imaginative ways. The bread cloths and towels are worked quickly using simple cross-stitch patterns. Fill the tins with fresh-from-the-kitchen Onion-Bacon Rolls, Easy Soft Pretzels, or purchased candies. Instructions for the tins and linens begin on page 210. Recipes are on pages 210 and 212–213.

Dressing goodies in their finest, these whimsical Jester Jar Covers can be made the right size for almost any jar. By solving the wrapping problem, they become welcome gifts themselves. Tuck Kiwi-Pear Preserves or Rhubarb-Raspberry Jam inside small jars, and pack an assortment of One-for-All Christmas Cookies into a larger one. The instructions, patterns, and recipes begin on page 213.

jester jar covers and treats

personalized popcorn bags

In the tradition of the finest gourmet shops, these Popcorn Gift Bags are the ultimate in presenting colorful Rainbow Popcorn, crunchy Nutty Nibble Mix, or microwave-popped Magic Popcorn. To personalize purchased gift bags, cut out cookie cutter shapes, back with clear cellophane, and embellish with paint-pen holiday messages. Let the entire family help with this project for a fun-filled afternoon. Instructions for the bags and recipes begin on page 216.

sweet holiday gift bags

As sweet as candy, these cross-stitched Santa and reindeer gift bags are sure to be treasured long after the candy is gone. The motifs are stitched on 18-count white Aida cloth then sewn to velveteen. Line the bags with plastic wrap and fill them to the brim with Marbled Bark and Marshmallow Fudge. The instructions for the bags and recipes begin on page 217.

In the wink of an eye, you can turn plain carry-out containers into clever wraps by decorating the sides with a candy-cane motif using a foam brush and red and white paint. To make the gift truly one-of-a-kind, fill the boxes with delicious spiced nuts. The instructions for the containers and the recipes for the nuts begin on page 220.

candy-cane containers

Come in from the cold and feel the warmth of a delightful cup of cocoa served in a decorated gingerbread man mug. The matching cookie jar is filled with popcorn balls, but any goody will do the trick. A painted gingerbread man napkin rests underneath. Instructions begin on page 221; the cookie recipe is on page 188.

gingerbread jar & mugs

heartwarming delights

Hearty Stone Soup, ladled into Parmesan-Herb Bread Bowls, warms both heart and soul. A variety of quick homemade breads, relishes, and Apple-Berry Cider complete the delicious menu. The Onion-Bacon Rolls (see recipe on page 212), Sweet Potato Bread, and Twist-o-Caraway Sticks are packaged in clever No-Sew Gift Bags created from Christmas print fabrics. The bags are constructed using fusible webbing and glue. The instructions and diagrams for the bags and all of the recipes begin on page 223.

jeweled tins

As shown on pages 202–203, it takes about 22½ inches of trim to go around a can once, approximately 1 yard to wrap a handle, 1½ yards for a large bow at the base of the handle, and 3 to 4 yards of wide ribbon for a large bow on lid.

Materials
18-millimeter round acrylic mirrors
18-millimeter red acrylic
 flower-shaped jewels
4-millimeter gold beads
Thick white crafts glue
22×11-millimeter green
 leaf-shaped jewels
7-inch-diameter colored cans with
 handles and lids, in desired
 heights
Red, green, and metallic braids
 and trims
Wide ribbons
Gift tags; large jingle bells
Thin florist's wire

Instructions
For jeweled can, glue a flower jewel atop an acrylic mirror. Glue a gold bead to center of each flower. Arrange groups of one mirrored flower and two leaves on top of lid, referring to photograph, *pages 202–203*. When leaves and flowers are spaced as desired, glue in place. Repeat pattern around base of tin, using additional jewels, mirrors, and beads. If desired, wrap trim around handle and tie loopy bows made from the trim at sides of handle.

For remaining cans, glue trims around bases of cans and edges of lids as desired. Make a large ribbon bow for each lid. Wire a jingle bell to bow, if desired. Wrap handles with remaining trims.

Use a scrap of trim to tie a gift tag to the handle of each decorated can.

easy soft pretzels

As shown on page 203.

Ingredients
1 10-ounce package refrigerated
 pizza dough
1 beaten egg
1 tablespoon water
 Coarse salt, onion salt,
 sesame seed, or poppy seed

Method
Unroll pizza dough onto an 18-inch piece of lightly floured waxed paper. Roll dough into a 16×10-inch rectangle. Cut dough into ten 1-inch-wide strips.

Shape each strip of dough into a circle, overlapping about 4 inches from each end and leaving ends free. Taking one end of dough into each hand, twist at point where dough overlaps. Carefully lift each end across to edges of circle opposite it. Tuck ends under to seal. Repeat with remaining strips. Place pretzels on an ungreased baking sheet, 1 inch apart.

Stir together egg and water. Brush the pretzels with the egg mixture. Sprinkle with salt, onion salt, sesame seed, or poppy seed. Bake in a 350° oven for 15 to 17 minutes or until light golden. Makes 10 pretzels.

holly towel and bread cloth

As shown on pages 202–203.

Materials

Fabrics for towel

½ yard of ⅞-inch-wide 14-count white Aida banding with red trim

Purchased red, white, or green guest towel

Fabric for bread cloth

18×18-inch piece of 18-count red, white, or green Davosa fabric

Threads

Cotton embroidery floss in colors listed in keys

Blending filament in colors listed in keys

White sewing thread

Supplies

Needle

Embroidery hoop

Instructions

For towel, tape or zigzag ends of banding to prevent fraying. With long edge at top, find center of banding. Count four squares to the right; begin stitching left edge of first holly motif there.

Work blended needle as specified on chart. Work backstitches and lazy daisy stitches using two plies of floss. Stitch three more motifs, one to the right of the first and two to the left, separating each with eight squares.

Center banding on one end of towel and trim to width of towel plus 1 inch. Turn under ½ inch along each cut end and pin. Machine-sew banding to towel.

For bread cloth, machine-zigzag around fabric, ¾ inch from edges. In one corner, measure 1¼ inches from zigzag stitching; begin stitching center berry of the design there. Work blended needle as specified in key over two threads of fabric. Use two plies of floss to work backstitches and lazy daisy stitches.

Repeat motif in each of the remaining three corners of fabric. For fringe, remove threads between cut edge and machine stitching.

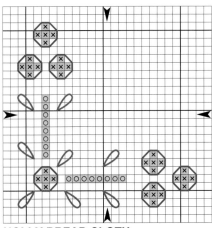

HOLLY BREAD CLOTH

HOLLY TOWEL

HOLLY BREAD CLOTH		
ANCHOR	DMC	
BLENDED NEEDLE		
9046	☒	321 Christmas red (3X) and 003 Kreinik red blending filament (1X)
923	⊡	699 Christmas green (3X) and 009HL Kreinik emerald blending filament (1X)
BACKSTITCH		
9046	╱	321 Christmas red– berries
LAZY DAISY		
923	⬭	699 Christmas green

Stitch count: 23 high x 23 wide

Finished design sizes:
14-count fabric – 1⅝ x 1⅝ inches
18-count fabric – 1¼ x 1¼ inches
8½-count fabric – 2¾ x 2¾ inches

HOLLY TOWEL		
ANCHOR	DMC	
BLENDED NEEDLE		
9046	☒	321 Christmas red (2X) and 003 Kreinik red blending filament (1X)
923	⊡	699 Christmas green (2X) and 009HL Kreinik emerald blending filament (1X)
BACKSTITCH		
9046	╱	321 Christmas red– berries
LAZY DAISY		
923	⬭	699 Christmas green

Stitch count: 9 high x 37 wide

Finished design sizes:
14-count fabric – ⅝ x 2⅝ inches
18-count fabric – ½ x 2 inches
8½-count fabric – 1 x 4⅜ inches

candy cane towel and bread cloth

As shown on pages 202–203.

Materials

Fabrics for towel
½ yard of 1¾-inch-wide 14-count white Aida banding with white trim

Purchased red, white, or green guest towel

Fabrics for bread cloth
Purchased red, white, or green bread cloth

Four 4×4-inch pieces of 8½-count waste canvas

Floss
Cotton embroidery floss in colors listed in key

Supplies
Needle; white sewing thread

Large red seed beads

Instructions

For towel, tape or zigzag ends of banding to prevent fraying. With long edge at top, find center of banding and center of chart; begin stitching first motif there. Work cross-stitches using two plies of floss. Work backstitches using one ply of floss. Work lazy daisy stitches and French knots using two plies of floss. Work three more motifs on each side of first one, separating motifs with 11 squares.

For bread cloth, machine-zigzag around square, ¾ inch from edges. Tape or zigzag edges of waste canvas to prevent fraying. Baste one piece of waste canvas diagonally across each corner of bread cloth with bottom center of canvas ½ inch above machine stitching.

Work cross-stitches and lazy daisy stitches using six plies of floss. Work backstitches using two plies of floss. Substitute one seed bead, attached with one ply of red floss, for each French knot.

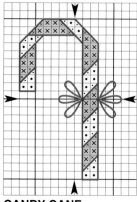

CANDY CANE

CANDY CANE		
ANCHOR	DMC	
002	⊡	000 White
9046	☒	321 Christmas red
BACKSTITCH		
9046	⁄	321 Christmas red– all stitches
LAZY DAISY		
923	⬭	699 Christmas green
FRENCH KNOT		
9046	●	321 Christmas red

Stitch count: 20 high x 12 wide
Finished design sizes:
14-count fabric – 1⅝ x ⅞ inches
18-count fabric – 1⅛ x ⅝ inches
8½-count fabric – 2⅜ x 1⅜ inches

Remove basting threads and trim canvas close to stitching. Wet canvas and pull individual canvas threads from under cross-stitches using tweezers.

onion-bacon rolls

As shown on page 203 and 209.

Ingredients
1 12-ounce package sliced bacon
1 large onion, chopped (1 cup)
½ cup chopped green pepper
½ teaspoon dried dillweed
½ teaspoon pepper

1 16-ounce loaf frozen bread dough, thawed
Milk
Poppy seed, fennel seed, or sesame seed

Method
For filling, in a medium skillet cook the bacon until crisp; remove bacon, reserving 1 tablespoon of the drippings in the skillet. Drain

the bacon on paper towels and crumble when cool.

Cook the onion, green pepper, dillweed, and pepper in the reserved drippings until the onion is tender, but not brown. Cool. Stir in the crumbled bacon.

Divide the bread dough into 30 portions. Roll each portion into a ball; roll or pat each ball into a 3-inch circle. Place a scant 1 tablespoon of the filling in the center of each circle. Bring up the edges of the dough around filling; seal the edges together.

Arrange the filled rolls with seam side down, on a greased baking sheet. Use a pastry brush to lightly brush top of each roll with milk. Sprinkle each roll with a pinch of poppy seed, fennel seed, or sesame seed.

Bake, uncovered, in a 375° oven for 15 to 20 minutes or until the rolls are golden. Serve warm. Makes 30 rolls.

To freeze, prepare and bake the rolls as directed above. Cool thoroughly on a wire rack. Transfer the rolls to a freezer container and freeze for up to 4 months.

To reheat, arrange the frozen rolls on an ungreased baking sheet. Bake, uncovered, in a 375° oven about 15 minutes or until the rolls are heated through.

jester jar covers

As shown on page 204, the small cover fits a jelly jar, medium cover fits a pint jar, and large cover fits a quart jar.

Materials

¾ yard each of 45-inch-wide fabric in two complementary Christmas prints (makes one large and one medium or small cover)
Ruler
Erasable fabric marking pen
Threads to match fabrics
¼-inch-wide elastic: 11 inches for large or medium cover; 7½ inches for small
Decorative ribbon or cord: one yard for large or medium cover; ⅔ yard for small cover
4 jingle bells in desired size and color for each cover

Instructions

Cut a 24×24-inch square from each fabric for a large jar cover, a 19×19-inch square from each fabric for a medium jar cover, or a 14×14-inch square from each fabric for a small jar cover. Using the diagram and appropriate measurements, *right*, as a guide for

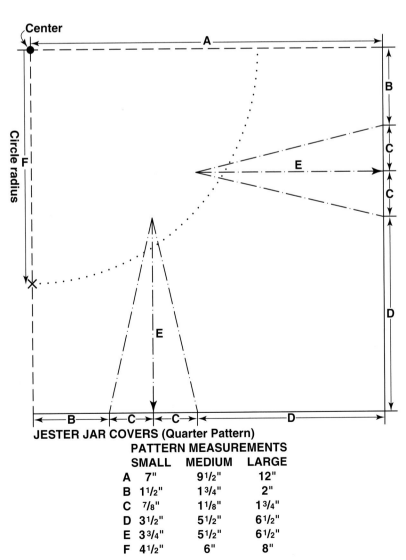

JESTER JAR COVERS (Quarter Pattern)

PATTERN MEASUREMENTS

	SMALL	MEDIUM	LARGE
A	7"	9½"	12"
B	1½"	1¾"	2"
C	⅞"	1⅛"	1¾"
D	3½"	5½"	6½"
E	3¾"	5½"	6½"
F	4½"	6"	8"

each cover, carefully measure and transfer the dart markings to the wrong side of each fabric square. Transfer the circle outline and X to the right side of one square.

Make a ½-inch-long vertical buttonhole at the X on marked fabric square; clip open. Stitch darts on both squares. Press the darts to the left on one square and to the right on the other. Using a ¼-inch seam allowance, sew squares together with right sides facing. Leave an opening for turning. Clip corners and turn right side out. Sew the opening closed and press.

To make circular casing, stitch two circles, one on each side of marked outline, each ¼ inch beyond markings. Insert elastic through buttonhole, overlap elastic ends; stitch. Sew a bell to each corner. Slip cover over jar. Tie cord or ribbon around elastic casing.

rhubarb-raspberry jam

As shown on page 204.

Ingredients

6 cups fresh or frozen sweetened sliced rhubarb

4 cups sugar

2 cups raspberries or one 12-ounce package frozen loose-pack raspberries

1 3-ounce package raspberry-flavored gelatin

Method

Combine rhubarb and sugar in a large kettle or Dutch oven. Let stand 15 to 20 minutes or until sugar is moistened. Bring to boiling. Boil, uncovered, for 10 minutes, stirring frequently.

Add the raspberries; return to boiling. Boil hard for 5 to 6 minutes or until thick, stirring frequently. Remove from heat. Add gelatin; stir until dissolved.

Ladle into half-pint freezer jars or into freezer containers, leaving ½-inch headspace. Seal and label the jars or containers. Let stand at room temperature several hours or until jam is set. Store in refrigerator or freezer. Makes about 5 half-pint gifts.

Gift label: Serve with toast, muffins, or scones. Store jam up to 3 weeks in refrigerator or up to 1 year in freezer.

kiwi-pear preserves

As shown on page 204.

Ingredients

8 kiwi fruits; 2 large ripe pears

4 cups sugar

½ of a 6-ounce package (1 foil pouch) liquid fruit pectin

½ teaspoon finely shredded lime or lemon peel

2 tablespoons lime or lemon juice

Method

Peel and chop kiwi (should measure 2½ cups). Peel, core, and chop pears (should measure 1½ cups).

In large bowl stir together fruits. Stir in sugar. Let stand 10 minutes. Combine pectin, lime peel, and lime juice. Add to fruit mixture; stir.

Ladle mixture into half-pint freezer jars, leaving ½ inch at top. Seal; label. Let stand several hours. Store in refrigerator or freezer. Makes about 6 half-pint gifts.

Gift label: Serve with muffins. Store up to 3 weeks in refrigerator or up to 1 year in freezer.

one-for-all christmas cookies

As shown on page 204.

Ingredients

  ¾ cup margarine or butter
1¾ cups all-purpose flour
  ½ cup sugar
  1 egg yolk
  ½ teaspoon vanilla
  ¼ teaspoon baking powder
  ¼ teaspoon flavoring

Method

Beat margarine with an electric mixer on medium to high speed about 30 seconds or until softened.

Add about half of the flour, sugar, egg yolk, vanilla, baking powder, and flavoring. Beat until combined. Then beat or stir in remaining flour. Do not chill dough unless otherwise directed.

For Spritz, use ¼ teaspoon almond extract for flavoring. If desired, tint dough with food coloring. Pack into a cookie press. Force onto an ungreased cookie sheet. Decorate cookies with candies or colored sugars. Bake in a 375° oven for 8 to 10 minutes or until edges are firm but not browned. Remove cookies. Cool on a wire rack. Makes about 42.

For Pecan Snowballs, use ¼ teaspoon almond extract for flavoring. After all flour is added, stir or knead in ½ cup finely chopped pecans, almonds, or walnuts. Shape dough into 1-inch balls. Place 1 inch apart on an ungreased cookie sheet. Bake in a 325° oven for 15–17 minutes or until edges are firm. Remove cookies; cool slightly on a wire rack. Place 1 cup sifted powdered sugar in a plastic bag. Gently shake a few warm cookies at a time in sugar. Cool completely on wire rack. Makes about 42.

For Cherry Nests, use ¼ teaspoon almond extract for flavoring. In a shallow dish use a fork to slightly beat 1 egg white with 1 tablespoon water. Shape dough into 1-inch balls. Dip balls into egg white mixture, then roll in 1½ cups very finely chopped hazelnuts (filberts), pecans, or walnuts. Place 2 inches apart on ungreased cookie sheet. Press a candied cherry half, cut side down, into center of each cookie. Bake in a 325° oven for 15–17 minutes or until edges are firm. Remove cookies; cool on a wire rack. Makes about 42 cookies.

For Candy Canes, use ¼ teaspoon peppermint extract for flavoring. For each cookie, shape 1 tablespoon of dough into a 4×½-inch log. Place logs 2 inches apart on ungreased cookie sheet. Shape logs into candy canes. Slightly flatten. Bake in a 325° oven about 15 minutes or until edges are firm and bottoms are lightly browned. Cool on cookie sheet for 1 minute. Remove cookies and cool completely on a wire rack. Decorate using red or white decorator icing to pipe diagonal lines on top of cookies. Makes about 30.

For Sugar Bells, use ¼ teaspoon almond extract for flavoring. Shape dough into two 6-inch rolls. Then roll each dough roll in red or green sugar to coat surface. Wrap each roll in waxed paper or clear plastic wrap. Chill for 2–24 hours. Cut dough into ¼-inch-thick slices. Place 1 inch apart on ungreased cookie sheet. Place a candy-coated milk chocolate piece on bottom half of each slice for bell clapper. Let dough slices stand for 1–2 minutes to soften for easier handling. Fold in sides of each slice. Pinch in sides to resemble bell shape. Bake in a 375° oven for 8–10 minutes or until edges are firm but not browned. Remove cookies; cool on a wire rack. Makes about 48.

For Holiday Checkerboards, use ¼ teaspoon almond extract for flavoring. Divide dough in half. Into one portion, knead ¼ teaspoon red food coloring. Into remaining portion knead ¼ teaspoon green food coloring. Shape each pink and green dough into four 10-inch-long ropes. For each checkerboard roll, place one pink rope next to one green rope, then place another green rope on top of first pink rope and another pink rope on top of first green rope. (You will have two checkerboard rolls total.) Wrap each roll in waxed paper or clear plastic wrap. Chill for 2–24 hours. Cut dough into ¼-inch-thick slices. Place 1 inch apart on an ungreased cookie sheet. Bake in a 375° oven for 8–10 minutes or until edges are firm. Remove cookies; cool on a wire rack. Makes about 80.

popcorn gift bags

As shown on page 205.

Materials
Metallic, coated, or heavyweight
    gift bags in desired colors
Large Christmas cookie cutters
Pencil; scissors or crafts knife
Clear cellophane; masking tape
Paint pens in desired colors

Instructions
For each bag, draw around desired cookie cutter onto center of one side of bag. Carefully cut out cookie cutter shape along pencil line, being careful to make no cuts outside of drawn lines.

Cut a rectangular piece of cellophane slightly larger than cutout. Tape cellophane securely to inside of bag directly behind cutout. Use paint pens to add names and decorations to each bag. Allow to dry.

magic popcorn

As shown on page 205.

Ingredients
1 3.5-ounce package microwave
   popcorn or 8 cups popped
   popcorn
Chocolate-Lover's Mix,
   Cheese-Tomato Mix, or Easy
   Herb Seasoning

Method
Prepare popcorn according to package directions. Immediately add desired flavoring mix to popcorn in microwave popping bag or conventionally popped popcorn in a paper bag. Close bag and shake to coat. Makes 6 to 8 servings.

Chocolate-Lover's Mix: Combine 1 cup milk chocolate pieces, ½ cup walnut pieces, and 2 tablespoons instant malted milk powder or presweetened cocoa mix.

Cheese-Tomato Mix: Combine 2 tablespoons grated Parmesan cheese and half a single-serving size envelope (4 teaspoons) instant tomato soup mix.

Easy Herb Seasoning: Use 1 teaspoon dry salad dressing mix such as ranch or Italian.

nutty nibble mix

As shown on page 205.

Ingredients
⅓ cup margarine or butter
1 tablespoon soy sauce
¾ teaspoon chili powder
⅛ teaspoon garlic powder
⅛ teaspoon ground red pepper
3 cups bite-size corn-and-rice
   square cereal
1 3-ounce can chow mein
   noodles
1 cup peanuts
1 cup shelled raw pumpkin seeds

Method
Mix margarine or butter, soy sauce, chili powder, garlic powder, and red pepper in a small saucepan. Cook and stir until margarine or butter melts.

Mix cereal, chow mein noodles, peanuts, and pumpkin seeds in a roasting pan. Drizzle margarine mixture over noodle mixture; toss.

Bake at 300° for 30 minutes, stirring every 10 minutes. Spread on foil to cool. Store in an airtight container. Makes 12 to 15 servings.

rainbow popcorn

As shown on page 205.

Ingredients

- 10 cups popped popcorn
- 1 cup margarine or butter
- ¾ cup sugar
- 1 3-ounce package desired flavor gelatin
- 3 tablespoons water
- 1 tablespoon light corn syrup

Method

Remove all unpopped kernels from popped corn. Place in a greased 17×12×2-inch baking pan. Keep warm in a 300° oven while making syrup mixture.

Butter bottom and sides of a heavy 2-quart saucepan. Combine margarine or butter, sugar, gelatin, water, and corn syrup. Cook mixture over medium heat until boiling, stirring constantly. Clip a candy thermometer to side of pan.

Continue cooking over medium heat for 20 minutes, stirring constantly until thermometer registers 255° (hard-ball stage). Pour syrup mixture over popcorn and stir gently to coat popcorn.

Bake in a 300° oven for 5 minutes. Stir once and bake for 5 minutes more. Turn popcorn mixture onto a large piece of foil. Cool completely. Break popcorn mixture into clusters. Store in an airtight container in a cool, dry place. Makes about 10 cups.

sweet holiday gift bags

As shown on page 206, each bag measures 10×6¼ inches.

Materials for one bag

Fabrics

12×8-inch piece of 18-count white cotton Aida cloth

22½×7¼-inch piece of velveteen in desired color

22×6¾-inch piece of desired lining fabric

Threads

Cotton embroidery floss in colors listed in key on page 219

Blending filament as listed in key on page 219

Supplies

Small red jingle bell

3 red seed beads

Tracing paper; tailors' chalk pencil

Thread to match velveteen

½ yard of ¼-inch-wide decorative gold braid

Fabric glue; seam ripper

Two 20-inch-long pieces of ¼-inch-wide satin ribbon in desired color

Safety pin

Instructions

Tape or zigzag the edges of the Aida cloth to prevent fraying. Find the center of one chart, *pages 218–219*, and the center of one piece of Aida cloth; begin stitching there.

Use two plies of embroidery floss to work the cross-stitches. Work blended needles using one ply of each color of embroidery floss as listed in the key, *page 219*. Work the backstitches, lazy daisy stitches, and French knots using

GIFT BAGS
PATTERN

Fold

sweet holiday gift bags — *continued*

one ply of embroidery floss or blending filament.

Press stitchery from the back. If stitching reindeer, tack jingle bell to collar as shown on the chart. If stitching Santa, sew beads to hat as shown on the chart.

Trace oval shape from pattern, *page 217*, onto paper; cut out. Fabric measurements include ½-inch seam allowances. Sew seams with right sides of fabric facing.

Trace around paper oval onto velveteen, centering top of oval 4 inches below one short edge. Cut out oval. Stitch ⅛ inch away from cut edge. Clip to stitching; finger press clipped edge to wrong side.

Center and draw around the oval pattern onto stitchery, adding ½ inch all around; cut out. Position stitched design inside of the oval from wrong side. Stitch around the oval opening in velveteen close to the edge to secure stitchery.

Fold velveeten rectangle in half to measure 11×6¾ inches. Sew long edges together for bag side seams. Repeat for lining, except leave opening along one side seam; do not turn.

To shape the bottom, fold one corner flat so the bottom and side seams meet. Run row of stitches perpendicular to seam lines, ⅝ inch from fold; trim corner. Repeat for the opposite corner and corners of lining.

Sew the bag to the lining around the top edge. Turn right side out through the opening in lining. Slip-stitch opening closed. Tuck lining into bag. Glue braid around oval opening.

To make casing and drawstring, sew around top of bag 2 inches and again 2⅜ inches below top edge.

Slit side seam of velveteen between rows of stitching. Using safety pin to carry ribbon, thread one ribbon piece in one side of casing and all the way around between velveteen and lining. Bring ribbon back out same slit; knot ends. Repeat, beginning on opposite side using remaining ribbon.

Santa stitch count: 93 high x 63 wide
Santa finished design sizes:
18-count fabric – 5¼ x 3½ inches
14-count fabric – 6¾ x 4½ inches
11-count fabric – 8½ x 5¾ inches

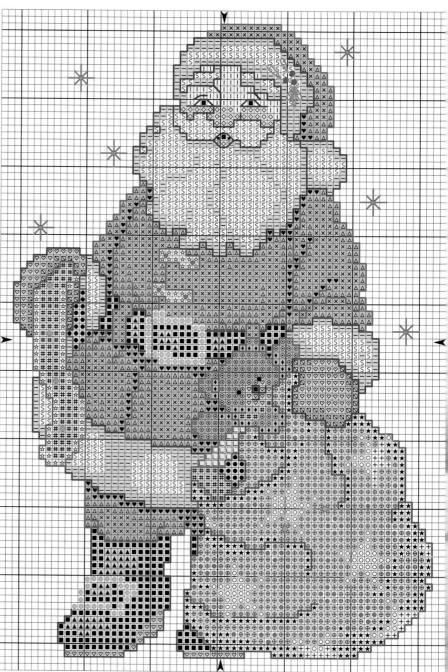

SANTA GIFT BAG

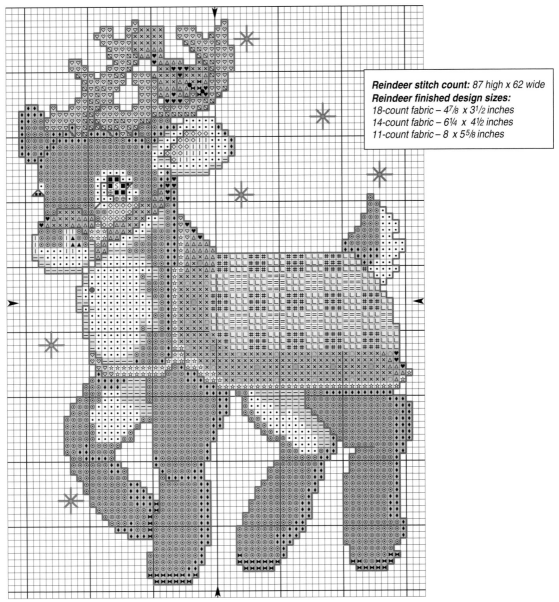

REINDEER GIFT BAG

Reindeer stitch count: 87 high x 62 wide
Reindeer finished design sizes:
18-count fabric – 4⁷/₈ x 3¹/₂ inches
14-count fabric – 6¹/₄ x 4¹/₂ inches
11-count fabric – 8 x 5⁵/₈ inches

SANTA AND REINDEER GIFT BAGS

ANCHOR		DMC
002	•	000 White
289	=	307 True lemon
403	■	310 Black
400	▲	317 Pewter
9046	△	321 True Christmas red
009	◇	352 Coral
398	−	415 Pearl gray
290	☆	444 Medium lemon
1005	♥	498 Dark Christmas red
891	♡	676 Old gold
226	#	702 Christmas green
256	L	704 Chartreuse
133	★	796 Royal blue
131	⊕	798 Delft blue
360	⋈	898 Coffee brown
881	I	945 Ivory
355	♦	975 Deep golden brown
035	×	3705 Watermelon
923	●	3818 Emerald
1048	⊙	3826 Dark golden brown
373	◲	3828 Hazel

ANCHOR		DMC
BLENDED NEEDLE		
002	S	000 White (2X) and 032 Kreinik pearl blending filament (1X)
289	O	307 True lemon (2X) and 028 Kreinik citron blending filament (1X)
290	+	444 Medium lemon (2X) and 028 Kreinik citron blending filament (1X)
BACKSTITCH		
400	╱	317 Pewter–reindeer's eyes and ear; Santa's coat, beard, face, and boots
360	╱	898 Coffee brown–reindeer, bird, teddy bear, Santa's coat
152	╱	939 Navy–Santa's bag
298	╱	972 Canary–reindeer's blanket
	╱	028 Kreinik citron blending filament–stars on Santa's bag
	╱	032 Kreinik pearl blending filament–snowflakes

ANCHOR		DMC
LAZY DAISY		
226	╱	702 Christmas green–Santa's hat
FRENCH KNOT		
403	●	310 Black–bird's eyes and teddy bear's eyes
SEED BEADS		
	●	00968 Mill Hill red seed beads–Santa's hat
	●	40479 Mill Hill pearl petite beads–snowflakes
	●	42011 Mill Hill Victorian gold petite beads–reindeer's blanket and Santa's buckles
	●	42013 Mill Hill red petite beads–Santa's bag and coat clasps
JINGLE BELLS		
	●	1090-01 Darice 6mm gold–reindeer's blanket and ties on Santa's bag
	●	Red jingle bell–reindeer

marbled bark

As shown on page 206.

Ingredients

- ¾ cup semisweet chocolate pieces
- 2 teaspoons shortening
- 4 ounces vanilla-flavored candy coating, chopped
- 2 teaspoons shortening

Method

In a small heavy saucepan melt together chocolate pieces and 2 teaspoons shortening. In another small heavy saucepan, melt together candy coating and 2 teaspoons shortening.

Drizzle melted chocolate in a 10-inch-square area on a baking sheet lined with waxed paper. Drizzle melted vanilla coating over chocolate, filling in spaces. Cool slightly. Run a knife or metal spatula through the mixture to achieve a marbled effect. Do not overmix. Chill for about 10 minutes or till almost set. Cut into desired shapes.

marshmallow fudge

As shown on page 206.

Ingredients

- 4 cups sugar
- 2 5-ounce cans (1¼ cups total) evaporated milk
- 1 cup butter
- 1 12-ounce package semisweet chocolate pieces
- 1 7-ounce jar marshmallow crème
- 1 cup chopped walnuts
- 1 teaspoon vanilla

Method

Line a 13×9×2-inch baking pan with foil; extend foil over edges. Butter foil; set aside. Butter sides of a heavy 3-quart saucepan. In it, combine sugar, milk, and butter. Cook and stir over medium-high heat to boiling. Clip candy thermometer to side of pan. Cook and stir over medium heat to 236°, soft-ball stage (about 12 minutes).

Remove from heat and remove thermometer. Add chocolate, marshmallow crème, nuts, and vanilla; stir until chocolate melts. Spread into pan. Score into squares while warm. When firm, cut into squares. Store in refrigerator. Makes about 3½ pounds (96 servings).

clever candy-cane containers

As shown on page 207, sizes will vary according to container.

Materials

Colored food container boxes or sacks
1-inch sponge brush
Acrylic paints: red and white

Instructions

Dip the tip of the sponge brush into white paint. Press the tip repeatedly straight down onto the container, following a curved candy-cane configuration and leaving spaces for the red paint. Allow to dry completely. Fill in the spaces with red paint using the same technique.

sweet spiced walnuts

As shown on page 207.

Ingredients

- 1 egg white
- 1 teaspoon water
- 5 cups walnut halves or pieces
- 1 cup sugar
- 1 teaspoon ground cinnamon
- ½ teaspoon salt
- ¼ teaspoon ground nutmeg
- ¼ teaspoon ground allspice

Method

Beat together the egg white and water in a large bowl with a fork. Add the walnuts and toss to coat. In a small bowl combine the sugar, cinnamon, salt, nutmeg, and allspice. Sprinkle the sugar mixture over the walnuts and toss to coat.

Spread the nuts in a greased 15×10×1-inch baking pan. Bake, uncovered, in a 325° oven for 20 minutes. Transfer to waxed paper to cool. Break into clumps. Makes 7 cups.

spicy pecans

As shown on page 207.

Ingredients

- 1 to 1½ teaspoons chili powder
- 1 teaspoon garlic salt
- 1 teaspoon curry powder
- ¼ teaspoon ground cumin
- ¼ teaspoon ground ginger
- ¼ teaspoon ground cinnamon
- 3 tablespoons olive oil or cooking oil
- 1 teaspoon Worcestershire sauce
- ¼ to ½ teaspoon bottled hot pepper sauce
- 3 cups pecan halves

Method

Combine the chili powder, garlic salt, curry powder, cumin, ginger, and cinnamon in a large skillet. Stir in oil, Worcestershire sauce, and bottled hot pepper sauce. Cook and stir over low heat for 5 minutes to mellow the flavors.

Place pecan halves in a large bowl; add spice mixture. Toss to coat evenly. Spread pecans in a single layer in a 15×10×1-inch baking pan. Bake in a 325° oven for 15 minutes, stirring occasionally. Spread on foil and cool completely. Makes 3 cups.

gingerbread jar & mugs

As shown on page 208.

Materials

Clear glass cookie jar and mugs
Liquitex Glossies high gloss
   acrylic enamel paints for glass:
   golden brown, green, white,
   red, and metallic gold

½-inch-wide flat paintbrush
Small round paintbrush
Tracing paper
Tape

Instructions

Wash and dry cookie jar and mugs thoroughly. Avoid touching the surfaces to be painted.

gingerbread jar & mugs — *continued*

For cookie jar, use flat brush and red paint to paint two rows of checkerboard pattern around the curved bottom edge of jar. Allow paint to dry. Using green paint, complete checkerboard pattern; allow to dry.

Trace large gingerbread man goody jar pattern, *right,* onto tracing paper; cut out. Tape pattern, slightly angled, to inside of cookie jar 1 inch from bottom. Using flat brush, golden brown paint, and pattern as a guide, paint gingerbread man on outside of jar. Repeat, painting gingerbread men at different angles. Allow paint to dry.

Paint evergreen wisps above the gingerbread men using flat brush, green paint, and the photograph, *page 208,* as a guide. When green paint is dry, brush white paint lightly over green for a snowy effect.

Outline each gingerbread man using round brush and white paint using a zigzag motion. Add white mouth and eyes to each. Paint small round noses and buttons red. Highlight buttons with white.

Dip eraser end of pencil in desired color paint and press onto glass repeatedly to make garland between greens as shown in photograph. Paint gold swirls at random between gingerbread men using round brush.

Allow the paint to dry 24 hours. Bake the cookie jar in oven at 325° for 35 minutes. Keep area well ventilated. After baking time, turn oven off and allow jar to cool in oven. When completely cool, paint is permanent.

For each mug, paint only one row of green and red checkerboard border, following method for cookie jar, *left.* Trace gingerbread man mug pattern onto tracing paper; cut out. Tape pattern at an angle to inside of mug ½ inch from bottom. Paint as for cookie jar.

Paint a second gingerbread man on the opposite side of the mug. Paint the details on gingerbread men and add swirls as for the cookie jar.

Bake mug, following directions given for cookie jar.

GINGERBREAD MAN GOODY JAR

GINGERBREAD MAN NAPKIN

GINGERBREAD MAN MUG

gingerbread man napkin

As shown on page 208.

Materials

Purchased red napkin
Transfer paper; transfer pen
Fabric paints: brown and white
½-inch flat paintbrush
Small round paintbrush
12 inches of ⅛-inch-wide green
   satin ribbon
Needle; green sewing thread

Instructions

Wash, dry, and iron napkin.

Trace gingerbread man napkin pattern, *opposite,* onto transfer paper using transfer pen. Following manufacturer's instructions, transfer gingerbread man outline to one corner of napkin and again to each side of the first.

Paint gingerbread men brown; allow to dry. Outline each gingerbread man in white, using a zigzag motion. Paint mouth and dot eyes and buttons white; allow to dry completely.

Cut ribbon into three 4-inch-long pieces; tie each in a bow. Tack a bow to the neck of each gingerbread man.

no-sew gift bags

As shown on page 209, large bag measures 16×6×2½ inches; small bag measures 10×3¾×1¾ inches.

Materials

For large bag

17×20-inch piece each of
   two coordinating Christmas
   print fabrics
16½×19½-inch piece of
   fusible web

For small bag

11×13-inch piece each of
   two coordinating Christmas
   print fabrics
10½×12½-inch piece of
   fusible web

For both bags

Pinking shears
Ruler
Fabric glue
Cord or ribbon as desired to
   tie bag closed

Instructions

For each bag, sandwich web between wrong sides of fabrics and fuse fabrics together following manufacturer's instructions. Using pinking shears, trim fused fabric to a 16×19-inch rectangle for large bag and a 10×12-inch rectangle for small bag. Determine which fabric is desired for outside of bag.

For large bag, make ¼-inch-long slits along one 19-inch-long side as follows: 4 inches in from left corner for A, 2½ inches in from A for B; 4 inches in from right corner for D, and 2½ inches from D for C (Step 1, *page 224*).

For small bag, make ¼-inch-long slits along one 12-inch-long side as follows: 2¼ inches in from left corner for A, 1¾ inches in from A for B; 2¼ inches in from right corner for D, and 1¾ inches in from D for C (Step 1, *page 224*). (Slits A, B, C, and D mark bottom of each fold line for assembling bag. Edge with slits becomes bag bottom.)

For each bag, with inside fabric up, press short sides of rectangle toward center along fold lines A and D (Step 2, *page 224*). Open rectangle out, and fold short sides in along fold lines C and D (Step 3, *page 224*). Bring fold A to fold B and fold C to fold D to make side pleats of bag (Step 4, *page 224*).

NO-SEW GIFT BAGS

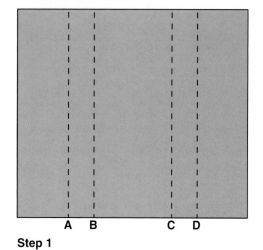

Step 1

Open rectangle out and press 2½ inches along the bottom edge to wrong side. Open fold back out and cut slits at A, B, C, and D to fold line. Shape bag, overlap side edges at back, and glue in place (Step 5, *below*). Lap front bottom flap over back bottom flap and glue in place (Step 6, *below*). Cut each side flap to a point using pinking shears and glue them to bag bottom (Step 7, *below*).

After filling bag, tie top with cord or ribbon.

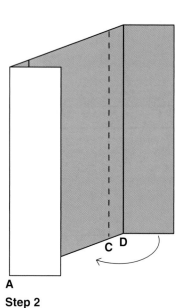

Step 2

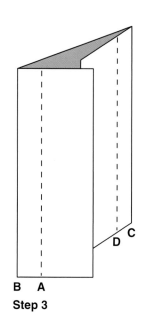

Step 3

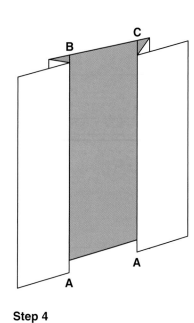

Step 4

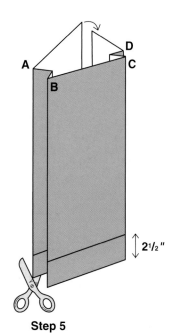

Step 5

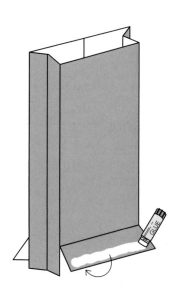

Step 6

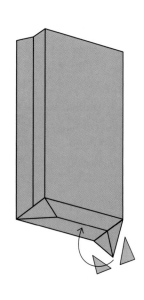

Step 7

parmesan-herb bread bowls

It's a good idea to serve these bread bowls with a shallow soup bowl liner. As shown on page 209.

Ingredients

- 1 16-ounce package hot roll mix
- ⅓ cup grated Parmesan cheese
- 1 teaspoon dried Italian seasoning, crushed
- 1½ cups hot water (120° to 130°)
- 2 tablespoons cooking oil
- 1 slightly beaten egg white
- 1 tablespoon water
- 2 tablespoons grated Parmesan cheese

Method

Combine flour mixture and yeast packet from hot roll mix with ⅓ cup Parmesan cheese and Italian seasoning in a large mixing bowl; mix well. Add hot water and oil. Stir until dough follows spoon around bowl. Turn dough onto a lightly floured surface. Knead until smooth (about 5 minutes). Cover dough and let rest 5 minutes.

Divide dough into 6 portions; form into balls. Roll each ball into a 6-inch circle. On lightly greased baking sheets, fit each circle of dough over bottom of an inverted, well-greased 10-ounce custard cup or individual casserole. Trim dough at edges of dishes. Smooth edges of dough, pressing against dishes. Brush with a mixture of egg white and 1 tablespoon water.

Bake in a 375° oven for 12 to 15 minutes or until golden. (If dough puffs up, press it down with a potholder.)

Carefully remove the bread from the custard cups with a narrow metal spatula. Turn each bowl right side up on the baking sheet. Brush the insides and rim of each bowl with the egg-water mixture and sprinkle with about 2 teaspoons of Parmesan cheese. Return to the oven and bake for an additional 5 minutes.

Transfer the bowls to a wire rack to cool. Store the cooled bowls in a clear plastic bag in the refrigerator for up to three days or freeze up to 3 months.

stone soup

Everyone brings something for the soup pot as the stone soup legend goes. As shown on page 209.

Ingredients

- 1 pound lean ground beef, lean ground pork, or lean ground raw turkey
- 1 medium onion, chopped
- 1 clove garlic, minced
- 4 cups water
- 4 teaspoons beef bouillon granules
- 1 teaspoon dried herb, crushed (basil, oregano, marjoram, or thyme)
- 6 contributed ingredients and additional water specified for each
  Salt and pepper

Method

Cook ground meat, onion, and garlic in a 5- or 6-quart soup pot until meat is browned and onion is tender. Drain fat. Add the 4 cups of water, bouillon granules, and dried herb.

Bring to boiling, reduce heat and simmer 20 minutes, stirring occasionally. If necessary, reduce heat and keep warm.

Meanwhile, calculate the total amount of additional water that will be needed for all six contributed ingredients.

Return the soup to boiling. Add any fresh vegetables and all of the additional water for the contributed ingredients. Reduce the heat and simmer, covered, for 20 minutes. Add any frozen vegetable, pasta, or grain. Simmer, covered, 10 minutes more. Add any undrained canned vegetables and simmer, covered, 10 minutes. Season to taste with salt and pepper. Ladle into bread bowls. Makes 6 servings.

Contributed ingredients: For each 1 cup of fresh vegetables, (sliced carrots, chopped celery, chopped green pepper, chopped onion, or cubed potatoes), add ¼ cup additional water.

For each 8 to 10-ounce package or 1½ cups of loose-pack frozen vegetables (mixed vegetables, corn, cut green beans, lima beans, peas, cauliflowerettes, or chopped broccoli), add ¼ cup additional water.

For each ½ cup pasta or grain (elbow macaroni, corkscrew macaroni, bowtie, wagon wheel, alphabet-shaped pasta, egg noodles, broken lasagna noodles, broken spaghetti, or for ¼ cup quick-cooking barley or dried lentils), add ½ cup additional water.

For each 8- or 16-ounce can of vegetables (tomato juice; undrained tomatoes, cut up; undrained corn, beans, peas, or carrots), do not add any additional water.

twist-o-caraway sticks

As shown on page 209.

Ingredients

- 1 beaten egg
- 1 tablespoon water
- 1 teaspoon country-style Dijon-style mustard or prepared mustard
- ¾ cup shredded Swiss cheese (3 ounces)
- ¼ cup finely chopped onion
- 2 teaspoons snipped parsley
- 1½ teaspoons caraway seed
- ½ teaspoon garlic salt
- ½ of a 17½-ounce package frozen puff pastry thawed

Method

Combine the egg, water, and mustard in a small bowl; set aside. In a medium bowl stir together the cheese, onion, parsley, caraway seed, and garlic salt.

Unfold the pastry sheet. Brush one side generously with egg mixture. Sprinkle cheese mixture lengthwise over half of rectangle. Fold the plain half over cheese, lining up edges and pressing to seal. Brush the top of the pastry with egg mixture. With a sharp knife, cut pastry crosswise into ½-inch-wide strips. Twist each strip several times and place 1 inch apart on a greased baking sheet, pressing the ends down.

Bake in a 350° oven for about 18 to 20 minutes or until lightly browned. Serve warm. Makes 18 bread sticks.

apple-berry cider

As shown on page 209.

Ingredients

- 8 cups apple cider or apple juice
- 1 10-ounce package frozen red raspberries or frozen sliced strawberries
- 4 inches stick cinnamon
- 1½ teaspoons whole cloves
- 1 large apple (optional)
- Cinnamon sticks (optional)

Method

Combine the apple cider or juice, the frozen raspberries or strawberries, cinnamon, and cloves in a large saucepan. Bring to boiling; reduce heat. Cover and simmer for 10 minutes. Strain through a sieve lined with a 100% cotton cheesecloth.

To serve, pour warm cider into 8 heat-proof glasses or cups. If desired, cut ⅛-inch-thick slices from apple, then cut stars or other holiday shapes freehand or using canapé cutters. Float a shape in each mug of cider and garnish with a cinnamon stick. Makes 8 (8-ounce) servings.

sweet potato bread

As shown on page 209.

Ingredients

- 1 15- to 16-ounce package nut quick bread mix
- 2 teaspoons ground cinnamon
- ¼ teaspoon ground nutmeg
- ¼ teaspoon ground ginger or ⅛ teaspoon ground cloves
- 1 cup water
- ½ cup drained and mashed canned sweet potatoes or canned pumpkin
- 1 beaten egg
- 2 tablespoons cooking oil
- Orange Icing (optional)

Method

Grease and lightly flour one 8×4×2-inch loaf pan or five 4½×2½×1½-inch loaf pans. Set the pans aside.

Stir together the quick bread mix, cinnamon, nutmeg, and ginger or cloves in a large mixing bowl. Add the water, sweet potato or pumpkin, egg, and oil. Stir just until all of the dry ingredients are moistened.

Pour the batter into prepared pan(s). Bake in a 350° oven until a toothpick inserted near the center(s) come out clean. Allow 60 to 65 minutes baking time for a large pan or 30 to 35 minutes baking time for small pans.

Cool the pan(s) on a wire rack for 10 minutes. Remove the loaves from the pans and cool completely on the wire rack. If desired, wrap loaves in clear plastic wrap and store overnight in a cool, dry place for easier slicing. Then, drizzle the loaves with orange icing before serving or giving. Makes 1 large loaf or 5 small loaves.

Orange Icing: In a small mixing bowl stir together 1 cup unsifted powdered sugar and enough orange juice (about 1 tablespoon) to make of drizzling consistency.

Gift label: Store in the refrigerator for up to 1 week or freeze for up to 3 months.

traditional christmas fare

Gathering together with family and friends is what makes the holidays eagerly awaited and long remembered. In this chapter we share delicious holiday fare—recipes to make with confidence and share with pride.

holiday yule log

Welcome your guests with the spirit of Christmas by serving our delightful and delicious yule log cake. Made jelly-roll style, this cake is filled with Coffee Cream Filling and topped with Rich Chocolate Frosting. Turn to page 244 for the recipe for this traditional holiday dessert.

victorian steamed pudding

A sweet orange-juice flavored frosting delicately covers our steamed pudding. A favorite Christmas dessert for generations, this pudding is steamed in a slow cooker and then unmolded and presented on an antique cake plate. The recipe begins on page 244.

christmas morning buffet

Put holiday rise-and-shine into your Christmas morning and gather the whole family around a brunch that's as festive and extraordinary as the day itself. Make French toast the star attraction with a luscious topping of strawberries or raspberries. (It's surprisingly quick to fix.) Then complement it with a spinach salad, garnished with bright Mandarin orange slices and a strawberry-orange salad dressing. For both recipes, turn to pages 245–246.

sweetly decorated treats

Candy can play dress-up too! Use pastel candy coating to add swirls of color to sleek Chocolate Covered Cherries. Our Lemon Crunch Candy is quick to make and sure to disappear fast! Recipes for both candies are on pages 246–247.

a wreath of vegetables

Vegetables are shaped into a wreath for snacking while wrapping gifts. We've added a shiny ribbon bow to make the wreath complete. Instructions for the dip and for arranging the vegetables are on page 247.

christmas dinner bells

Let a melody of heavenly bells add its own sweet harmony to your family's Christmas Eve supper. The fare is a trio medley that includes Oyster Stew with Vegetables, Christmas Bell Bread (a yeast recipe that rings with orange peel and cinnamon flavors) and Apricot Bavarian Crème with Raspberry Sauce. Crocheted bells serve as lacy grace notes tied to golden flatware and holiday packages, and later to the branches of your tree. Then repeat the sounding joy all over your tabletop with a scattering of antique or new bells and bell-trimmed greeting cards. Recipes begin on page 248, crochet bell instructions on pages 249–251.

237

snowman celebration

You've built the grandest snowman—so pull up to the table and warm up with some Make-Ahead Minestrone and Tortilla Roll Ups. Big Soft Ginger Cookies and White Hot Chocolate make the day extra cozy. Keep those snowmen coming with a tableful of snowman friends printed on the tablecloth and a sidekick snowman made from a stack of marshmallows. Recipes begin on page 252.

238

christmas tea party

In Wonderland, the table is always set for teatime. Here, it's readied as an extra-festive occasion for Christmas guests. The spread offers an assortment of scrumptious appetizers from purchased petit fours to orange scones and finger sandwiches that you can prepare in the wink of an eye. Recipes begin on page 255.

This is it—the tallest, darkest, and richest chocolate cake of the season. Triple your pleasure by robing it in Chocolate Buttercream and Chocolate Glaze. Top it off with chocolate leaves and fresh raspberries. The recipe for this wonderful cake is on pages 257–258.

chocolate brandy cake

sweet treats

Candy, as sweet as can be, has always been a delicious part of Christmastime. This candy collection features easy Chocolate-Almond Truffles, Grandma's Fudge, and two flavors of heavenly divinity. Recipes and easy step-by-step tips start on page 258.

holiday yule log

As shown on page 230.

Ingredients

- 1 cup all-purpose flour
- ¼ teaspoon salt
- 5 egg yolks
- 2 tablespoons dry or cream sherry
- 1 cup granulated sugar
- 5 egg whites
- ¼ teaspoon cream of tartar
  Powdered sugar
  Coffee Cream Filling
  Rich Chocolate Frosting

Method

Grease and lightly flour a 15×10×1-inch jelly-roll pan; set aside. Stir together flour and salt in a small bowl. Beat egg yolks and sherry in a large bowl with electric mixer on high speed 5 minutes or until thick and lemon-colored. Gradually add ½ cup of the granulated sugar, beating until sugar is almost dissolved.

Wash beaters. Beat egg whites and cream of tartar in a very large bowl on medium to high speed until soft peaks form (tips curl). Gradually add remaining granulated sugar, 2 tablespoons at a time, beating on medium to high speed until stiff peaks form (tips stand straight). Fold 1 cup of the egg white mixture into egg yolk mixture. Fold egg yolk mixture into remaining egg white mixture. Fold in flour mixture; spread in the prepared pan.

Bake in a 375° oven for 12 to 15 minutes or until top springs back. Immediately loosen cake from pan. Invert cake onto a towel sprinkled with powdered sugar. Roll up warm cake and towel jelly-roll style, starting from a short side. Cool on a wire rack.

Gently unroll cake. Spread Coffee Cream Filling onto cake to within 1 inch of edges. Roll up cake without towel, jelly-roll style, starting from one of the short sides. Cut a 2-inch slice from one end of cake. Place slice at side of log to form a branch. Frost with Rich Chocolate Frosting. Using the tines of a fork, score the cake lengthwise to resemble tree bark. Makes 10 servings.

Coffee Cream Filling: Beat 1 cup whipping cream, ¼ cup sifted powdered sugar, and 1½ teaspoons instant coffee crystals in a mixing bowl until soft peaks form. Makes about 2 cups.

Rich Chocolate Frosting: Heat and stir 2 ounces unsweetened chocolate and 2 tablespoons margarine or butter in a saucepan until the chocolate melts. Remove from heat and stir in 2 cups sifted powdered sugar, ½ teaspoon vanilla, and 2 to 3 tablespoons milk to make frosting. Makes 1¼ cups.

victorian steamed pudding

As shown on page 231.

Ingredients

- 1¼ cups all-purpose flour
- 1 teaspoon baking powder
- ½ teaspoon baking soda
- ½ teaspoon ground cinnamon
- ½ teaspoon ground nutmeg
- 2 eggs
- ¾ cup packed brown sugar
- ½ cup shortening
- 2 medium carrots, sliced
- 1 medium apple, peeled, cored, and cut into eighths
- 1 medium potato, peeled and cut into pieces

- ¾ cup raisins
- 2 tablespoons orange liqueur (optional)
- 1 3-ounce package cream cheese
- ¼ cup margarine or butter
- ½ teaspoon finely shredded orange peel
- 1 cup sifted powdered sugar
- 2 tablespoons orange juice

Method

Combine flour, baking powder, baking soda, ground cinnamon, and ground nutmeg in a large mixing bowl; set aside.

Place eggs, brown sugar, and shortening in a blender container or food processor bowl. Cover; blend or process until smooth.

Add the sliced carrots; blend or process until chopped. Add the peeled apple; blend or process until chopped. Add the peeled potato; blend or process until finely chopped. Stir the carrot-apple-potato mixture and the raisins into dry ingredients.

Pour batter into a greased and floured 6½-cup tower mold (without the tube); cover tightly with greased foil.

Set mold inside crockery liner of a 3½-, 4-, or 6-quart crockery

cooker. Cover and cook on high-heat setting for 4 hours.

Remove mold from cooker. Cool 10 minutes.

Unmold pudding. If desired, brush pudding with orange liqueur. Let pudding stand 20 to 30 minutes before serving.

For pudding sauce, in bowl beat cream cheese, margarine or butter, and orange peel until light and fluffy. Slowly beat in powdered sugar. Stir in orange juice until smooth. Drizzle some of the cream cheese sauce over pudding. Pass remaining sauce. Makes 6 to 8 servings.

strawberry french toast

As shown on pages 232–233.

Ingredients

- 5 eggs
- ¾ cup milk
- 1 teaspoon vanilla extract
- 8 slices French bread, cut 1½ inches thick
- 5 cups loose-pack frozen strawberries or raspberries
- ⅔ cup sugar
- ½ teaspoon cinnamon

Method

Break the eggs into a large mixing bowl and stir them until they are all one color. Stir in the milk and the vanilla.

Dip the French bread slices into the egg mixture for about 30 seconds on each side. Place the bread slices on a baking sheet and let them stand for about 10 minutes until the egg mixture is absorbed.

Heat oven to 450°. Grease a 13×9×1½-inch glass baking dish. Spread frozen strawberries evenly over bottom of dish.

In a small bowl combine sugar and cinnamon. Sprinkle ½ cup of the sugar mixture over the strawberries. With a spatula carefully place bread slices over the strawberries. Sprinkle remaining sugar over the bread. Bake for 15 minutes or until

bread is golden brown. (Bake for 5 minutes more, if necessary.)

To serve, use a spatula to place one slice of bread on a plate, then spoon some strawberries and syrup on top. Makes 8 servings.

orange-spinach toss

As shown on pages 232–233.

Ingredients

- 8 cups torn, prewashed spinach or mixed salad greens
- 1 11-ounce can Mandarin orange sections
- ¼ of an 8-ounce container (¼ cup) soft-style cream cheese with strawberries
- ⅓ cup orange juice
- ½ cup cashews or dry-roasted peanuts

Method

Place salad greens in a large salad bowl. Open the Mandarin oranges and drain the liquid. Add the drained orange sections to the spinach. Carefully toss. Set aside.

For salad dressing, put the cream cheese in a small mixing bowl. Add orange juice and stir to combine with a wire whisk or fork. Pour dressing over spinach and oranges. Toss again.

Sprinkle cashews or dry-roasted peanuts over salad before serving. Makes 8 servings.

chocolate covered cherries

As shown on page 234.

Ingredients

- 60 maraschino cherries with stems
- 3 tablespoons butter, softened
- 3 tablespoons light-colored corn syrup
- 2 cups sifted powdered sugar
- 1 pound chocolate-flavored candy coating, chopped
- 2 ounces pastel vanilla-flavored candy coating (optional) Pastel-Colored Candy Coating

Method

Drain cherries on paper towels. Line a baking sheet with waxed paper; set baking sheet aside.

In a small mixing bowl combine the butter and corn syrup. Stir in powdered sugar. Knead the mixture until smooth (chill if the mixture is too soft to handle). Shape about ½ teaspoon powdered sugar mixture around each cherry. Place coated cherries, stem sides up, on prepared baking sheet; chill about 1 hour (do not chill too long or sugar mixture will begin to dissolve).

In a heavy medium saucepan melt chocolate-flavored candy coating over low heat, stirring constantly. Holding cherries by stems, dip one at a time into the coating. If necessary, spoon coating over cherries to coat. (Be sure to completely seal cherries in coating to prevent juice from leaking.) Let excess coating drip off. Place cherries, stem sides up, on prepared baking sheet.

Chill until coating is firm. (Check bottoms of cherries to see if well sealed. If necessary spread bottoms with additional melted chocolate to seal.) If desired, in a heavy small saucepan melt the pastel vanilla-flavored candy coating over low heat, stirring constantly. Using a decorating bag fitted with a small round tip, decorate dipped cherries with dots, stripes, zigzags, swirls, or a combination. Place cherries in a tightly covered container in the refrigerator. Let candies ripen in the refrigerator for 1 to 2 weeks before serving. (Ripening allows powdered sugar mixture around cherries to soften and liquefy.) Bring to room temperature before serving. Makes 60 pieces.

Pastel-Colored Candy Coating: Melt additional vanilla flavored candy coating and stir in food coloring paste, a little at a time, until desired color is achieved.

lemon crunch candy

As shown on page 234.

Ingredients

- 1 pound vanilla-flavored candy coating, cut up
- ¾ cup crushed hard lemon, orange, strawberry, cherry, or peppermint candies

Method

Line a baking sheet with foil; set aside. In a heavy medium saucepan melt candy coating over low heat, stirring constantly. Remove saucepan from heat. Stir in crushed candies. Pour melted mixture onto the prepared baking sheet. Spread mixture to about a ⅜-inch thickness.

Chill candy about 30 minutes. (Or, let candy stand at room temperature for several hours.) Use foil to lift candy from baking sheet; carefully break candy into pieces. Place in airtight container and store at room temperature for up to 2 weeks. Makes about 1¼ pounds (20 servings).

horseradish dip and vegetable wreath

As shown on page 235.

Ingredients

- 1 cup regular or light mayonnaise or salad dressing
- ½ cup regular or light dairy sour cream
- 3 tablespoons snipped fresh chives
- 1 tablespoon prepared horseradish
- 1 teaspoon Dijon-style mustard
- 1 clove garlic, minced
- ⅛ teaspoon pepper
  Assorted salad greens
  Assorted vegetables, such as green, red, and/or yellow sweet pepper strips; jicama slices; carrots; and zucchini and/or yellow summer squash

Method

In a small mixing bowl stir together the mayonnaise or salad dressing, sour cream, chives, horseradish, Dijon-style mustard, garlic, and pepper. Cover and chill in the refrigerator for 2 to 24 hours. To store, transfer to an airtight container and store in refrigerator for up to 2 days. This recipe makes about 1⅔ cups of dip (28 1-tablespoon servings).

To serve, transfer the dip to a small bowl. Place the bowl in the center of a lettuce-lined basket or glass platter. Using cookie cutters in desired shapes, cut the sweet

pepper strips and jicama slices into fun, festive shapes. Using a vegetable peeler, cut the carrots and zucchini and/or yellow summer squash into thin ribbon strips. Arrange all the vegetables among the lettuce to resemble a wreath.

apricot bavarian crème with raspberry sauce

As shown on page 236.

Ingredients

- ½ cup sugar
- 1 envelope unflavored gelatin
- 1 5½-ounce can apricot nectar
- 1 cup whipping cream
- 1 teaspoon vanilla
- 1 8-ounce carton low-fat vanilla yogurt
- 1 10-ounce package frozen raspberries, thawed
- 2 tablespoons powdered sugar
- 1 tablespoon orange juice

Method

Using a saucepan, combine sugar and gelatin. Stir in apricot nectar. Cook and stir over medium heat until sugar and gelatin dissolve.

Stir in the whipping cream and vanilla. Gradually whisk the vanilla yogurt into the gelatin mixture until well combined.

Pour mixture into lightly oiled ⅓ cup individual bell-shaped molds. Cover and chill for 8 to 24 hours or until firm.

To serve, unmold into a serving dish. Top with Raspberry Sauce. Makes 6 servings.

For the raspberry sauce, combine the thawed raspberries, powdered sugar, and the orange juice in a blender container or a food processor bowl.

Cover and blend or process until smooth. Press sauce through a sieve to remove seeds and discard any seeds.

christmas bell bread

As shown on pages 236–237.

Ingredients

- 2½ to 3 cups all-purpose flour
- 1 package active dry yeast
- ⅔ cup milk
- ¼ cup sugar
- ¼ cup margarine or butter
- ¼ teaspoon salt
- 1 egg
- ½ teaspoon finely shredded orange peel
- ¼ cup sugar
- 1½ teaspoons finely shredded orange peel
- ¼ teaspoon ground cinnamon
- 1 tablespoon melted margarine or butter
  Orange Icing
  Candied cherries, halved

Method

In a small mixing bowl, stir together 1¼ cups of the flour and the yeast. Set aside. In a small saucepan, heat and stir the milk, the ¼ cup sugar, the ¼ cup margarine or butter, and the salt until warm (120° to 130°) and the margarine is almost melted. Add milk mixture to flour mixture; add egg and ½ teaspoon orange peel.

Beat with an electric mixer on low speed for 30 seconds, scraping bowl frequently. Beat on high speed for 3 minutes. Using a spoon, stir in as much remaining flour as you can.

Turn dough out onto a lightly floured surface. Knead in enough

of the remaining flour to make a moderately stiff dough that is smooth and elastic (6 to 8 minutes total). Shape into a ball. Place in a lightly greased bowl; turn once to grease surface. Cover and let rise in a warm place until double (about 60 minutes). (Or, cover and let rise in refrigerator overnight.)

Punch dough down. Turn out onto a lightly floured surface. Remove one piece of dough, about the size of a walnut, and set aside. Cover both portions of dough and let rest for 10 minutes.

Combine the ¼ cup sugar, 1½ teaspoons orange peel, and the cinnamon. Roll out larger portion of dough to a 10-inch circle. Transfer to a greased baking sheet. Brush with some of the melted margarine. Sprinkle with the sugar mixture.

To shape bell, form smaller piece of dough into a ball; moisten the bottom with water and place it on the bottom of the circle to form the clapper. Fold in the sides of the circle, overlapping slightly at the top. Brush bell and clapper with the remaining melted margarine. Cover and let rise in a warm place until almost double (about 30 minutes). (Allow longer if dough has been chilled.) Bake in 350° oven for 15 minutes. Cover with foil and bake for 10 minutes more or until golden brown. Transfer to wire rack to cool.

Drizzle or spread with Orange Icing and arrange candied cherry halves to garnish. Makes 1 bell bread with 16 to 20 servings.

Orange Icing: Combine 1 cup sifted powdered sugar and ½ teaspoon vanilla. Stir in enough orange juice (2 to 3 teaspoons) to make an icing of drizzling consistency. Makes about ½ cup.

oyster stew with vegetables

As shown on pages 236–237. Use 5-quart Dutch oven to double recipe.

Ingredients
- ½ of a 16-ounce package frozen mixed broccoli, cauliflower, and carrots (about 2 cups)
- 1 small onion, cut into thin wedges
- ½ cup water
- ½ teaspoon instant chicken bouillon granules
- ⅛ teaspoon ground white pepper
- 1 bay leaf
- 2 13-ounce cans (3½ cups total) evaporated skimmed milk
- 1 pint shucked oysters or two 8-ounce cans whole oysters

Method
Cut up any large vegetables. In a 3-quart saucepan combine the vegetables, onion, water, bouillon granules, white pepper, and the bay leaf. Bring to a boil. Reduce heat. Cover and simmer for 5 to 7 minutes or until the vegetables are crisp-tender. Do not drain.

Stir in evaporated milk. Heat all the way through. Add undrained oysters to vegetable mixture. Cook over medium heat for about 5 minutes or until edges of oysters curl, stirring frequently. (If using canned oysters, just heat through.) Remove bay leaf. Makes 6 servings.

crocheted antique bell

Shown on page 237, the bell measures 3 inches tall. Crochet abbreviations are on page 320.

Materials
Size 9 steel crochet hook
J.P. Coats Metallic Knit-Cro-Sheen (100-yard ball): white (1G)
½-inch-diameter wood bead
Thick white crafts glue

Instructions
Ch 6, join with sl st to form ring.

Rnd 1: Ch 4, * dc in ring, ch 1 *. Rep bet *s 18 more times. Join last ch-1 in third ch of first ch-4.

Rnd 2: Ch 3, dc in ch-1 sp, * dc in dc, dc in ch-1 sp *. Rep bet *s 18 more times. Join in top of first ch-3.

Rnd 3: Ch 4, sk next dc, * dc in dc, ch 1, sk next dc *. Rep bet *s 18 more times. Join last ch-1 in third ch of first ch-4—20 filet sps.

Rnd 4: Ch 5, * dc in next dc, ch 2 *. Rep bet *s around. Join last ch-2 in third ch of first ch-5.

Antique Bell

Inspiration Bell

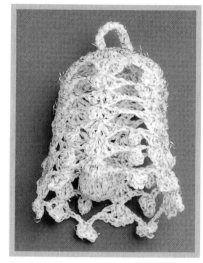

Joyful Bell

crocheted antique bell — *continued*

Rnd 5: Rep Rnd 4.

Rnd 6: Ch 5, dc in dc, ch 2, dc in dc, 2 dc in ch-2 sp, dc in dc, ch 2, * dc in dc, ch 2, dc in dc, ch 2, 2 dc in ch-2 sp, dc in dc, ch 2 *. Rep bet *s 3 more times. Join last ch-2 in third ch of first ch-5.

Rnd 7: Sl st in ch-2 sp, ch 4, trc, ch 3, holding last st on hook, in same sp work 2 trc, yo, thread through all 3 sts—2 trc-cl made; ch 7, * sk to center bl of open filet, 2 trc-cl, ch 3, 2 trc-cl in same sp, ch 7 *. Rep bet *s 3 more times. Join last ch-7 in trc of first cl, sl st in next 2 chs.

Rnd 8: Ch 3, dc, ch 3, 2 dc-cl in same st, ch 3, sk to fourth ch of ch-7 of prev rnd, then 6 dc in same sp, ch 3; * 2 dc-cl in center ch of next ch-3, ch 3, 2 dc-cl in same sp, ch 3, sk to center ch of next ch-7, 6 dc in same sp, ch 3 *. Rep bet *s 3 more times. Join last ch-3 in top of first ch-3.

Rnd 9: Sl st past the 2 sets of 2 dc-cl to center ch of ch-3; * ch 4, 3 trc-cl, only work each trc in first 3 dc, yo, thread through all 4 sts, ch 5, 3 trc-cl in next 3 dc, ch 4, sc in center ch of ch-3 *.

Rep bet *s 4 more times. Join last ch-4 in base of first ch-4.

Rnd 10: Ch 7, * 1 dc, ch 3, dc in third ch of ch-5, ch 7, sc in next sc *. Rep bet *s 4 more times. Join last ch-7 in base of first ch-7.

Rnd 11: * Ch 5, sc in next dc, (ch 4, sc in fourth ch from hook—picot made). Rep bet ( )s 2 more times, sc in next dc, ch 5, sc in next sc *. Rep bet *s around. Fasten off.

HANGING LOOP: Attach thread on top of bell, ch 12, sl st to opposite side in ring, ch 1, turn, sc over ch to beg. Sl st in first ch, fasten off. Weave threads into work.

CLAPPER: Ch 4, work 6 dc in fourth ch from hook, join in top of first ch-4.

Rnd 2: Ch 3, dc in same sp, 2 dc in each dc around. Join in top of first ch-3.

Rnd 3: Ch 3, dc in each dc around. Join in top of first ch-3. Insert bead.

Rnd 4: Stretch crochet work over bead, ch about 1½ inches, leaving a 2-inch thread to tie to hanging loop when bell is stiffened and finished.

STIFFENING: Use two parts white glue mixed with one part water for a stiffening solution. Wash crochet work in cold-water detergent; rinse well. Press almost dry in terry-cloth towel. Stack several small paper cups, making stack slightly taller than bell. Cover stack with plastic wrap, inserting one more cup in bottom of stack to hold plastic wrap in place. For rounded top on bell, place several cotton balls on top of cup before covering with plastic wrap. Stretch damp crochet over stack. Paint stiffening solution on work, beginning at hanging loop and working down. Saturate crochet. Place on heavy cardboard covered with wax paper. If bell has points, pin them to cardboard using rust-proof pins. Allow to partially dry; twist bell and remove it from cups, wipe away excess stiffening solution, and place back on cups. (This helps prevent webbing of solution between openings of crochet.) When completely dry, remove cups; twist plastic wrap away from inside of bell.

FINISHING: When bell is dry, insert the crochet hook inside bell from top. Pull clapper thread through, wind around hanging loop several times, then secure in place.

crocheted inspiration bell

As shown on page 237, the bell measures 3 inches tall.

Materials

Size 9 crochet hook
J.P. Coats Metallic Knit-Cro-Sheen
(100-yard ball): white (1G)
½-inch-diameter wood bead
Thick white crafts glue

Instructions

Ch 6, join with sl st to form ring.

Rnd 1: Ch 4, * dc in ring, ch 1 *. Rep bet *s 10 more times. Join last ch-1 in third ch of first ch-4—12 dc, with ch-1 bet.

Rnd 2: Ch 5, * dc in dc, ch 2 *. Rep bet *s 10 more times. Join last ch-2 in third ch of first ch-5.

Rnd 3: Ch 3, 2 dc in ch-2 sp, * dc in dc, 2 dc in ch-2 sp *. Rep bet *s 10 more times. Join in top of first ch-3—36 dc.

Rnd 4: Ch 4, trc in same sp, ch 5, sk next 5 dc, holding last st on hook of each trc, 2 trc in next dc, yo, thread through all 3 sts—2 trc-clusters made, ch 6, sl st in trc-cl joining—ch-lp made, ch 5, * sk next 5 dc, 2 trc-cl in next dc, ch 6, sl st in trc-cl joining—ch-6 lp made, ch 5 *. Rep bet *s 4 more times. Join last ch-5 in top of first ch-4, ch 6, sl st in base of same ch-6, sl st to third ch of next ch-5.

Rnd 5: * Ch 2, (2 trc-cl in ch-6 lp, ch 3, 2 trc-cl in same lp, ch 3, 2 trc-cl in same lp, ch 2), sc in third ch of next ch-5 of prev rnd *. Rep bet *s 5 more times. Join last ch-2 in base of first ch-2. Sl st to second trc-cl, and sc in top of cl.

Rnd 6: * Ch 8, sl st in top of next center trc-cl *. Rep bet *s around. Join last ch-8 in base of first ch-8.

Rnd 7: * Ch 5, sk 2 ch, sc in next ch, ch 5, sk 2 ch, sc in next ch, ch 5, sk 2 ch, sc in sc. Rep bet *s around. Last lp: Ch 2, dc in base of first ch-5; hook in center of lp. *Note:* Because the hook is in the center of lp you are ready to begin next rnd.

Rnd 8: * Ch 5, sc in next lp *. Rep bet *s around. Last lp: Ch 2, dc in base of first ch-5. Hook in center of lp.

Rnd 9: * Ch 2, sc in next lp *. Rep bet *s around. Join last ch-2 in base of first ch-2.

Rnd 10: Sl st in next 2 chs and next sc. Ch 4, trc in same sp, ch 9, * sk (2 ch, sc, 2 ch, sc, 2 ch), then 2 trc-cl in next sc, ch 6, sl st in base of same ch-6, ch 9 *. Rep bet *s 5 more times. Last ch-9 is joined in top of first ch-4, ch 6, sl st in base of ch-6, sl st to fifth ch of ch-9 of prev rnd.

Rnd 11: Rep Rnd 5, except sc in fifth ch of ch-9 of prev rnd. Join in base of first ch-2. Fasten off.

Make hanging loop and clapper, stiffen the bell, and finish as directed for Crocheted Antique Bell, *opposite.*

crocheted joyful bell

As shown on page 237, the bell measures 3 inches tall.

Materials

Size 9 steel crochet hook
J.P. Coats Metallic Knit-Cro-Sheen
(100-yard ball): white (1G)
½-inch-diameter wood bead
Thick white crafts glue

Instructions

Ch 6, join with sl st to form ring.

Rnd 1: Ch 4, * dc in ring, ch 1 *. Rep bet *s 10 more times. Join last ch-1 in third ch of first ch-4—12 dc with ch-1 bet.

Rnd 2: Ch 5, * dc in dc, ch 2 *. Rep bet *s 10 more times. Join last ch-2 in third ch of first ch-5.

Rnd 3: Ch 3, 2 dc in ch-2 sp, * dc in dc, 2 dc in ch-2 sp *. Rep bet *s 10 more times. Join in top of first ch-3.

Rnd 4: * Ch 1, sk 2 dc, (dc, ch 1) 5 times in next dc, sk 2 dc, sc in next dc *. Rep bet *s 5 more times. Join last ch-1 in base of first ch-1.

Rnd 5: Sl st in third dc, then ch 4, (dc, ch 1) 4 times in same sp; * (dc, ch 1) 5 times in third dc of next shell *. Rep bet *s 4 more times. Join in third ch of first ch-4.

Rnd 6: Rep Rnd 5.

Rnd 7: Rep Rnd 5, except ch 2 bet shells.

crocheted joyful bell — *continued*

Rnd 8: Sl st to third dc, ch 4, (dc, ch 1) 4 times in same sp, ch 4, hdc in third ch from hook, ch 2, sl st in base of hdc, ch 1–picot made, * (dc, ch 1) 5 times in third dc of prev rnd, ch 4, picot *. Rep bet *s 4 more times. Join last ch-1 to third ch of first ch-4.

Rnd 9: Ch 5, (dc, ch 1) 4 times in same sp, ch 5, hdc in third ch from hook, ch 2, sl st in base of hdc, ch 2–picot made, *(dc, ch 1) 5 times in third dc of prev rnd, ch 5, picot; rep bet *s 4 more times. Join last ch-1 in third ch of first ch-5.

Rnd 10: Sl st to third dc, * ch 4, in same sp (dc, ch 1, dc, ch 2, hdc in second ch from hook, ch 2, sl st in base of hdc–picot made, ch 1, dc, ch 1 dc) ch 5, hdc in second ch from hook, ch 2, sl st in base of hdc, ch 3 *. Rep bet *s 5 more times. Fasten off.

Make the loop and clapper, stiffen, and finish as directed on *page 250.*

tortilla roll ups

As shown on pages 238–239.

Ingredients

- 3 8- to 10-inch red and/or green colored flour tortillas
- 1 8-ounce tub cream cheese with garden vegetables (soft-style)
- 1 6-ounce package thinly sliced cooked turkey or ham
- 6 lettuce leaves
- 1 medium red pepper, cut into thin strips or 2 medium carrots, cut into julienne strips

Method

Spread one side of each tortilla with 1 well-rounded tablespoon cream cheese. Top with turkey or ham, a lettuce leaf, and some red pepper or carrot strips. Roll up tortillas tightly. May wrap and store in refrigerator up to 24 hours. Serves 6.

white hot chocolate

As shown on page 239.

Ingredients

- 3 cups half-and-half or light cream
- 2/3 cup vanilla-flavor baking pieces or vanilla-flavor candy coating, chopped
- 3 inches stick cinnamon
- 1/2 teaspoon ground nutmeg
- 1 teaspoon vanilla
- 1/4 teaspoon almond extract
  Peppermint sticks, optional

Method

Combine 1/4 cup of the half-and-half or light cream, vanilla-flavor pieces or vanilla-flavor coating, stick cinnamon, and nutmeg in a medium saucepan. Whisk over low heat until the vanilla-flavor pieces or the coating is melted. Remove the stick cinnamon.

Add the remaining half-and-half or light cream. Whisk till heated through. Remove from the heat. Stir in the vanilla and almond extract.

Serve the hot chocolate warm in mugs. Garnish with peppermint sticks, if desired. Makes 5 (6-ounce) servings.

make-ahead minestrone

As shown on pages 238–239.

Ingredients

- 3 14½-ounce cans beef broth
- 2 15-ounce cans canellini beans or small white beans, rinsed and drained
- 1 14½-ounce can Italian-style stewed tomatoes
- 1 1½-ounce can vegetable juice
- 1 6-ounce can tomato paste
- 2 teaspoons sugar
- 1 teaspoon dried Italian seasoning, crushed
- 1½ cups loose-pack frozen mixed vegetables (such as an Italian blend)
- 2 cups fresh spinach leaves, cut in strips
- 2 cups cooked pasta (1 cup uncooked, elbow macaroni or snowman pasta) Finely shredded Parmesan cheese

Method

In a large kettle combine broth, beans, tomatoes, vegetable juice, tomato paste, sugar, and Italian seasoning. Bring to boiling. Add mixed vegetables. Reduce heat. Cover and simmer for 10 minutes. Remove from heat; cool slightly.

Transfer to storage container. Refrigerate, covered, overnight. (Or, to serve immediately, add spinach and cooked pasta; heat through.)

To serve, return soup to kettle and reheat over medium heat. Stir in spinach and cooked pasta. Heat through. Ladle into bowls. Sprinkle with Parmesan cheese. Makes 8 main-dish servings.

big-soft ginger cookies

As shown on pages 238–239.

Ingredients

- 1 cup butter or margarine
- 1 cup sugar
- 2 teaspoons baking soda
- 2 teaspoons grated ginger root (or 1 teaspoon ground ginger)
- 1 teaspoon ground nutmeg
- ½ teaspoon ground cloves
- 2 eggs
- ⅔ cup molasses
- 4 cups all-purpose flour Lemon Icing

Method

In large mixing bowl beat butter with electric mixer on medium to high speed about 30 seconds or until softened. Add sugar, soda, ginger root, nutmeg, and cloves; beat until combined. Beat in eggs and molasses until combined, scraping sides of bowl occasionally. Beat in as much of the flour as you can with the mixer. Stir in any remaining flour with a wooden spoon.

Drop dough a scant ¼ cup at a time, 3 inches apart, onto an ungreased cookie sheet. Bake in 350° oven 12 to 14 minutes or until edges are firm. Cool on the cookie sheet for 1 minute. With a wide metal spatula, remove cookies to a wire rack. Spoon Lemon Icing over warm cookies to glaze tops, or drizzle icing in a zigzag pattern, write names, or draw snowflakes or other designs on the cookies. Makes 22 to 24 cookies.

Lemon Icing: In a small bowl combine 2 cups sifted powdered sugar, 2 tablespoons lemon juice, and enough milk (about 1 to 2 teaspoons) to make an icing of drizzling consistency.

friendly snowman tablecloth

As shown on pages 238–239.

Materials

Waxed paper
Washable light blue felt fabric in desired size
Fabric Paint: White, black, red, blue, yellow, and orange
Disposable plastic plates
Potatoes in three sizes
Sharp knife
Pencil with new eraser
Old clothespin

Instructions

Cover work surface with waxed paper. Lay the fabric on the covered surface.

Cut largest potato in half. Spread white paint on a plastic plate and dip potato in paint. Stamp tablecloth where desired making bottom of snowmen.

Cut the next size potato in half. Repeat for centers of snowmen. Repeat using the smallest potato for the heads.

Cut one of the remaining potato halves away leaving the shape of a hat. Print with black paint. Using a pencil eraser, dip pencil in black for eyes and bright colors for buttons. Take clothespin apart and use the end to paint noses and sides to paint arms. Allow to dry.

marshmallow snowman

As shown on page 239.

Materials

3 jumbo marshmallows
White frosting of choice
2 pretzel sticks
3 red hots
1 star sprinkle
Toothpicks
Black food coloring

Method

Place a small dab of frosting between the marshmallows and stack one atop the other. Poke a pretzel stick into opposite sides of the middle marshmallow to make snowman's arms.

Use small dabs of frosting to secure red hots down center of snowman for buttons and a star sprinkle for the nose.

Dip toothpick into black food coloring. Poke toothpick into top marshmallow to make the eyes and mouth.

current-orange scones

As shown on page 240.

Ingredients

- ½ cup buttermilk or sour milk
- ½ cup currants or chopped raisins
- 1 package piecrust mix (for 2-crust pie)
- 1 tablespoon sugar
- 1 teaspoon finely shredded orange peel
- 1½ teaspoons baking powder
- ⅛ teaspoon baking soda

Method

Combine the buttermilk and currants or chopped raisins in a small mixing bowl; let stand for 5 minutes. Meanwhile, stir together piecrust mix, sugar, orange peel, baking powder, and baking soda in a medium mixing bowl. Make a well in the center. Add buttermilk mixture to dry ingredients all at once.

Using a fork, stir just until dough clings together. (The dough will be sticky.)

On a well-floured surface, knead dough gently for 10 to 12 strokes. Roll or pat into an 8-inch circle; cut into 8 or 10 wedges. Transfer to a lightly greased baking sheet, allowing space between the wedges. Bake, uncovered, in a 425° oven for 12 to 15 minutes or until golden. Serve warm. Makes 8 or 10 scones.

Note: To make sour milk, add milk to 1½ teaspoons lemon juice to equal ½ cup. Let stand for at least 5 minutes.

chocolate-truffle tarts

As shown on page 240.

Ingredients

- ½ of an 11-ounce package piecrust mix or 1 stick piecrust mix
- ¼ cup finely chopped pecans or hazelnuts
- 2 tablespoons sugar
- 4 ounces semisweet chocolate
- ¼ cup whipping cream
- 3 tablespoons butter or margarine
- 1 beaten egg yolk
- 2 tablespoons desired liqueur or whipping cream
- ⅓ cup white baking pieces with cocoa butter, melted (optional) Fresh fruits (such as raspberries or cherries), fruit preserves, nuts, or edible flowers (such as violas)

Method

Prepare piecrust mix according to package directions, except add

the ¼ cup nuts and the sugar to the dry mix. Shape into twenty-four ¾-inch balls.

Press into bottom and up sides of 24 ungreased 1¾-inch muffin cups. Bake in a 450° oven for 6 to 8 minutes or until edges begin to brown. Cool in pans on a wire rack. Remove from pans.

For filling, in a heavy saucepan combine chocolate, ¼ cup whipping cream, and butter or margarine. Cook and stir over low heat until chocolate is melted. Gradually stir about half of the hot mixture into the egg yolk. Return all of the mixture to the saucepan. Cook and stir just until mixture starts to bubble. Remove from heat.

Stir in the liqueur. Transfer the chocolate mixture to a small bowl; chill for 1½ to 2 hours or until the mixture is cool and

smooth, stirring occasionally. (The butter may separate but will blend in when the mixture is stirred.)

Beat the chilled chocolate mixture with an electric mixer on medium speed about 2 minutes or until light and fluffy. If desired, spoon the chocolate mixture into a decorating bag fitted with a large star tip (about ½ inch opening). Pipe or spoon the mixture into the baked tart shells. Cover and chill for up to 24 hours.

Before serving, let stand at room temperature for 15 to 20 minutes. If desired, drizzle the tarts with white chocolate and top with fruits, preserves, nuts, or edible flowers. Makes 24 tarts.

mini-bagels with ham and lemon-caper cream

As shown on page 241.

Ingredients

- ⅓ cup mayonnaise or salad dressing
- 1 tablespoon capers, drained
- ½ teaspoon finely shredded lemon peel
- ½ teaspoon Dijon-style mustard
- ⅛ teaspoon white pepper
- 9 Mini-bagels, halved
  Lettuce leaves or curly endive
- 8 ounces ham or smoked turkey, thinly sliced

Method

Stir together the mayonnaise or salad dressing, drained capers, shredded lemon peel, Dijon-style mustard, and white pepper in a small mixing bowl.

Line mini-bagels with lettuce leaves or curly endive.

Using 8 ounces total, arrange thinly sliced ham or smoked turkey on lettuce.

Top with 1 teaspoon of the mayonnaise mixture. If desired, garnish with fresh dill. Serve at once. Makes ⅓ cup mayonnaise mixture (18 servings).

pineapple-carrot tea bread

As shown on page 240.

Ingredients

- 2¼ cups all-purpose flour
- 1 package active dry yeast
- 1 8-ounce can crushed pineapple (juice pack)
- ¼ cup sugar
- ¼ cup margarine or butter
- ½ teaspoon salt
- 1 egg
- 1 teaspoon vanilla
- ½ cup shredded carrot

Method

Lightly grease an 8×4×2-inch loaf pan; set aside. In a large mixing bowl stir together ¼ cup of the flour and the yeast; set aside.

Drain the pineapple, reserving ⅓ cup of the juice. In a saucepan, heat and stir reserved pineapple juice, sugar, margarine or butter, and salt just until warm (120° to 130°) and the margarine is almost melted. Add to flour mixture.

Add egg and vanilla. Beat with an electric mixer on low to medium speed for 30 seconds, scraping bowl occasionally. Beat on high speed for 3 minutes.

Stir in pineapple and carrot. Using a spoon, stir in remaining flour (batter will be sticky).

Spoon the batter into prepared pan. Cover and let rise in a warm place until almost double (45 to 60 minutes). Bake in a 375° oven for 35 to 40 minutes or until golden, covering with foil the last 10 minutes, if necessary. Remove bread from pan. Cool on wire rack. Makes 1 loaf (16 servings).

tortilla roll-ups with honey-vegetable vinaigrette

As shown on page 241.

Ingredients

12 6-inch flour tortillas
1 tablespoon salad oil
1 tablespoon vinegar
1 tablespoon honey
1 teaspoon course-grain brown
  mustard
1½ cups Chinese cabbage,
  chopped
½ cup shredded carrot
  Boston lettuce leaves

Method

Warm the tortillas by placing in tin foil in a 350° oven for about 10 minutes or until heated through. Meanwhile, stir together salad oil, vinegar, honey, and brown mustard in a medium mixing bowl. Add chopped Chinese cabbage and shredded carrot; toss gently to coat.

Place the lettuce leaves atop each warm tortilla. Spoon about 2 tablespoons cabbage mixture atop each tortilla.

Roll up jelly-roll style; slice the roll into 1-inch-thick pinwheels. Makes about 1½ cups of filling (about 7 appetizers).

chocolate brandy cake

For this sweet indulgence, choose a top-grade chocolate. Then even those who opt for "just a sliver" will get their just reward. As shown on page 242.

Ingredients

8 ounces bittersweet or
  semisweet chocolate, cut up
2 cups all-purpose flour
1 teaspoon baking soda
¼ teaspoon salt
1 cup sugar
2 eggs
1 cup cooking oil
⅓ cup brandy
¾ cup sour milk
½ cup brandy
1 recipe Chocolate Buttercream
  Frosting
1 recipe Chocolate Glaze
1 teaspoon water
1 recipe Chocolate Leaves
  Fresh raspberries (optional)

Method

In a small heavy saucepan melt chocolate over low heat, stirring often. Cool. In a small mixing bowl stir together flour, baking soda, and salt; set aside.

In a large mixing bowl combine sugar, eggs, oil, and ⅓ cup brandy; beat with an electric mixer on low speed until combined. Beat on medium speed for 3 minutes. Beat in melted chocolate. Add flour mixture and sour milk alternately to beaten mixture, beating on low speed after each addition just until combined. Pour batter into

3 greased and floured 9×1½-inch round baking pans. Bake in a 350° oven about 20 minutes or until a toothpick inserted near the centers comes out clean.

Cool in pans on wire racks for 10 minutes. Remove cakes from pans. Cool thoroughly on racks, bottoms up. With a long-tined fork, poke holes in the bottoms of the cakes. Sprinkle each layer with 4 teaspoons of the brandy.

To frost cake, reserve about ¼ cup of the Chocolate Buttercream Frosting, *page 258.* Place 1 cake layer on a serving platter. Spread with some of the remaining

chocolate brandy cake — *continued*

frosting. Repeat layers twice, spreading about ¾ cup frosting smoothly onto top of cake. Spread sides of cake with remaining frosting. Refrigerate cake about 20 minutes or until frosting is set.

Carefully spread Chocolate Glaze over top of the cake, allowing glaze to drip down the sides. Stir the water into reserved frosting. Pipe frosting onto top of cake in a decorative pattern. Pull the tip of a spatula or knife in diagonal lines 1 inch apart across the piped lines (see photograph, *below*). Decorate with Chocolate Leaves and fresh raspberries, if

After piping the thinned frosting atop cake, pull the tip of a spatula in diagonal lines through the piping and glaze.

desired. Chill to store. Let stand at room temperature 1 hour before serving. Makes 16 servings.

Chocolate Buttercream Frosting: In a small mixing bowl beat 1 cup softened butter until fluffy. Gradually add 3¾ cups sifted powdered sugar and 1 cup unsweetened cocoa powder, beating well. Slowly beat in ½ cup milk, 3 tablespoons brandy or milk, and 1½ teaspoons vanilla. Slowly beat in an additional 4 cups sifted powdered sugar. Beat in additional milk or powdered sugar, if needed to achieve spreading consistency. Makes 5¾ cups frosting.

Chocolate Glaze: In a small saucepan over low heat, melt 2 ounces bittersweet or semisweet chocolate, cut up, with 2 tablespoons margarine or butter, stirring frequently. Remove from heat; stir in ¾ cup sifted powdered sugar and 2 tablespoons hot water. Stir in additional hot water, if necessary, ½ teaspoon at a time, until smooth. Cool slightly (about 5 minutes). Makes ½ cup glaze.

Chocolate Leaves: Melt 6 ounces semisweet chocolate or

white baking bar; cool. Stir in 3 tablespoons light corn syrup until combined. Turn mixture onto a large sheet of waxed paper. Let stand at room temperature about 6 hours or until dry.

Gently knead for 10 to 15 strokes or until smooth and pliable. To make a lighter-colored chocolate, knead some white chocolate into dark chocolate. If the mixture is too soft, chill in the refrigerator about 15 minutes or until easy to handle. Or, if desired, knead in enough powdered sugar to make the mixture stiff. Store unused chocolate in a sealed plastic bag at room temperature for 3 to 4 weeks. (It will stiffen during storage. Knead the mixture until it is pliable before using.)

To make the leaves, shape a portion of the chocolate mixture into a ball. Flatten slightly; place between 2 sheets of waxed paper dusted with powdered sugar.

Roll to ⅛-inch thickness. Using small hors d'oeuvre or cookie cutters, cut the chocolate mixture into leaf shapes. Carefully lift the cutouts from the waxed paper and place atop and around the cake. If desired, place the smaller leaves on top of the larger leaves.

easy chocolate-almond truffles

As shown on page 243.

Ingredients

- 1 11½-ounce package milk-chocolate pieces
- ½ cup whipping cream
- ¼ teaspoon almond extract
- ⅔ cup toasted ground almonds
- 4 2-ounce squares vanilla-flavored candy coating
- ½ cup semisweet chocolate pieces, melted

Method

In a heavy saucepan, combine milk-chocolate pieces and whipping cream. Cook over low heat for 4 to 5 minutes or until chocolate melts, stirring frequently. Remove from heat. Cool slightly. Stir in almond extract. Beat with an electric mixer on low speed until smooth. Cover and refrigerate 1 hour or until firm.

Shape chocolate mixture into ¾-inch balls; roll in the ground almonds. Place on baking sheet lined with waxed paper. Freeze for 30 minutes. Meanwhile, in a heavy medium saucepan, melt candy coating over low heat, stirring constantly. Quickly dip truffles into melted candy coating, allowing excess coating to drip off. Place truffles on waxed paper and let stand about 30 minutes or until coating is set. Decoratively drizzle the melted semisweet chocolate over tops of truffles. Store in a tightly covered container in the refrigerator. Makes about 2½ dozen truffles.

Shape truffle mixture into balls; roll in ground almonds. Place on waxed paper-lined baking sheet to freeze.

Quickly dip the truffles into the melted candy coating, allowing excess coating to drip off.

Place truffles on a lined baking sheet and let stand about 30 minutes or until coating is set.

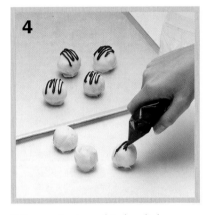

When coating is set, drizzle melted semisweet chocolate over the tops of the truffles.

cherry divinity

As shown on page 243.

Ingredients

2½ cups sugar
½ cup light corn syrup
½ cup water

2 egg whites
½ teaspoon cherry extract
1 or 2 drops red food coloring
½ cup finely chopped candied cherries

Method

Mix sugar, corn syrup, and water in a heavy 2-quart saucepan. Cover and stir over medium-high heat until the mixture boils. Clip a candy thermometer to side of pan. Reduce heat to medium; continue cooking, without stirring, until thermometer registers 260°, hard-ball stage (10 to 15 minutes).

Remove saucepan from heat; remove thermometer. In a large mixing bowl, beat egg whites with a sturdy, freestanding electric mixer on medium speed until stiff peaks form (tips stand straight). Gradually pour hot mixture in a thin stream over whites, beating on high speed about 3 minutes; scrape sides of

Beat egg whites with a freestanding electric mixer on medium speed until stiff peaks form.

Gradually pour hot mixture in a thin stream over whites, beating on high speed about 3 minutes.

Add the extract and coloring, then beat on high until mixture, when beaters are lifted, falls in a ribbon.

Drop the mixture, by spoonfuls, onto the waxed paper. If it stays mounded, it has been beaten sufficiently.

cherry divinity —
continued

bowl occasionally. Add cherry extract and food coloring. Continue beating on high just until candy starts to lose its gloss. When beaters are lifted, mixture should fall in a ribbon that mounds on itself. This should take 5 to 6 minutes.

Drop a spoonful of candy mixture onto waxed paper. If it stays mounded, the mixture has been beaten sufficiently. Immediately stir in cherries. Quickly drop remaining mixture from a teaspoon onto waxed paper. If mixture flattens, beat ½ to 1 minute more; check again. If mixture is too stiff to spoon, beat in a few drops hot water until candy is a softer consistency. Store tightly covered. Makes about 40 pieces.

mint divinity

As shown on page 243.

Ingredients
2½ cups sugar
½ cup light corn syrup
½ cup water
2 egg whites
½ teaspoon mint extract
1 or 2 drops green food coloring

Method
Mix sugar, corn syrup, and water in a heavy 2-quart saucepan. Cover and stir over medium-high heat until the mixture boils. Clip candy thermometer to side of pan. Reduce heat to medium; continue cooking, without stirring, until thermometer registers 260°, hard-ball stage (10 to 15 minutes).

Remove saucepan from heat; remove thermometer. In a large mixing bowl, beat egg whites with an electric mixer on medium speed until stiff peaks form (tips stand straight). Gradually pour hot mixture in a thin stream over egg whites, beating on high about 3 minutes; scrape sides of bowl occasionally. Add mint extract and food coloring. Continue beating on high just until candy starts to lose its gloss. When beaters are lifted, mixture should fall in a ribbon. This should take 5 to 6 minutes.

Drop a spoonful of candy mixture onto waxed paper. If it stays mounded, the mixture has been beaten sufficiently. Quickly drop remaining mixture from a teaspoon onto waxed paper. If mixture flattens, beat ½ to 1 minute more; check again. If mixture is too stiff to spoon, beat in a few drops hot water until candy is a softer consistency. Store tightly covered. Makes about 40 pieces.

grandma's fudge

As shown on page 243.

Ingredients

- 3 tablespoons margarine or butter
- 3 tablespoons unsweetened cocoa powder
- 2½ cups sugar
- ¼ cup plus 2 tablespoons evaporated milk
- 1 teaspoon light corn syrup

Method

In a 2-quart heavy saucepan, melt margarine or butter. Add unsweetened cocoa powder; stir until combined. Add sugar, evaporated milk, and light corn syrup. Cook over medium-high heat until mixture is boiling, stirring constantly with a wooden spoon to dissolve sugar. (This should take about 5 minutes.) Avoid splashing the candy mixture onto sides of pan.

When the mixture starts to boil, carefully clip a candy thermometer to the side of saucepan. Reduce heat to medium-low. The mixture should continue to boil at a moderate, steady rate over the entire surface.

Cook, stirring frequently, for 10 to 15 minutes or until the thermometer registers 230°.

Remove the candy thermometer. Pour the fudge mixture into a large mixing bowl, but do not scrape the saucepan.

Place the thermometer in the bowl. Cool until the thermometer registers 100° and the mixture is thick. (Depending on the room temperature, this can take between 1 and 2 hours, so check the thermometer frequently.) Do not scrape the bowl or stir during the cooling process.

Meanwhile, line a baking sheet with waxed paper. (Beginning fudge makers may want to line a 9×5×3-inch loaf pan with aluminum foil, extending the foil over the edges of the pan; butter the foil.) Set aside.

Using a wooden spoon, beat the cooled mixture about 7 minutes or until the fudge becomes like a soft frosting. The mixture should start to thicken and hold a swirl, yet still be glossy. Immediately drop the fudge mixture by teaspoonfuls onto buttered foil or waxed paper (with the help of an assistant). If the fudge starts to set before all of the candy is dropped, stir in ½ teaspoon hot water and continue dropping the fudge. (Beginning fudge makers may want to pour the mixture into the loaf pan instead of dropping it.) When the fudge becomes firm, lift it out of the pan and cut it into squares.

Cover the fudge and store in a cool, dry place up to one week. Makes about 30 pieces.

When mixture starts to boil, clip a candy thermometer to the pan; boil at steady rate over entire surface.

Use a wooden spoon to beat cooled mixture about 7 minutes or until fudge is like soft frosting.

Drop mixture by spoonfuls onto baking sheet or pour mixture into pan instead.

the first christmas

*S*ymbols of the season—stars, the manger scene, and more—are found in this heavenly chapter. Behold the glory of the first miraculous Christmas, by creating holiday heirlooms using techniques that range from quilting to paper marbleizing.

cross-stitched nativity

Depicting the birth of Christ in the lowly stable, this cross-stitched Nativity is stitched over two threads of 28-count ivory Jobelan fabric using subtle colors and neutral accents. The figures are finished with taffeta and gold trims and stand in a purchased crèche. The pieces may also be finished as lovely ornaments by attaching a gold hanger to the top of each. Instructions and charts for the Nativity begin on page 272.

265

A stellar accent for your holiday displays, these marbleized paper stars are a project the whole family will enjoy. Even your little one can swirl paint atop liquid starch to help make the magnificent marbled designs. Step-by-step photographs are on page 278. After the paint has dried on the paper, follow our folding and cutting diagrams on page 277 to complete four-, five-, or six-pointed stars.

elegant marbleized stars

button box ornaments

Shiny pearl and metallic buttons combine to make beautiful star ornaments. The buttons are sewn onto a backing and then embellished with tassels and gold cords. Instructions are on page 279.

folk art pillow

The Wise Men came from afar bearing gifts, and this folk art pillow captures the wonder of that eventful night. This quickly-worked pillow narrates its tale with rich-hued felts that are appliquéd using running stitches. Complete instructions are on pages 280–281.

bethlehem star

Crocheted to resemble
the star in the sky so
many years ago, this
beautiful version is made
from white cotton thread.
The star is stiffened to
hang as the star attraction
or to adorn your tree.
Instructions are on pages
281–282.

cozy star quilt

Cuddle up for the night and watch the stars with your cozy star quilt and matching pillow. These imperfectly shaped stars are all pieced using scraps of printed and plain fabrics. Instructions and patterns are on pages 282–283.

sparkling chrismons

Symbols of the Christian faith, the chrismons, *below*, are worked on plastic canvas with metallic needlepoint yarn. These lovely ornaments are sure to be found on evergreens celebrating the season in churches everywhere. You can easily make multiples of these quick-to-stitch gems to grace your own Christmas tree. Instructions and charts are on pages 284–285.

cross-stitched nativity

As shown on pages 264–265.

Materials for 1 each of 5 nativity figures

Fabrics

Five 12×11-inch pieces of 28-count ivory Jobelan fabric

¼ yard of moiré taffeta fabric in desired color; ¼ yard of fleece

¼ yard of lightweight fusible interfacing

8×6-inch piece of ivory felt

Threads

Cotton embroidery floss in colors listed in key

Metallic gold thread

Supplies

Fabric marking pencil

Tracing paper

Matboard; fabric glue

5 yards of narrow flat or round contrasting trim (1 yard for each figure)

5 yards of narrow gold metallic flat trim (1 yard for each figure)

Polyester fiberfill

Paper-backed iron-on adhesive

Instructions

Tape or zigzag edges of fabric to prevent fraying. For each figure, find center of chart and of one piece of fabric; begin stitching there. Use two plies of floss to work cross-stitches over two threads of fabric. Work backstitches, straight stitches, and French knots using one ply. Work blended needle as indicated on key. Press finished stitchery from back.

Use marking pencil to outline design shape, approximately ⅜ inch from edge of stitching. Cut fleece piece to cover back of stitching; baste in place along marked outline.

For angel, use outline on pattern, *opposite*, as a guide to draw pattern on tracing paper; cut out. Trace shape on matboard; cut out. Glue layer of fleece to matboard shape. Trim fleece-lined angel to

---

NATITY

ANCHOR		DMC
387	S	Ecru
002	•	000 White
1026	L	225 Pale shell pink
1017	⊙	316 Medium antique mauve
978	◇	322 Pale navy
1047	✶	402 Pale mahogany
358	◘	433 Dark chestnut
310	×	434 Medium chestnut
1046	▽	435 Light chestnut
1045	▢	436 Dark tan
362	◫	437 Medium tan
933	◥	543 Pale beige brown
168	△	597 Light turquoise
392	✗	640 Dark beige gray
891	⦶	676 Light old gold
295	‖	726 Light topaz
890	▣	729 Medium old gold
1016	♡	778 Pale antique mauve
130	⊕	809 True Delft blue
907	◮	832 Medium bronze
945	◳	834 Pale bronze
379	⊞	840 Medium beige brown
378	⊘	841 True beige brown
1041	⋈	844 Deep beaver gray
897	♥	902 Deep garnet
1035	●	930 Dark antique blue
4146	⋮	950 Light rose beige
360	◆	3031 Deep mocha
903	☆	3032 Medium mocha
391	⊟	3033 Pale mocha
886	▷	3047 Light yellow beige
292	◠	3078 Pale lemon
382	■	3371 Black brown
896	✳	3721 Dark shell pink
1018	▲	3726 True antique mauve
120	⊠	3747 Pale periwinkle
1009	+	3770 True ivory
1008	△	3773 Medium rose beige
778	☐	3774 Pale rose beige
1050	#	3781 Dark mocha
899	◎	3782 Light mocha
393	▼	3790 Deep beige gray

ANCHOR		DMC
1019	▶	3802 Deep antique mauve
851	✦	3808 Deep turquoise
779	★	3809 Dark turquoise
168	◩	3810 True turquoise
890	◆	3829 Deep old gold
	◈	284 Metallic gold thread

BLENDED NEEDLE

360 905	▥	839 Dark beige brown (1X) and 3021 Deep brown gray (1X) – cradle

BACKSTITCH

	╱	284 Metallic gold thread – halos, angel's wings, hair, banner, and bottom of gown
352	╱	300 Deep mahogany – rope on donkey
1019	╱	315 Dark antique mauve – donkey's blanket
358	╱	433 Dark chestnut – shepherd's eyebrows
897	╱	902 Deep garnet – shepherd's mouth and sheep's mouth
1035	╱	930 Dark antique blue – lettering on angel's banner
360	╱	3031 Deep mocha – Mary's hair (2X)
896	╱	3721 Dark shell pink – Joseph's, Mary's, and angel's mouths
382	╱	3371 Black brown – all remaining stitches

STRAIGHT STITCH

891	╱	676 Light old gold – hay
897	╱	902 Deep garnet – Joseph's sash

FRENCH KNOT

002	●	000 White – donkey's and lamb's eyes
897	●	902 Deep garnet – Joseph's sash
382	●	3371 Black brown – Mary's, baby's, and Joseph's eyes

ALGERIAN EYELET

	✳	284 Metallic gold thread – angel's hair

ANGEL

Angel stitch count: 106 high x 75 wide
Angel finished design sizes:
28-count fabric – 7 1/2 x 5 3/8 inches
22-count fabric – 9 5/8 x 6 7/8 inches
36-count fabric – 5 7/8 x 4 1/4 inches

cross-stitched nativity — *continued*

¾ inch beyond basting. Clip into seam allowance and position angel over matboard; glue allowance to back. Glue contrasting trim around outside edge, followed by gold metallic trim. Using pattern, cut piece from felt and glue to back. If desired, glue ribbon to back of angel and tie to crèche.

For the remaining figures, use stitched pieces as guides to cut back pieces from moiré taffeta. With right sides facing, stitch the figure fronts to the backs on basting line, leaving bottom edge open. Trim seam allowance to ¼ inch. Trim away all fleece in seam allowance. Clip curves and turn right side out.

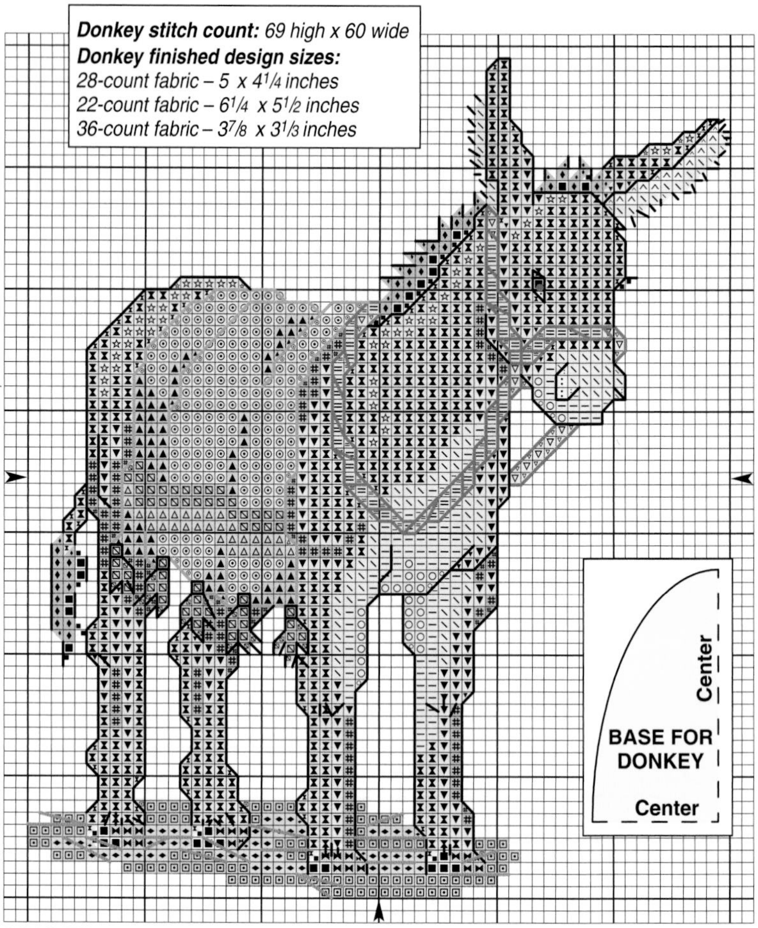

Donkey stitch count: 69 high x 60 wide
Donkey finished design sizes:
28-count fabric – 5 x 4¼ inches
22-count fabric – 6¼ x 5½ inches
36-count fabric – 3⅞ x 3⅓ inches

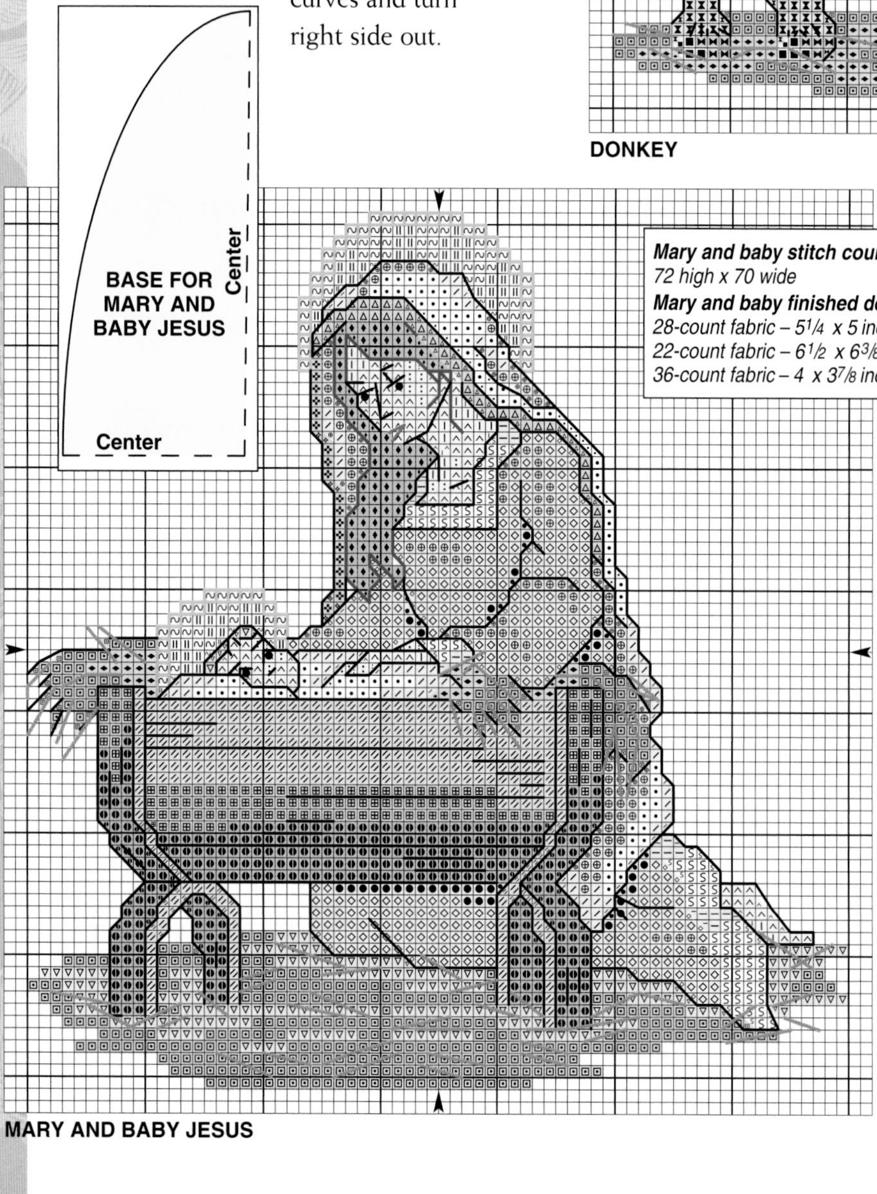

BASE FOR DONKEY
Center
Center

DONKEY

BASE FOR MARY AND BABY JESUS
Center
Center

Mary and baby stitch count:
72 high x 70 wide
Mary and baby finished design sizes:
28-count fabric – 5¼ x 5 inches
22-count fabric – 6½ x 6⅜ inches
36-count fabric – 4 x 3⅞ inches

Turn under ¼ inch along bottom edge and baste. Stuff figure with polyester fiberfill.

Trace base patterns, *above, left,* and *opposite;* cut out. Cut shapes from matboard. Fuse taffeta to right side of matboard, following the manufacturer's directions on iron-on adhesive. Trim fabric ½ inch beyond the matboard; clip and glue to the wrong side. Whipstitch the bases to bottoms of figures. Remove basting threads at bottom edge if visible.

Glue contrasting trim along seam line of sides and top of each figure. Repeat with metallic gold trim. Glue gold trim around bottom edge.

MARY AND BABY JESUS

Joseph stitch count: *102 high x 53 wide*
Joseph finished design sizes:
28-count fabric – 7¼ x 3¾ inches
22-count fabric – 9¼ x 4⅞ inches
36-count fabric – 5⅔ x 3 inches

BASE FOR
JOSEPH AND
SHEPHERD
WITH SHEEP
Center
Center

JOSEPH

Shepherd stitch count: *94 high x 52 wide*
Shepherd finished design sizes:
28-count fabric – 6¾ x 3¾ inches
22-count fabric – 8½ x 4¾ inches
36-count fabric – 5¼ x 2⅞ inches

SHEPHERD WITH SHEEP

elegant marbleized stars

As shown on page 266, stars measure from 2 to 8½ inches across, depending on size of paper used to create star.

Materials

Plastic table covering or
  newspapers
Two large rectangular baking
  dishes or plastic dishpans
Liquid laundry starch
Custard cups or small containers
Acrylic paint in desired colors
Artist's brushes; white bond paper
Marbleizing tools (see page 278)
Newspaper strips
Gold metallic paint

Instructions

Cover work surface with plastic covering or newspapers. To marbleize paper, pour the starch into one baking dish to a depth of 2 inches. Fill remaining dish with cool water.

In custard cups, dilute each paint color with water until it just barely drips from a brush. Allow paint to gently drop from ends of brushes onto surface of starch until the surface of the starch is nearly covered.

Create a pattern in the paint. Drag a comb, made by inserting plastic picks into a block of plastic foam, or similar tool through the paint for a pattern of wavy lines.

For an arched pattern, comb paint in one direction and then in the perpendicular direction. For a pebble pattern, leave paint drops as they are. For a feather pattern, use an ice pick to make parallel lines back and forth through paint, alternating direction. For a star burst pattern, use ice pick to gently pull points of paint outward from round drops. For a swirl pattern, swirl ice pick in a circular motion through paint.

Hold piece of paper to be marbleized by opposite corners and bend it lightly so it sags slightly in the center. Lay it gently atop the paint, but do not allow it to sink below the surface. Immediately lift the paper back out of the starch mixture. Holding paper over dish, allow it to drip for about 10 seconds.

Rinse paper in water dish. Lift paper out of water and allow it to drip for about 15 seconds. When most of water has dripped off, lay it flat on a paper-towel-covered work surface to dry.

Add additional paint for next paper, if desired. To remove paint from starch before adding new colors, skim with newspaper strips.

For each star, when paper is completely dry, smooth it by ironing on the wrong side. (Cover ironing board with a protective cloth.) Cut paper into squares.

For four-pointed star, refer to folding diagram, *opposite.* Fold the square in half twice to make a smaller square (Step 1). Fold A to B to make a triangle (Step 2). Cut as indicated by the dotted line. Open out star and make a sharp crease along each fold, creasing each point of star outward and each inner corner inward.

For five-pointed star, refer to folding diagram, *opposite.* After folding the square in half, locate the center of the folded edge and an imaginary line four-fifths of the distance from center of folded edge to left edge (Step 1). Fold A to imaginary line, using center of folded edge as pivot point (Step 2). Next, fold C to A (Step 3). Fold B around back to meet opposite point D (Step 4) and cut as indicated by dotted line. Open out star and crease points and inner corners as for four-pointed star.

For six-pointed star, refer to folding diagram, *opposite.* After folding the square in half, locate the center of the folded edge (Step 1). Fold the piece into thirds, using the center of the folded edge as the bottom point (Step 2). Next, fold the resulting shape in half, matching C to D, and cut as indicated by the dotted line (Step 3). Open out; crease points and inner corners as for the four-pointed star.

Paint a metallic gold border along the edges of each star.

FOUR-POINTED STAR

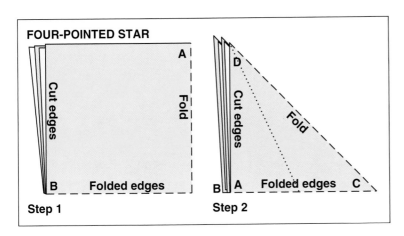

Step 1

Step 2

FIVE-POINTED STAR

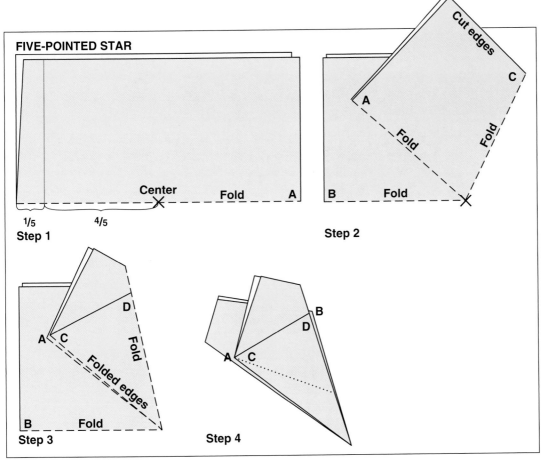

Step 1

1/5   4/5

Step 2

Step 3

Step 4

SIX-POINTED STAR

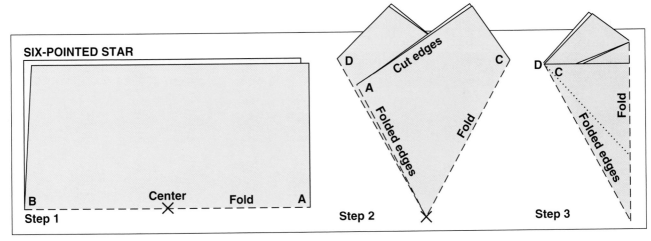

Step 1

Step 2

Step 3

Step-by-Step Marbleizing

You'll find lots of uses for marbleized paper during the holiday season. It makes beautiful paper ornaments like the folded stars on page 266. Dip larger sheets for gift wrap or try heavier paper for Christmas cards.

You probably already have most of the supplies you need to make beautiful marbleized paper. Gather a large bottle of liquid starch; several colors of acrylic paints; two large flat baking dishes or dishpans; a few custard cups, small bowls, or empty margarine containers; paintbrushes; plus a variety of tools to create patterns in the paint.

Fill one baking dish or dishpan with starch to a depth of 2 inches; fill the second one with cool water. In custard cups or other small containers, dilute each paint color until it just barely drips from a brush. Then drip colors on top of the starch until the surface is nearly covered.

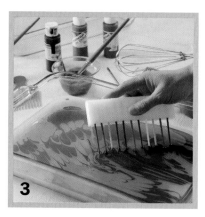

Create a pattern in the starch using one of the methods on page 276, or experiment with a feather, nut pick, ice pick, coiled rubber cord, wire whisk, fork, or wide-toothed hair comb. Move desired tool through paint in straight lines, at geometric angles, in circles, or in rays. Even if you leave the dots undisturbed, no two patterns will be the same.

Hold a piece of paper by opposite corners and bend it gently so the paper sags slightly. Lay it gently on top of the paint, but do not allow the paper to sink below the surface. Immediately lift paper back out of the starch. Hold it over the dish and allow the paint to drip off for 10 seconds.

Rinse the paper in the dish of plain water. Lift the paper out of the water and allow it to drip for about 15 seconds or until most of the water has dripped off. Lay the paper, paint side up, flat on a paper towel-covered work surface to dry.

button box ornaments

As shown on page 267, ornaments measure 4×4 inches and 4½×4½ inches.

Materials for one ornament

Silver and gold metallic
perforated paper
Card stock
Silver and gold metallic
wrapping paper
Thick crafts glue
Tracing paper
Silver and gold metallic thread
Tapestry needle
20 to 60 assorted gold, silver,
clear, or pearl buttons for
each ornament
Silver or gold metallic or beaded
tassels (optional)
Silver and gold cord

Instructions

Glue the perforated paper to the
card stock and then to the wrong
side of the matching wrapping
paper. Trace the star patterns,
right, onto tracing paper and cut
out. Cut the stars as desired from
the paper-covered card stock.

Sew buttons onto the perforated
paper side of stars to cover, using
matching thread.

Cut 24 inches of matching
cord for the hanging loop. Tack
the center of the cord to the back
of the star at the top point. Knot
the ends. Tack the tassel to the
bottom of the star. If desired, glue
another layer of the wrapping
paper to the back of the star to
cover the threads; trim to match
the shape.

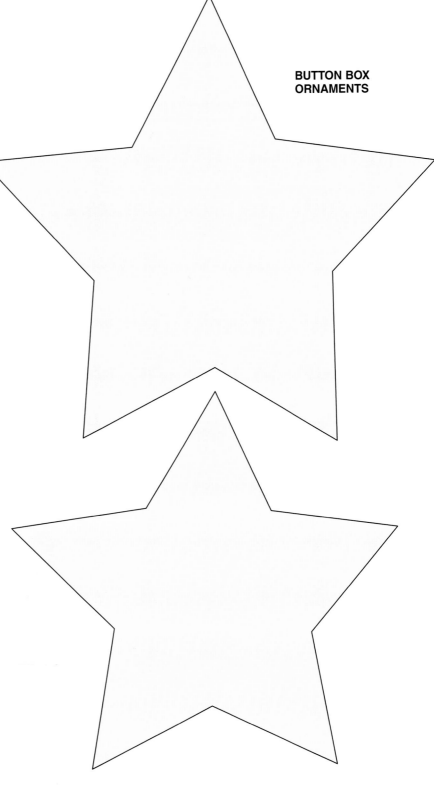

**BUTTON BOX
ORNAMENTS**

folk art pillow

As shown on page 268, pillow measures 18×17 inches.

Materials

Tracing paper; pinking shears

7×9-inch piece of paper-backed iron-on adhesive

7×9-inch piece of dark blue-and-black print cotton fabric

6×12-inch piece of cinnamon brown felt

4×8-inch piece of green felt

2×4-inch piece of cranberry red felt

6×6-inch piece of gold felt

4×4-inch piece of tan felt

3×3-inch piece of light heather gray felt

1×3-inch piece of ivory felt

16½×17½-inch piece of cranberry red felt

Straight pins; needle
Sewing threads: black, green, dark brown, gray, tan, and gold
3 gold or brown-toned, ¼- to ½-inch-diameter buttons
⅛×12-inch strips each of green felt, red felt, and dark blue fabric
17½×18½-inch piece of black felt
16-inch-square pillow form

Instructions

Trim edges of large red and black felt pieces using pinking shears; set aside.

Enlarge patterns, *opposite,* onto tracing paper and cut out. Following the manufacturer's instructions, fuse paper-backed adhesive to back of blue-and-black print cotton fabric. Cut the sky background piece from blue print. Cut fence boards and camel from brown felt. Cut curved ground pieces from green felt. Cut king's body from red felt. Cut star, crown, and infant's basket from gold felt. Cut cow, king's feet, and infant's and king's heads from

tan felt. Cut donkey's head and forelock from gray felt. Cut infant's body from ivory felt.

Position large red rectangle on work surface with 17½-inch measurement running horizontally. Following pattern diagram for placement, and marking center, remove paper backing from blue fabric and fuse in place on red felt pillow top. Use placement diagram to position remaining pieces; pin in place. Pin donkey's forelock to top of head.

To sew each piece in place, use doubled strand of sewing thread. Using running stitches ⅛ inch from outer edges, stitch around fused sky piece with black thread. With green running stitches, sew green ground pieces in place. Use dark brown running stitches to sew fence boards, camel, king's body, and infant's body in place. Use gray running stitches to sew donkey's head in place, catching forelock along top. Use tan running stitches for cow, infant's

and king's head, and king's feet. Sew crown in place with gold running stitches. Use gold buttonhole stitches to sew infant's basket and star in place.

Work face detail on donkey and cow using dark brown thread. Also using dark brown, sew buttons at Xs on star.

Cut two ⅛×12-inch strips each of green felt, red felt, and dark blue fabric. Treating strands of each color as one strip, braid. Tack top of braid at center top edge of camel's head. Tack again at back of camel's neck, then to center left edge of king's clothing. Allow unbraided ends to hang.

Center pillow top on black felt, wrong sides facing. Sew front to back, machine-stitching 1 inch from pinked edge of red felt. Do not leave opening. Slit pillow back vertically between top and bottom stitching. Insert pillow form and hand-sew the opening closed.

bethlehem star

As shown on page 269. Crochet abbreviations are on page 320.

Materials

1 ball of white J & P Coats Knit-Cro-Sheen
Size 5 or 6 steel crochet hook
Crafts glue; piece of cardboard; plastic kitchen wrap; T-pins

Instructions

Rnd 1: Ch 6; join with sl st to form a ring. Ch 1, work 12 sc in ring; join with sl st in first sc.

Rnd 2: Ch 4 (counts as dc, ch 1), dc in next sc; * ch 1, dc in next dc; rep from * around, ending ch 1; join with sl st in third ch of beginning ch-4. 12 dc.

Rnd 3: Ch 7 (counts as tr, ch 3), tr in next dc; * ch 3, tr in next dc; rep from * around, ending ch 3, join with sl st in fourth ch of beginning ch-7. 12 ch-3 sps.

Rnd 4: In first ch-3 sp [sl st, ch 3 (counts as dc)], 5 dc in same sp; 6 dc in each ch-3 sp around; join with sl st in third ch of beginning ch-3. 72 sts.

Rnd 5: For first point—sc in next st, hdc in next st, 2 dc in next st, in next st (tr, ch 5, tr), 2 dc in next st, hdc in next st, sc in next st, sl st in next 2 sts; for second point—sc in next st, hdc

bethlehem star — *continued*

in next st, 2 dc in next st, in next st (tr, ch 2, tr), 2 dc in next st, hdc in next st, sc in next st, sl st in next 2 sts; for third point—cont as est working (tr, ch 6, tr); for fourth point—work as for second point; for fifth point—work as for first point; for sixth point—work as second point; for seventh point—cont as est working (tr, ch 7, tr); for eighth point—sc in next st, hdc in next st, 2 dc in next st, in next st (tr, ch 2, tr), 2 dc in next st, hdc in next st, sc in next st, sl st in next st.

Rnd 6: Sl st in sl st and next sc, sc in hdc, hdc in dc, dc in dc, dc in tr, in sp (3 tr, ch 3, 3 tr), dc in tr, dc in dc, hdc in dc, sc in hdc, sl st in each of next 4 sts, sc in

each of next 4 sts, in sp (3 sc, ch 1, 3 sc), sc in each of next 4 sts, sl st in each of next 4 sts, sc in next st, hdc in next st, dc in each of next 2 sts, in sp (3 tr, ch 4, 3 tr), dc in each of next 2 sts, hdc in next st, sc in next st, sl st in each of next 4 sts, sc in each of next 4 sts, in sp (3 sc, ch 1, 3 sc), sc in each of next 4 sts, sl st in each of next 4 sts, sc in next st, hdc in next st, dc in each of next 2 sts, in sp (3 tr, ch 3, 3 tr), dc in each of next 2 sts, hdc in next st, sc in next st, sl st in each of next 4 sts, sc in each of next 4 sts, in sp (3 sc, ch 1, 3 sc), sc in each of next 4 sts, sl st in each of next 4 sts, sc in next st, hdc in next st, dc in each of next 2 sts, in sp (3 tr, ch 6, 3 tr), dc in each of

next 2 sts, hdc in next st, sc in next st, sl st in each of next 4 sts, sc in each of next 4 sts, in sp (3 sc, ch 1, 3 sc), sc in each of next 4 sts, sl st in each of next 2 sts; join with sl st in first sl st and fasten off.

FINISHING: Dilute glue slightly with water or follow directions on stiffener. Dip star until saturated with glue mixture. Squeeze out excess. Cover cardboard with plastic wrap; secure with tape on back. Shape star on plastic wrap using T-pins to hold crochet, pulling out points and keeping spacing even. Allow to dry, remove pins, and gently pull plastic wrap away from star. Thread a piece of crochet thread through top point as a hanger.

Materials

Fabric yardages are for 45-inch-wide fabrics unless otherwise indicated.
Tracing paper
Quilters' template material
¼ yard each of 12 different plaid fabrics

cozy star quilt

As shown on page 270, quilt measures 58½×65½ inches.

¼ yard each of 12 different coordinating solid fabrics
1¼ yards of lavender-gray fabric
2¼ yards of red solid fabric
1¼ yards of red plaid fabric
2¼ yards of 60-inch-wide backing fabric
Clear nylon sewing thread
Polyester batting; eighty 1-inch buttons in assorted colors
Threads to match buttons

Instructions

Enlarge and trace pattern pieces, *opposite.* Cut apart on solid lines. Draw around pieces on template

material adding ¼-inch seam allowances. From each of the 12 plaid fabrics, cut pieces A, B, C, D, E, and F, turning grainline of plaid at random. From each of the 12 solid fabrics, cut pieces 1, 2, 3, 4, and 5.

For sashing, cut sixteen 3½×10½-inch lavender vertical strips, fifteen 3½×12½-inch lavender horizontal strips, and twenty 3½×3½-inch squares from assorted solids.

For border, cut two 4½×70-inch strips and two 4½×62-inch strips from the solid red fabric. Cut red

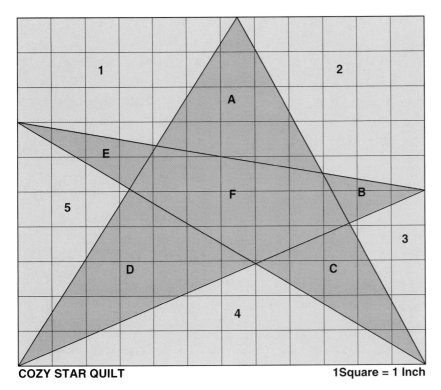

COZY STAR QUILT　　　　　　　　　　　　　**1Square = 1 Inch**

one 3½×3½-inch square to each
short end of one 12½-inch long
sashing strip, then sew another
sashing strip to right side of
right-hand square. Continuing to
work from left to right, sew a
third square, another sashing, and
a fourth square. Make five. Sew
horizontal sashing between rows
of blocks and at top and bottom,
matching seam lines. Sew a red
border strip to each side, mitering
corners. Layer quilt top, batting,
and backing (pieced as necessary).
Baste. Machine quilt along seam
lines of sashing.

Trim batting and back ½ inch
beyond quilt top. Sew enough
3-inch-wide binding strips together
to fit around edge of quilt. Pin
binding to quilt top, right sides
together; stitch through all layers
using ¼-inch seam. Miter corners.
Turn binding to back and turn
under ¼ inch along raw edge.
Slipstitch in place.

Add buttons to corners of each
sashing square.

plaid into 3-inch-wide bias binding
strips. All measurements include
¼-inch seam allowances. Sew the
seams with the right sides facing.

For each block, referring to
diagram, *above,* sew background
pieces 1 and 2 to A. Sew 4 and 5
to D, 3 to B, and C and E to F.
Next, stitch piece B3 to piece EFC.
Sew 1A2 to top and 5D4 to
bottom to finish one block. Make

11 more blocks.

Arrange blocks in four rows
of three blocks each. For each
row, sew long side of one vertical
10½-inch sashing strip to each
side of left hand block. Sew the
second block to right sashing.
Continuing to work from left to
right, sew another sashing, third
block, and another sashing.

For horizontal sashing, sew

stars and buttons
pillow

As shown on page 270, pillow measures 20×23 inches.

Materials

Fabric yardages are for 45-inch-wide
fabrics unless otherwise indicated.
Tracing paper
Quilters' template material
1½ yards of desired plaid fabric
　　for back and ruffle

¼ yard of desired plaid fabric
　　for star
¼ yard of coordinating solid fabric
¼ yard of blue-gray fabric
Four 3½×3½-inch squares of
　　assorted solid fabrics

Clear nylon sewing thread
Narrow piping cord; polyester
　　fiberfill
Sixteen 1-inch buttons in
　　assorted colors
Threads to match buttons

Instructions

Enlarge and trace pattern, *page 283*, and make templates as for Cozy Star Quilt. Cut pieces A, B, C, D, E, and F from star plaid, and pieces 1, 2, 3, 4, and 5 from solid. Cut two 3½×10½-inch vertical sashing strips and two 3½×12½-inch horizontal sashing strips from blue-gray. Complete a star block as for quilt, *page 283*, surrounded by sashing strips.

For the ruffle, cut enough 7½-inch-wide plaid strips to measure 4 yards. Sew short ends together to make a circle. Press ruffle in half lengthwise with the wrong sides facing.

Position piping cord inside ruffle along folded edge; stitch close to piping using zipper foot. Sew a gathering thread through both layers of ruffle close to raw edges. Pin ruffle to pillow; adjust gathers evenly. Baste ruffle in place.

Use pillow top as pattern to cut plaid pillow back. Sew pillow front to back, right sides facing, using ½-inch seam allowance. Leave opening for turning. Trim seams and clip corners. Turn pillow right side out and stuff with fiberfill. Slipstitch opening closed.

sparkling chrismons

As shown on page 271.

Materials

Fabric

1 sheet of 7-count plastic canvas

Thread

Rainbow Gallery Plastic Canvas
   Metallic Needlepoint Yarn:
   26 yards of No. 10 pearl and
   24 yards of No. 7 gold

Supplies

Thirty-five 4-millimeter gold beads
5 yards of fine gold metallic
   thread
Tapestry needle
Manicure scissors

Instructions

Cut pieces from sheet of plastic canvas using charts, *opposite*. Use scissors to cut away inner portions of chrismons where necessary.

Work continental, long, and straight stitches all using one ply of needlepoint yarn. Overcast all edges using gold yarn.

Use thread to attach beads. If the bead symbol lies over an intersection, bring the needle up as for the continental stitch, slip bead on the needle, then insert needle back through the canvas as if completing a continental stitch. If symbol is between the stitches, bring the needle up in hole, slip bead on, and insert needle back through canvas in same place. Knot all ends, then weave in tails. Cut a 5-inch length of gold yarn for each ornament and secure at top of ornaments for hangers.

NEEDLEPOINT CHRISMONS

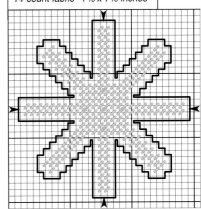

07 Rainbow Gallery Metallic gold plastic canvas yarn

10 Rainbow Gallery Metallic pearl plastic canvas yarn

STRAIGHT STITCH

07 Rainbow Gallery Metallic gold plastic canvas yarn – crown, fish, descending dove

BEADS

Gold beads – 1/8- inch diameter

Cross and Chi
stitch count: 26 high x 26 wide

Cross and Chi
finished design sizes:
7-count fabric – 3¾ x 3¾ inches
14-count fabric – 1⅞ x 1⅞ inches

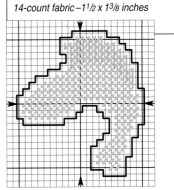

CROSS AND CHI

Triangle and Trefoil
stitch count: 22 high x 24 wide

Triangle and Trefoil
finished design sizes:
7-count fabric – 3⅛ x 3⅜ inches
14-count fabric – 1⅝ x 1¾ inches

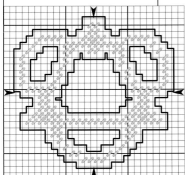

TRIANGLE AND TREFOIL

Chi-Rho stitch count: 33 high x 17 wide

Chi-Rho finished design sizes:
7-count fabric – 4¾ x 2⅜ inches
14-count fabric – 2⅜ x 1¼ inches

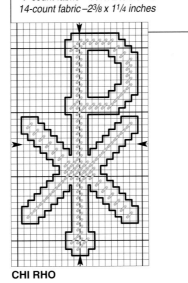

CHI RHO

Fish stitch count: 21 high x 19 wide

Fish finished design sizes:
7-count fabric – 3 x 2¾ inches
14-count fabric – 1½ x 1⅜ inches

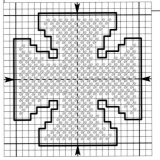

FISH

Crown stitch count: 16 high x 24 wide

Crown finished design sizes:
7-count fabric – 2¼ x 3⅜ inches
14-count fabric – 1⅛ x 1¾ inches

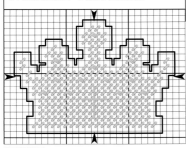

CROWN

Decending Dove
stitch count: 28 high x 21 wide

Decending Dove
finished design sizes:
7-count fabric – 4 x 3 inches
14-count fabric – 2 x 1½ inches

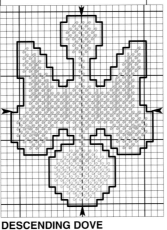

DESCENDING DOVE

Cross Pat'ee stitch count: 19 high x 19 wide

Cross Pat'ee finished design sizes:
7-count fabric – 2¾ x 2¾ inches
14-count fabric – 1⅜ x 1⅜ inches

CROSS PAT'EE

all I want for christmas

Always a blessing, children bring special joy at Christmastime. These delightful toys and yuletide trims are created to bring jolly giggles and grins from all the little ones on your holiday list. They'll love you for making their holiday so very, very merry.

Gingerbread people made of wood and paint open their arms to wish that special boy or girl a Merry Christmas. Make these wooden treats even more unique by personalizing them with the child's name written with a paint pen. Instructions and patterns are on page 296.

faux gingerbread friends

joyful gift bag santa

Santa is always filled with joy, but our Santa, filled with sweet candies, is extra special. His body, secured with a red and gold drawstring, holds holiday treats safe inside. Full-size patterns and instructions begin on page 297.

Who could resist kissing this magical frog? Freddy has personality-plus and is made from muslin, then painted with shimmering green paint. His fancy satin shirt, vest, trousers, and beret make this frog a prince of a fellow. Full-size patterns and instructions start on page 300.

freddy the frog prince

christmas twins

Little Signa and Bjorn are all dressed up for Christmas in their best holiday bib and tucker. The petite twins are made from cross-stitch fabric with tiny motifs cross-stitched on their charming removable clothing. Instructions, patterns, and charts begin on page 306.

lovable elf santa

Know who's naughty or nice? This little fellow does! And judging by his pleased expression, he has loads of Christmas wishes to fill. Santa's clothes are made from fabrics rich with pattern, color, and texture, making him a mantel standout. His chubby-cheeked face and hands are stitched in felt. Best of all, jointed arms and legs let you pose him any way you like. The instructions and patterns are on pages 309–314.

She'll stay warm and toasty dressed in her candy cane scarf, mittens, and hat knit from soft red and eggshell-color yarns. The hat has a jolly bell tassel and the scarf has long fancy fringes. If red and white doesn't match your winter wear, choose two of your own favorite hues. Instructions are on pages 315–316.

candy cane scarf set

gingerbread noah's ark

Children of all ages will gather around to hear the story of Noah and the Ark—and to share the tastes and smells of the spicy gingerbread. The ark is constructed with flat pieces of gingerbread and then piped with colorful frosting. Dozens of pairs of animals can be made two by two using favorite animal cookie cutters. Instructions and patterns start on page 316.

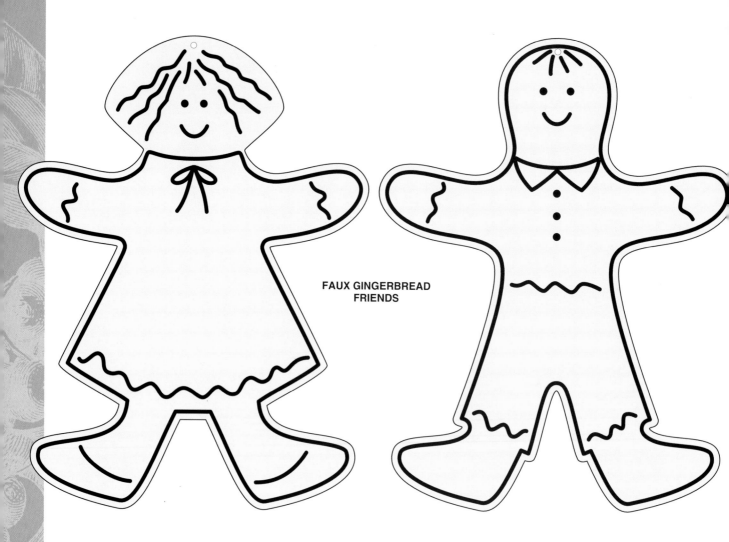

FAUX GINGERBREAD FRIENDS

faux gingerbread friends

As shown on page 288, each ornament measures 5×3⅞ inches.

Materials

For both ornaments

Tracing paper; carbon paper; ballpoint pen

8×7-inch piece of ⅛-inch Baltic birch plywood

Scroll saw; drill with ⅛-inch bit

Fine grit sandpaper

Acrylic paints: dark brown and light brown

Crystals fabric paint

White fabric paint pen

¼- and ½-inch paint brushes

Polyurethane spray

12 inches of ⅛-inch-diameter red satin ribbon

Instructions

Trace patterns, *above*, onto tracing paper. Place the carbon paper between the pattern and wood; transfer body outline, tracing over line with ballpoint pen. Cut out ornament with scroll saw. Drill hole in top for hanger. Sand surfaces smooth.

Paint the entire ornament dark brown. While fronts are still damp, blend light brown around the edges to resemble baked edges of cookies; allow to dry. Brush several coats of crystals paint over the front. When crystals paint is dry, use white paint pen to draw "icing" detail as desired, using the photograph, *page 288*, for ideas. Spray with polyurethane spray to seal.

Thread ribbon through hole in top of ornament; knot ends.

joyful gift bag santa

As shown on page 289, Santa measures 26 inches long.

Materials

Yardages are for 45-inch-wide fabrics

Tracing paper

⅓ yard of red wide-wale corduroy

¼ yard of black polished cotton fabric

¼ yard of ecru cotton fabric

4×4-inch piece of muslin

4×4-inch piece of paper-backed iron-on adhesive

8×14-inch piece of white satin

10×20-inch piece of gold metallic netting

Pins; polyester fiberfill

Three 1×5-inch strips of white short-nap fake fur

Fabric marking pen

Thread to match fabrics

⅔ yard of red 1-inch-wide double-fold bias tape

Ten ⅜-inch-diameter gold jingle bells

Black ultra-fine tip permanent marker

2 yards of gold and red cording

Two 5-millimeter black beads

Thick white crafts glue

1½-inch-diameter white pom-pom

Cosmetic powder blush

Instructions

Trace patterns, *right* and *pages 298–299*, onto paper and cut out. Fold corduroy, black polished cotton, and ecru cotton fabrics in half with right sides facing. Use fabric marker to draw around leg and arm patterns twice and hat pattern once on corduroy. Draw around boot pattern twice on black cotton, and mitten pattern twice onto ecru cotton. Do not cut out pieces.

For head, fuse iron-on adhesive square to muslin square following manufacturer's instructions. Draw around face pattern on muslin; cut out. Cut satin into two 8×7-inch pieces. Remove paper backing from face. Referring to head pattern, position face on right side of one satin piece; fuse in place. Machine-stitch around face using narrow zigzag stitches and black thread. Turn piece over and position head pattern on back, aligning stitched face outline with face outline on head pattern. Draw around head pattern. Position satin piece with face atop the other, right sides together.

For all pieces, cut out ¼ inch beyond stitching. Sew on drawn lines on doubled fabrics, leaving openings as marked on patterns; clip curves. Turn right side out and set aside.

Fold gold netting in half to measure 10×10 inches with fold at bottom. Center legs between layers, with top edges of legs against netting's folded edge. Sew across folded edge of netting ¼ inch away from fold to secure leg tops.

Measure 1¼ inches down from top edges of folded netting and insert arm on each side, matching top edges of arms with side raw edges of netting. Sew ¼-inch seam down each netting side, leaving top 1¼ inches on each side unstitched.

Turn netting bag right side out. Cut two strips of bias tape to measure length of top edge of bag plus ½ inch. Turn under each end of tape ¼ inch; stitch to netting's raw edge. Fold each strip over top edge of bag; stitch.

Stuff mittens to within ½ inch of opening. Stuff arms; sew openings closed. Slip a mitten over end of each arm and whipstitch wrist edges of mittens to arms. Trim fur strip for each wrist to fit; glue around mitten.

Stuff boots; stitch across openings to close. Stuff each leg to within ½ inch of opening. Turn under ¼ inch along raw edges. Using a doubled thread and running stitches, run a

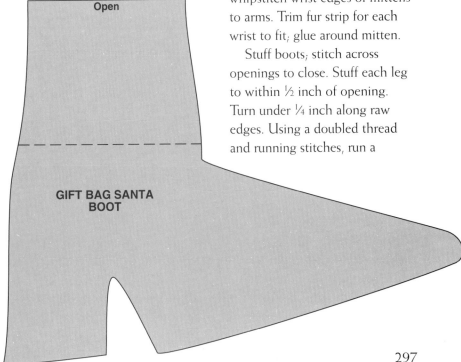

Open

GIFT BAG SANTA BOOT

joyful gift bag santa —

continued

gathering thread along each fold. Insert boot tops into bottom of legs and pull gathering threads to close legs around boots. Adjust gathers and tack leg edges to boots. Sew five bells around gathered bottom edge of each pant leg.

Cut cord into two equal lengths for drawstring. Beginning at one side of bag, thread one cord all the way around through both bag top casings and out again at starting point. Knot ends together. Repeat with remaining cord, beginning on opposite side.

Stuff head; sew opening closed. Using black thread, sew black beads in place for eyes. Pull thread tight between eyes to define bridge of nose. Using same thread, straight-stitch eyebrows. Enter and exit through head top to hide thread ends. Use black marker to add detail to inner eyes and nostrils as desired.

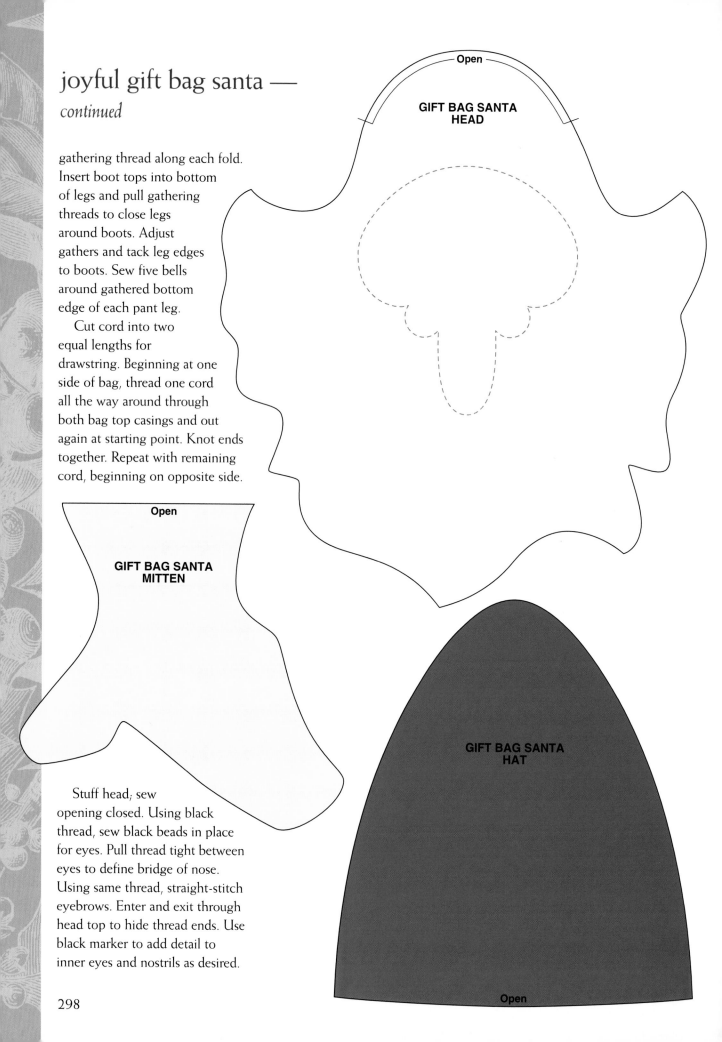

Open

GIFT BAG SANTA HEAD

Open

GIFT BAG SANTA MITTEN

GIFT BAG SANTA HAT

Open

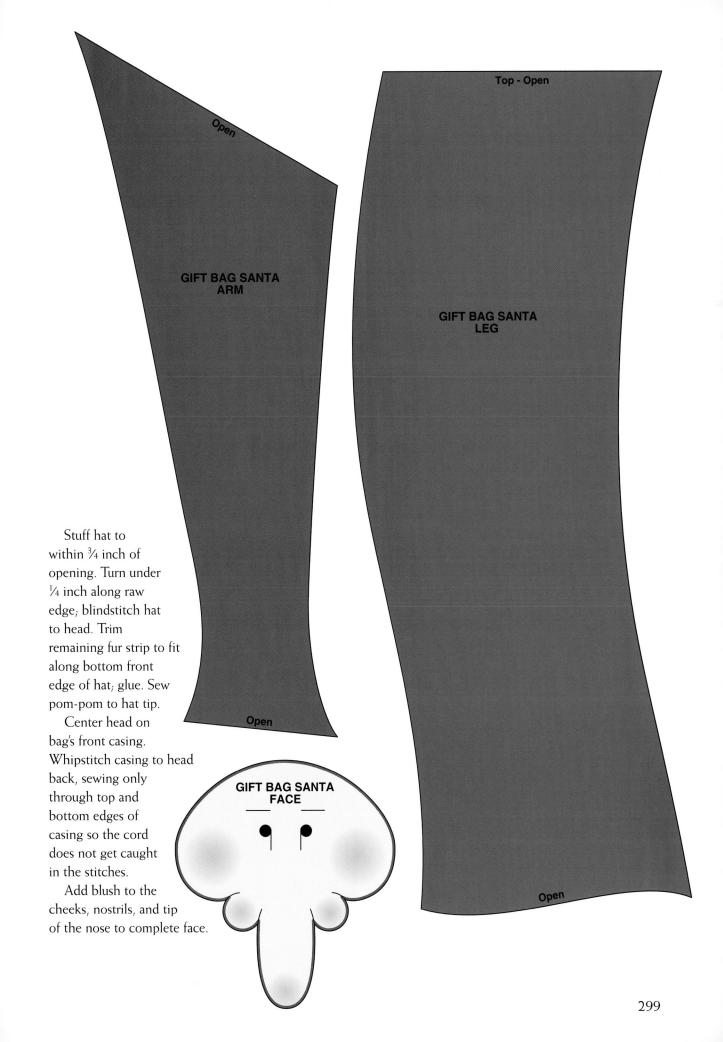

GIFT BAG SANTA ARM

Open

Open

Top - Open

GIFT BAG SANTA LEG

Open

Stuff hat to within ¾ inch of opening. Turn under ¼ inch along raw edge; blindstitch hat to head. Trim remaining fur strip to fit along bottom front edge of hat; glue. Sew pom-pom to hat tip.

Center head on bag's front casing. Whipstitch casing to head back, sewing only through top and bottom edges of casing so the cord does not get caught in the stitches.

Add blush to the cheeks, nostrils, and tip of the nose to complete face.

GIFT BAG SANTA FACE

freddy the frog prince

As shown on page 290, frog prince is approximately 13 inches long and sits 7½ inches tall.

Materials

Tracing paper
¼ yard of 45-inch-wide
  unbleached muslin
¼ yard of 45-inch-wide dark
  gold satin
¼ yard of 45-inch-wide light
  gold taffeta
¼ yard of 45-inch-wide
  purple satin
¼ yard of 45-inch-wide dark
  purple velvet
1½×13-inch piece of fusible
  interfacing
Threads to match fabrics
Polyester fiberfill
Polyfill pellet beads
Two 12-millimeter wood beads
Wood putty
Delta Ceramcoat acrylic paints:
  black and empire gold
Delta Starlite Dye Shimmering
  Fabric Color: leaf green, ivory,
  and hunter green
Delta Fabric Dye Brush-On Fabric
  Color: red
Artists' brushes

Large darning needle
Light green carpet thread
Hot-glue gun; hot glue
Two 16-millimeter antique gold
  buttons; 4 small snaps
7×1½-inch strip of fusible
  interfacing
Ribbon to tie around neck

Instructions

Trace patterns, *pages 301–305,* onto tracing paper and cut out. Patterns and measurements include ¼-inch seam allowances. All seams are sewn with right sides of fabric facing, unless otherwise specified. Clip curved seams as necessary.

Cut all frog body parts from muslin fabric.

Cut shirt pieces from gold satin, pants from purple satin, jacket and hat pieces from purple velvet, and jacket and a 5½-inch circle for hat lining from light gold taffeta. In addition, cut two 1½×3¼-inch shirt cuffs from gold satin, two 1½×4½-inch pant cuffs from purple satin, and a 1½×7-inch band and 5½-inch circle for hat from purple velvet.

For frog, sew arm seams and legs together in pairs, leaving both ends open. Turn limbs right side out. Sew hands and feet together in pairs leaving top straight edges unstitched; turn and press. Make small tuck in top of each hand and foot; stitch across. Turn under ¼ inch along lower open edge of each arm;

insert the tucked edge of the hand and topstitch, securing hand in arm. Repeat for legs and feet. Stuff limbs firmly with fiberfill; set aside.

Sew darts in head front and back, body front, and throat, using ¼-inch seam allowances. Sew head front to throat piece along mouth edge; sew body front to throat along neck edge. Sew body back center seam, leaving opening for stuffing. Next, join head back to body back at neck.

Sew body front to back around shoulders and head. Put each arm inside body, directly below shoulder, matching raw edges. Sew body side seams, securing arms. Matching raw edges, sew legs in place on body front. Sew base to body with legs and arms inside, taking care not to catch limbs in stitching. Turn body right side out through back opening. Stuff head and then top three-fourths of body firmly with polyester fiberfill. Fill remainder of body with polyfill beads and sew opening closed.

For eyes, fill one hole in each bead with wood putty. When dry, sand smooth. With the remaining hole facing down, use eye diagram as a guide to draw eye onto front of each bead. Paint eye leaf green with empire gold irises, black pupils, and black eye outlines. Highlight pupils with dots of white.

Paint frog leaf green. Blend ivory into throat. Blend red into cheeks and knees. Shade approximate spots for eyes and along neckline using hunter green.

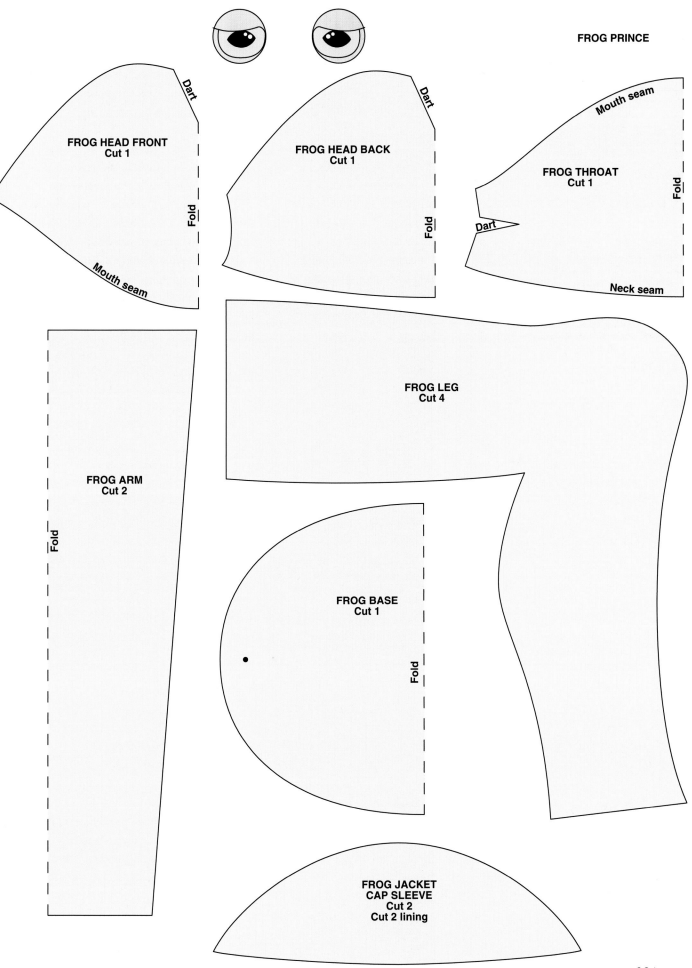

FROG PRINCE

FROG HEAD FRONT
Cut 1

Dart

Fold

Mouth seam

FROG HEAD BACK
Cut 1

Dart

Fold

FROG THROAT
Cut 1

Mouth seam

Fold

Dart

Neck seam

FROG LEG
Cut 4

FROG ARM
Cut 2

Fold

FROG BASE
Cut 1

Fold

**FROG JACKET
CAP SLEEVE**
Cut 2
Cut 2 lining

301

freddy the frog prince — *continued*

Paint the thin line along the mouth seam for smile, curving line up at the corners.

Thread needle with a double strand of carpet thread; knot. Stitch back and forth several times between eye placement points to indent eye sockets. Pull thread taut and knot. Hot-glue each eye in place.

For shirt, sew backs to front at shoulders. Gather sleeve tops to fit arm openings; stitch. Press cuffs in half lengthwise, wrong sides facing. Gather each sleeve bottom to fit cuff. Matching doubled edge of cuff to gathered sleeve bottom edge, stitch. Fold cuffs down.

Sew collar pieces together, leaving straight neck edge open. Turn right side out and press. Sew collar to shirt neck, matching raw edges. Turn under ¼ inch along outside edge of shirt facing; stitch. Sew facing to neck over collar. Turn facing to inside, with collar standing up, and press. Sew underarm/side seams. Turn under the bottom and back opening edges ¼ inch and stitch to hem. Sew three snaps down the shirt back opening.

For pants, sew pieces together along one side from crotch to waist for front seam. Repeat to make back seam, stopping 2 inches below the waist to allow for the back opening.

Fuse interfacing to wrong side of waistband. Press waistband in half lengthwise, wrong sides facing. Stitch across doubled ends of waistband ¼ inch from edges; turn and press. Gather the pants waist to fit the waistband; stitch.

Press cuffs in half lengthwise, wrong sides facing. Gather pant legs to fit cuffs. Sew cuffs to pant legs as for shirt. Sew inner leg/crotch seam. Turn pants right side out. Turn under ¼ inch

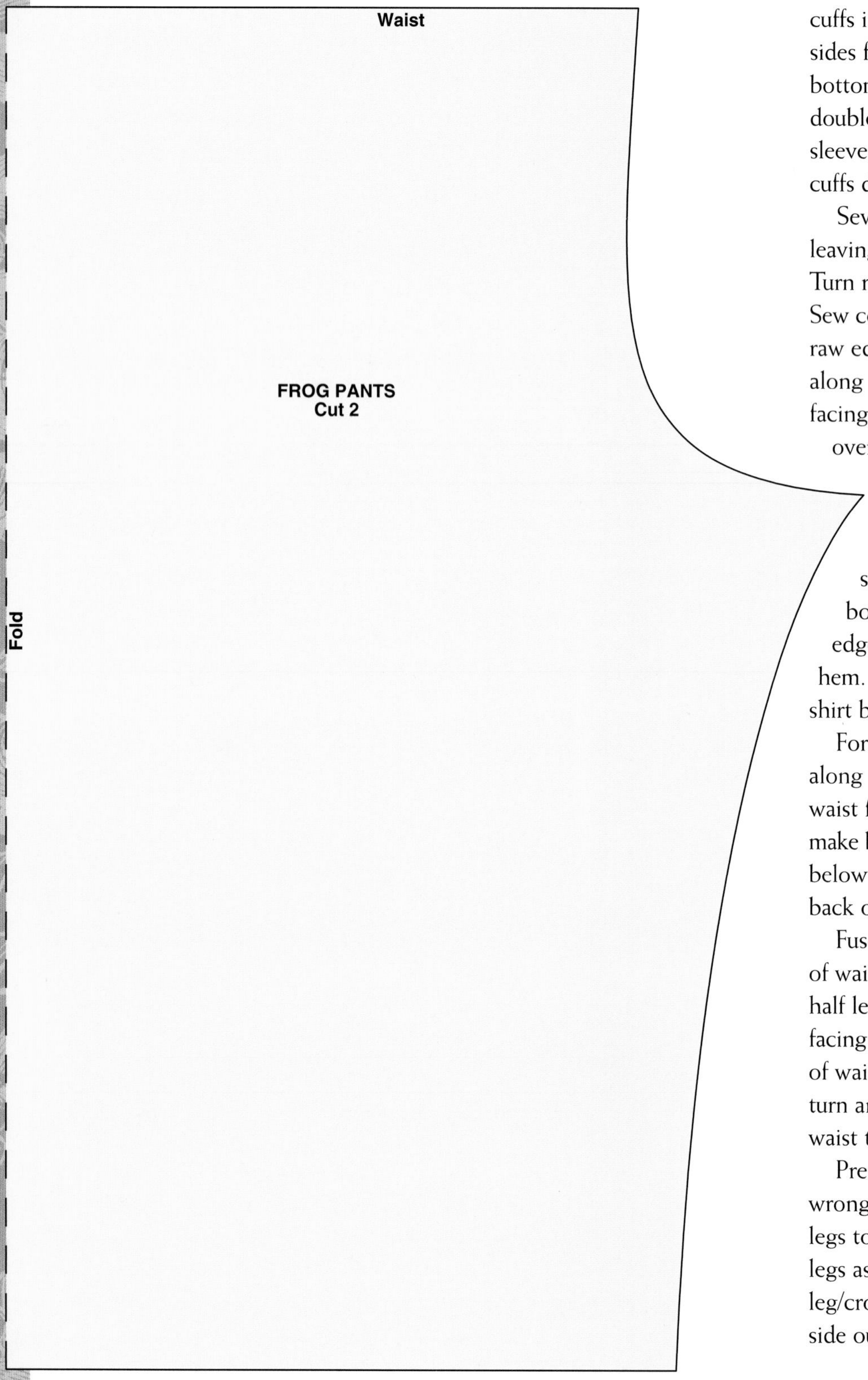

Waist

FROG PANTS
Cut 2

Fold

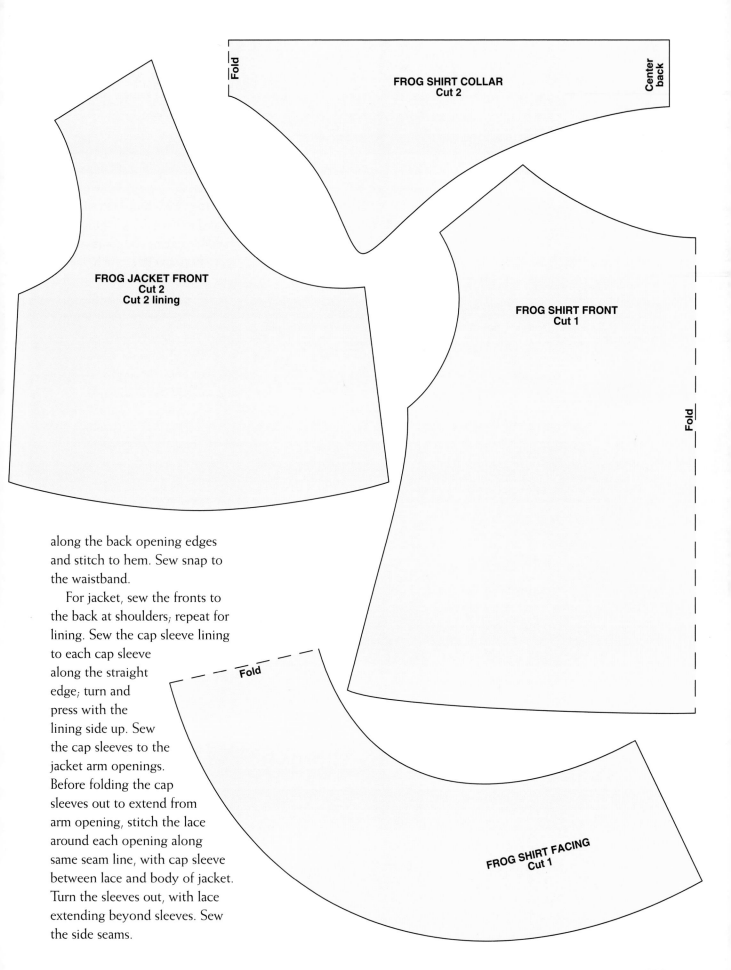

FROG SHIRT COLLAR
Cut 2

Fold

Center back

FROG JACKET FRONT
Cut 2
Cut 2 lining

FROG SHIRT FRONT
Cut 1

Fold

Fold

FROG SHIRT FACING
Cut 1

along the back opening edges and stitch to hem. Sew snap to the waistband.

For jacket, sew the fronts to the back at shoulders; repeat for lining. Sew the cap sleeve lining to each cap sleeve along the straight edge; turn and press with the lining side up. Sew the cap sleeves to the jacket arm openings. Before folding the cap sleeves out to extend from arm opening, stitch the lace around each opening along same seam line, with cap sleeve between lace and body of jacket. Turn the sleeves out, with lace extending beyond sleeves. Sew the side seams.

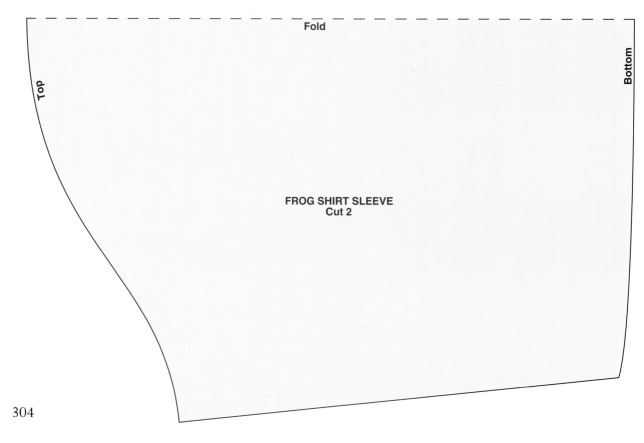

FROG SHIRT BACK
Cut 2

Center back

freddy the frog
prince — *continued*

Press under ¼ inch along lining side seam raw edges. With right sides facing, sew lining to jacket around all edges. Turn jacket right side out through side openings in lining. Press seams with lining side up. Hand-stitch lining side openings closed. Sew one button to each side of jacket front.

For hat, sew short ends of hatband together. Press hatband in half lengthwise with wrong sides facing. Position lining circle atop hat circle with wrong sides facing. Gather edge of doubled layer to fit hatband. Sew gathered hat top to outer raw edge of hatband. Turn under ¼ inch along remaining hatband edge and whipstitch to inside of hat along seam line.

Dress frog; tie ribbon around neck of shirt with bow in front.

Fold

Top

Bottom

FROG SHIRT SLEEVE
Cut 2

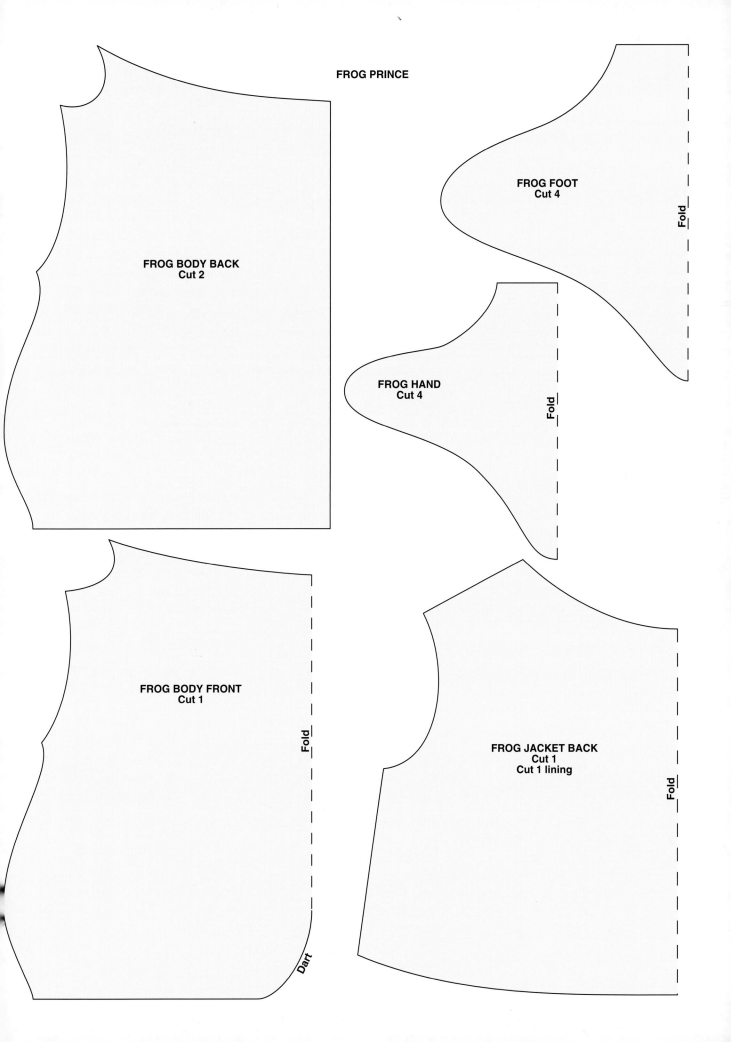

FROG PRINCE

FROG BODY BACK
Cut 2

FROG FOOT
Cut 4

Fold

FROG HAND
Cut 4

Fold

FROG BODY FRONT
Cut 1

Fold

Dart

FROG JACKET BACK
Cut 1
Cut 1 lining

Fold

christmas twins

As shown on page 291, dolls measure 6 inches tall.

Materials

Fabrics for boy
Two 8×10-inch pieces of 28-count ivory Jobelan fabric
Two 5×6-inch pieces of 28-count tan Jobelan fabric
5×8½-inch piece of tan fabric
5½×9-inch piece of red fabric
Two 4¼×3-inch pieces of dark green fabric

Fabrics for girl
Two 8×10-inch pieces of 28-count ivory Jobelan fabric
6×10¼-inch piece of 28-count tan Jobelan fabric
4×4½-inch piece of 28-count tan Jobelan fabric
5×9-inch piece of red fabric
1⅞×2½-inch piece of tan fabric
3¾×13-inch piece of dark green fabric
1×26½-inch piece of dark green fabric

Threads
Cotton embroidery floss in colors listed in key on page 308
Two additional skeins of deep mahogany (DMC 300) floss

Supplies
Tracing paper
Water-soluble marking pen
Light box or brightly lit window
Embroidery hoop; needle
Threads to match fabrics
3¼-inch-wide piece of cardboard
Polyester fiberfill
Cosmetic blush and small brush
⅛-inch-wide elastic
Four ¼-inch-diameter snaps

Instructions

Trace body and clothing patterns, *opposite,* onto tracing paper and cut out. Use patterns to cut dress bodice and sleeves from 5×9-inch piece of red fabric, vest back and lining from 5×8½-inch piece of tan fabric, and shirt and shirt sleeves from 5½×9-inch piece of red fabric. Vest fronts are cut after stitching is completed. Patterns for clothes and measurements include ¼-inch seam allowances as necessary. Sew all seams with the right sides of fabric facing. Sew Jobelan fabric using very small machine stitches.

Tape or zigzag raw edges of Jobelan to prevent fraying.

For body, stitch lengthwise center of each 8×10-inch Jobelan piece using contrasting basting thread. Match center of body pattern to basting thread on each piece and mark outline using fabric marker. Holding each fabric piece to light source, marked side up, slide body pattern behind fabric and realign outline. Mark shoe tops and body stitching lines.

Cross-stitch shoes below shoe top lines, making each shoe the same number of rows and stitches. Center nose on body front face, leaving 30 threads between top of nose and top of head. Stitch face according to chart, above. Use two plies of floss to work cross-stitches over two threads of fabric. Work backstitches and straight stitches using one ply of floss over two threads of fabric.

For each body piece, match center of pattern to basting thread on wrong side of fabric. Place against light source to trace body lines from right side of fabric to wrong side; remove pattern. Pin fronts to backs with right sides facing. Hold fabric to light source to match centers, lines, dots, and shoe tops.

Sew fronts to backs along outlines, leaving opening for turning. Restitch inner legs and inside curves. Remove basting threads and fabric marker lines; press. Cut bodies a scant ¼ inch beyond stitching, leaving wider seam allowances at opening. Clip curves; turn right side out.

Stuff limbs, leaving top ¾ inch of legs and top ½ inch of arms unstuffed. Stitch across limb tops along dotted lines. Stuff head and body, leaving ½ inch of body bottom unstuffed; sew opening closed. Stitch along body bottom dotted lines.

For boy's hair, wrap deep mahogany floss 20 times around 3¼-inch cardboard. Slide loops off card and spread center of wrapped floss to measure 1 inch. Machine stitch across center to make part. Hand-stitch part to head top using floss. Pull loops down; hand-stitch to nape of neck. Spread loops as necessary to cover back of head.

For bangs, use floss from same skein as boy's hair. Wrap floss five times around three fingers. Cut

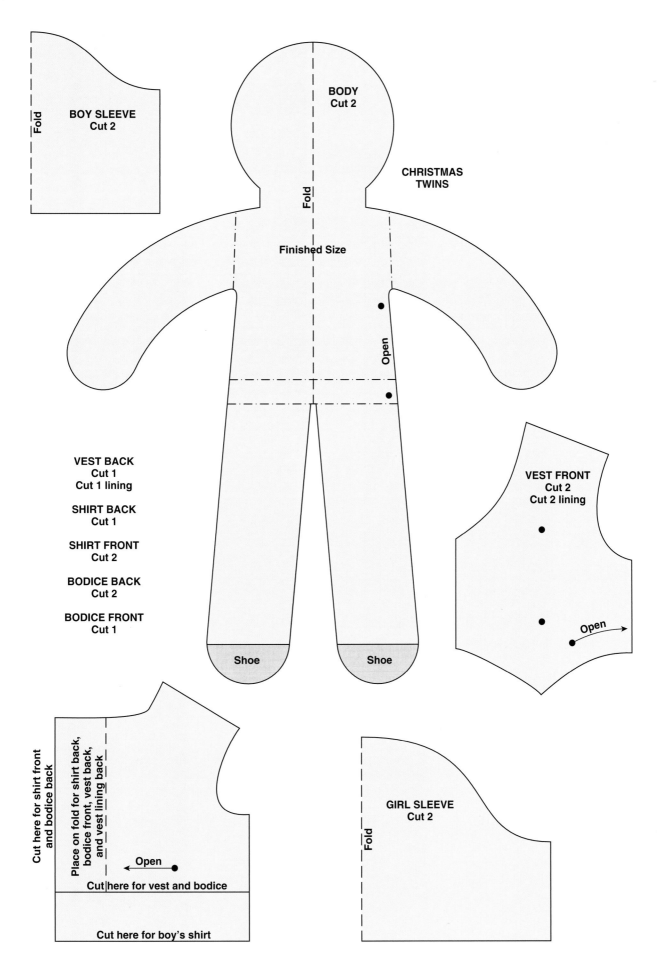

BOY SLEEVE
Cut 2

Fold

BODY
Cut 2

CHRISTMAS TWINS

Fold

Finished Size

Open

VEST BACK
Cut 1
Cut 1 lining

SHIRT BACK
Cut 1

SHIRT FRONT
Cut 2

BODICE BACK
Cut 2

BODICE FRONT
Cut 1

VEST FRONT
Cut 2
Cut 2 lining

Open

Shoe

Shoe

Cut here for shirt front and bodice back

Place on fold for shirt back, bodice front, vest back, and vest lining back

Open

Cut here for vest and bodice

Cut here for boy's shirt

GIRL SLEEVE
Cut 2

Fold

christmas twins — *continued*

off, tie around center, and cut loops. Use point of pin to separate strands. Hand-stitch bangs to front part; trim to shape.

For girl's hair, spread center of full skein of deep mahogany floss to measure 1½ inches. Stitch across center to make part. Hand-stitch part to head top using floss. Gather loops at each side below ear level; tie with scrap of floss for pigtails. Make bangs as for boy.

Make rosy cheeks using blush and small brush.

For pinafore bib design, find center of 4×4½-inch piece of Jobelan and center of chart, *below;* begin stitching there.

For pinafore skirt design, find the center of chart and point 5⅛ inches in from one short end and 2 inches above bottom edge of fabric; begin stitching there.

For each vest front design, find center of 4×5-inch piece of Jobelan and center of chart, *below;* begin stitching there.

Work clothing stitchery using same guidelines as for bodies. Trim the bib to 2½×1⅞ inches, centering design and leaving ½ inch of fabric beyond top and sides of border. Trim skirt to 4×9¼ inches, allowing ¾ inch of fabric below bottom of border. Position vest front pattern over

one tree, matching dots to tree top and bottom; cut out. Flip pattern and repeat for second vest front. Set pieces aside.

For boy's shirt, turn under ¼ inch twice along center front edges to hem; stitch. Sew fronts to back at shoulders. Stitch around neck ¼ inch from edge. Clip to stitching, press under along seamline, and edgestitch. Gather sleeve tops to fit armholes; stitch. Turn under ¼ inch twice along sleeve bottoms to hem; stitch. Sew sleeve/side seams. Hem shirt bottom as for sleeves. Sew two snaps to center front.

For boy's pants, turn up ¼ inch twice along one short edge of each 4¼×3-inch pant piece. Stitch to hem. Lay pant pieces together right sides facing. Mark point 1¾ inches below the unhemmed top edges on one side. Sew pieces together from top edge to mark using ¼-inch

CHRISTMAS TWINS		
ANCHOR	**DMC**	
352	▽	300 Mahogany
1005	●	498 Christmas red
212	✕	561 Dark seafoam
210	I	562 Medium seafoam
132	▲	797 Royal blue
BACKSTITCH		
403	╱	310 Black–eyes
914	╱	407 Cocoa–nose
1005	╱	498 Christmas red–mouth
212	╱	561 Dark seafoam–vest, bib, and skirt border

Pinafore Skirt Border stitch count: 9 high x 46 wide
Pinafore Skirt Border finished design sizes:
28-count fabric – ⅝ x 3¼ inches
36-count fabric – ½ x 2½ inches
22-count fabric – ⅞ x 4⅛ inches

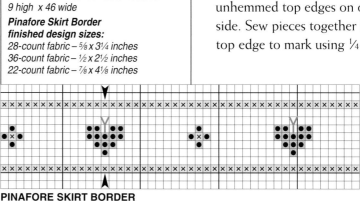

PINAFORE SKIRT BORDER

Face stitch count: 8 high x 12 wide
Face finished design sizes:
28-count fabric – ½ x ⅞ inch
36-count fabric – ⅜ x ⅝ inch
22-count fabric – ¾ x 1 inch

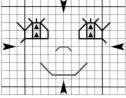

FACE

Pinafore Bib stitch count: 14 high x 13 wide
Pinafore Bib finished design sizes:
28-count fabric – 1 x 1 inch
36-count fabric – ⅞ x ¾ inch
22-count fabric – 1¼ x 1⅛ inches

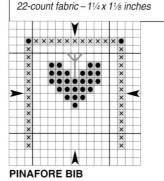

PINAFORE BIB

Vest stitch count: 13 high x 11 wide
Vest finished design sizes:
28-count fabric – 1 x ¾ inch
36-count fabric – ¾ x ⅝ inch
22-count fabric – 1⅛ x 1 inches

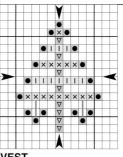

VEST

seam allowance to make center front seam. Open piece out. Press top raw edge as for hem. Lay elastic within fold and sew casing closed. Secure one elastic end, pull elastic to fit waist, and secure opposite end. Sew center back seam as for center front seam. Sew leg inseams.

For boy's vest, sew fronts to back at side seams. Repeat for lining. Sew vest to lining leaving open between dots. Clip curves and trim seams, leaving wider seam allowance at opening. Turn to right side, press, and sew the opening closed. Hand-sew shoulder seams.

For girl's dress bodice, turn under ¼ inch twice along center back edges to hem; stitch. Sew fronts to back at shoulders. Finish neck and sew in sleeves as for shirt.

Press sleeve bottoms as for hem. Lay elastic within fold and sew casing closed. On each sleeve, secure one end of elastic, pull elastic to fit arm, and secure opposite end. Sew sleeve/side seams.

To finish dress, hem one long edge of 3¾×13-inch skirt strip in same manner as other hems. Press under ¼ inch on short ends. Gather top edge to fit bodice bottom edge; stitch. Beginning at hem, sew 1½-inch center back seam. Sew snaps to bodice back.

For pinafore, press 1×26½-inch waistband and strap piece in half lengthwise. Press both long raw edges under to meet first fold. Cut 20-inch long waistband and two 3¼-inch-long straps. Hem pinafore skirt sides and bottom in same manner as other hems. Gather the top edge to measure

3¼ inches. Center gathered top along waistband and encase edge in fold, allowing waistband ends to extend for ties. Topstitch along waistband, securing skirt. Knot ends of ties.

Sew the bib to the lining leaving bottom open. Turn, press, and sew opening closed. Position the bib bottom edge, centered, behind waistband. Stitch bib to skirt along previous topstitching.

Sew folded strap edges together. Turn the ends under and hand-stitch each to the wrong side of the bib top. Fit straps over the shoulders and under the waistband, with straps even with skirt backs. Sew the straps in place along previous waistband stitching.

Press all pieces lightly and dress the dolls.

lovable elf santa

As shown on page 292, seated Santa measures 14 inches tall.

Materials

Fabric measurements are for 45-inch-wide fabric.

Tracing paper
¼ yard of peach felt
¼ yard of unbleached muslin
¼ yard of black-and-red mini-check polar fleece (hat and jacket)
7×20-inch piece of ivory short nap fur or fleece (jacket sleeves and trim)
¼ yard of green knit fabric (pants and scarf)
Brown paper
Sewing threads to match fabric, including black
Fabric glue

Polyester fiberfill
Two round-headed brass fasteners
Acrylic paints: black, red, and yellow
Small flat artist's brush
Long soft-sculpture needle
Brown eye shadow
¼ yard of black-and-red mini-check fabric (lower leg)
Dental floss
Ten 10-millimeter wood beads
⅔ yard of 1-inch-wide decorative woven trim
White wool roving
⅞-inch-diameter jingle bell
Tiny seed pods or pinecones
Purchased dark red doll boots, with the soles approximately 2¾ inches long

6×6×12-inch doll chair
Cream paper
Gold and black pens

Instructions

Trace only clothing, body, head back, and forehead pieces on *pages 311–314* onto tracing paper; cut out.

Cut head back and forehead from peach felt, body from muslin, hat and jacket from polar fleece, and pants from green knit. In addition, cut two 4½×7-inch sleeve rectangles and one 2×20-inch jacket trim strip from fur and a 4×20-inch scarf rectangle from green knit.

lovable elf santa — *continued*

Transfer the head front profile, *page 313*, and the upper arm, lower arm, upper leg, lower leg, and toe and heel guide patterns, *page 314*, onto brown paper to make templates; cut out.

Patterns include the necessary seam allowances. Sew all clothing seams with right sides of fabric facing and use ¼-inch seam allowances, unless otherwise indicated. Follow the individual instructions closely for stitching the body and head pieces.

For the head, draw around head front profile template onto double thickness of peach felt; do not cut out. Stitch center front seam along drawn line. Cut out head ⅛ inch away from stitching and along drawn lines around perimeter. Turn head front right side out. Dot inside of nose with glue and stuff with small piece of fiberfill. Set the head aside.

Paint brass fasteners black. When dry, push the fasteners into face for eyes. Bend the prongs to hold the fasteners in place.

Turn under ¼ inch along inner curve of forehead and glue to secure. Position forehead over top of face with folded edge along dotted line (refer to pattern piece). The forehead piece should cover the top one-fourth of the eye, creating eyelids.

Run a thin line of glue along the center front seam on the face behind the forehead area only; press forehead to the face. To shape the eyelids, work running stitches using pale peach sewing thread along the dotted line over each eye.

Sew the head front to the back, right sides facing, using a ⅛-inch seam allowance; leave open at bottom as indicated for turning. Turn head right side out and stuff with fiberfill, adding extra fiberfill to cheeks. Sew opening closed.

Using the soft-sculpture needle and a single strand of black sewing thread, insert needle from the back of the head and out near the corner of one eye. Referring to the face diagram, *page 313*, work straight stitches around each eye. For the mouth, work long straight stitches as shown in diagram using a double strand of black thread. Define the bridge of the nose by stitching back and forth several times between the inner corners of the eyes using pale peach thread. Blush cheeks using thinned red paint. Rub brown eye shadow over the eyelids.

For the body, sew the front to the back, leaving the neck edge open. Turn body right side out and stuff firmly, stopping ½ inch from top. Turn under ¼ inch along opening; sew opening closed.

For arms and legs, draw twice around upper arm and upper leg template onto double thickness of muslin, twice around lower arm template onto double thickness of peach felt, and twice around lower leg template onto black-and-red mini-check fabric; do not cut out. Stitch along drawn lines leaving open as indicated on pattern pieces. Cut out each piece ⅛ inch beyond stitching and turn all shapes right

side out, except lower legs. Stuff upper arm, lower arm, and upper leg, then sew openings closed. Backstitch along finger division (dot-and-dash) lines on lower arm.

Flatten each foot part of lower leg, wrong side out, with top and bottom seams matching. Place toe template on toe edge of flattened foot. Draw around template curve reversing template for opposite foot. Stitch along drawn line. Cut out each foot ⅛ inch away from stitching. For each heel, match center back and bottom seams and flatten, forming a triangular configuration. Place heel template on triangle ½ inch down from point. Draw around heel curve, stitch, and cut as for toe. Turn lower legs right side out and stuff. Sew openings closed. Using black thread, backstitch toe divisions as shown on toe template.

Overlap each lower arm over end of one upper arm, matching Xs. Using needle threaded with double strand of dental floss, push needle through overlapped area at X. Slide bead onto needle and push needle back through to other side. Slide another bead onto needle, pull floss tight, and push it through arm once again. Sew back and forth through arm and beads four more times and knot floss. Whipstitch tops of arms to body at shoulders, matching Xs.

Join lower legs to upper legs as for arms. Using needle and dental floss, sew jointed legs to body as follows: Push needle through lower body from left to right, entering and exiting at Xs. Next, push needle through X at top of jointed leg in same manner. Slide

bead onto the needle and push
back through leg and body. Push
needle through remaining jointed
leg at X. Slide another bead onto
needle and push back through
body. Sew back and forth through
body, legs, and beads several
times and knot floss.

For pants, sew inseam from A
to B on each piece. Turn one
piece right side out; slip leg into
other pant leg, matching seams.
Sew pieces together along curved
seam. Turn right side out; put on
Santa. Hand-sew pants to Santa's
waist, gathering as necessary.
Gather each pant leg ⅛ inch from
the bottom edge to fit leg. Glue
6 inches of embroidered trim
around the gathered edge,
covering gathering stitches. Cut
away the excess trim, turn
under the raw edge, and glue
in place.

For jacket, fold each
sleeve rectangle in half
lengthwise. Sew the long
edges together, stopping
2 inches from one end
(sleeve top). Turn each
sleeve right side out
and slide onto arm
with seam along
underarm. Pull
sleeve top over
shoulder and
around arm;
whipstitch to
body.

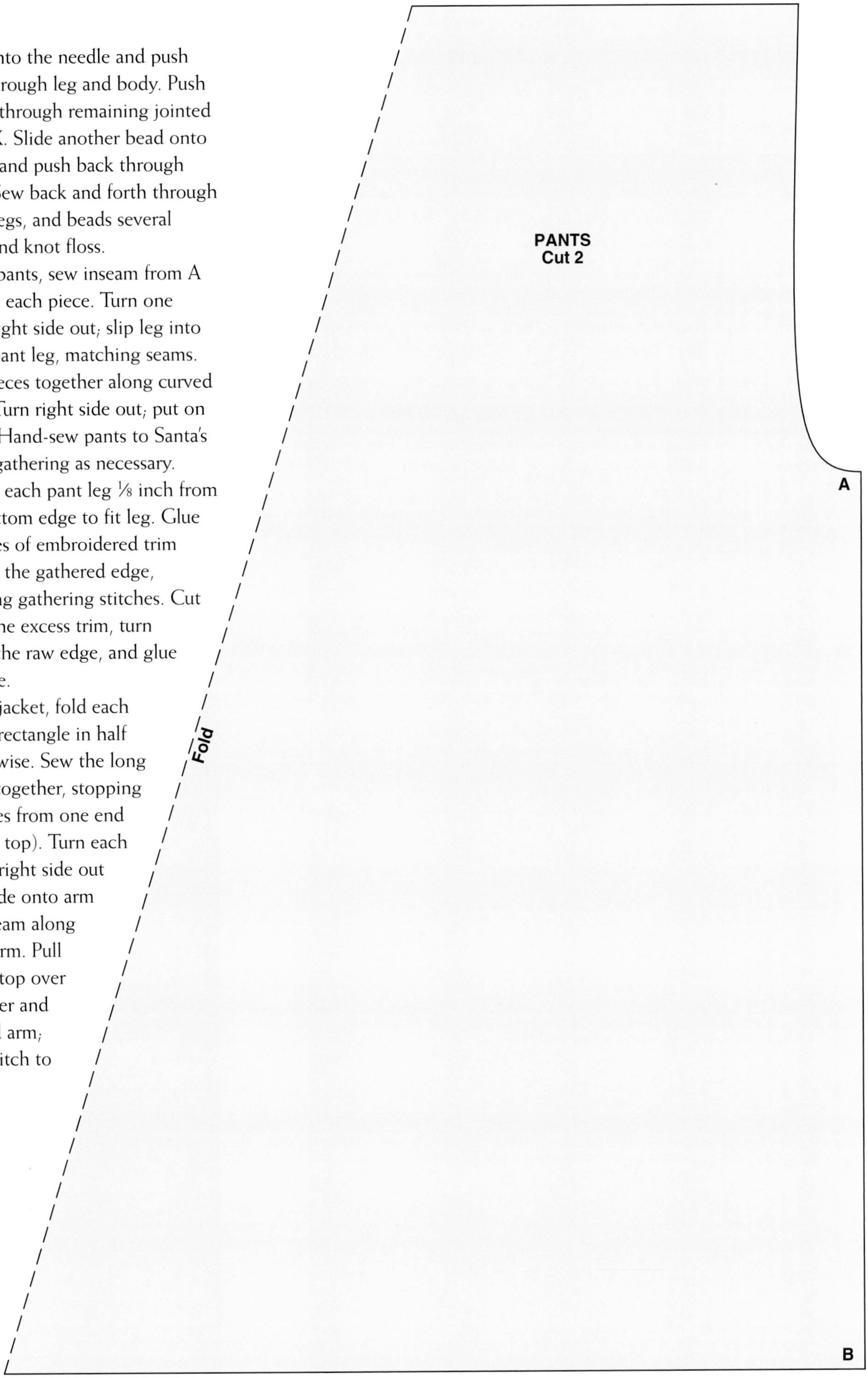

PANTS
Cut 2

Fold

A

B

lovable elf santa — *continued*

Cut jacket from A to B on dashed line to make neck opening. Sew side seams from bottom to dot; turn jacket right side out. Join short ends of 2×20-inch fur strip. Sew one long edge to bottom edge of jacket. Turn fur to inside and whipstitch raw edge to seam. Put the jacket on Santa, pulling arms through side openings. Turn under ¼ inch along side opening edges and glue to sleeves at shoulders and underarms. Glue embroidered trim around each sleeve bottom. Fringe short ends of scarf; set scarf aside.

For head and beard, position head at top of neck, tipped slightly to figure's right side. Hand-sew the head in place. Dab glue under chin, around sides of face, and at back of neck. Pull out small tufts of wool roving and glue three or four tufts under chin and along sides of face.

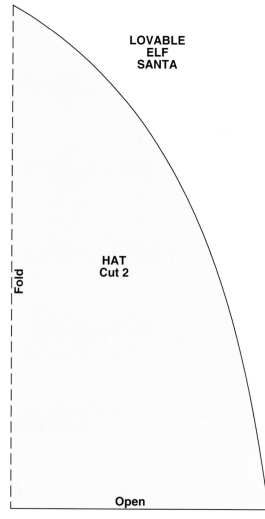

LOVABLE
ELF
SANTA

Fold

HAT
Cut 2

Open

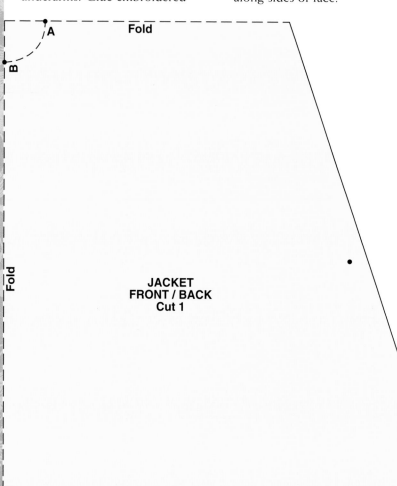

A

Fold

B

Fold

JACKET
FRONT / BACK
Cut 1

Glue larger tuft to head back, covering neck. Glue small bits of wool over eyes for the eyebrows. Twist a tuft of the wool and glue it under the nose for mustache.

For hat, sew front to back, leaving bottom open. Stuff hat lightly; sew jingle bell to point. Position the hat on the head and slip-stitch in place. Glue the tiny seed pods or pinecones around front bottom edge.

For list, cut 3×15-inch strip of cream paper. Write names on paper to make Santa's list.

Tie scarf around neck, put boots on feet, and set Santa in chair.

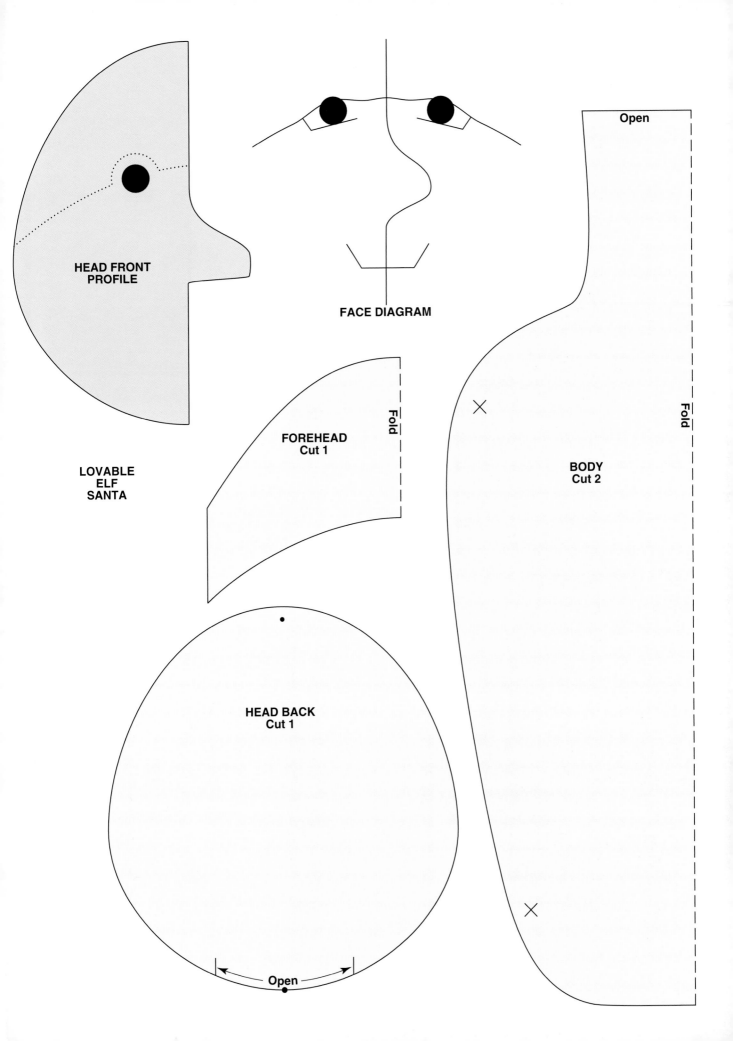

HEAD FRONT
PROFILE

FACE DIAGRAM

Open

LOVABLE
ELF
SANTA

FOREHEAD
Cut 1

Fold

BODY
Cut 2

Fold

HEAD BACK
Cut 1

Open

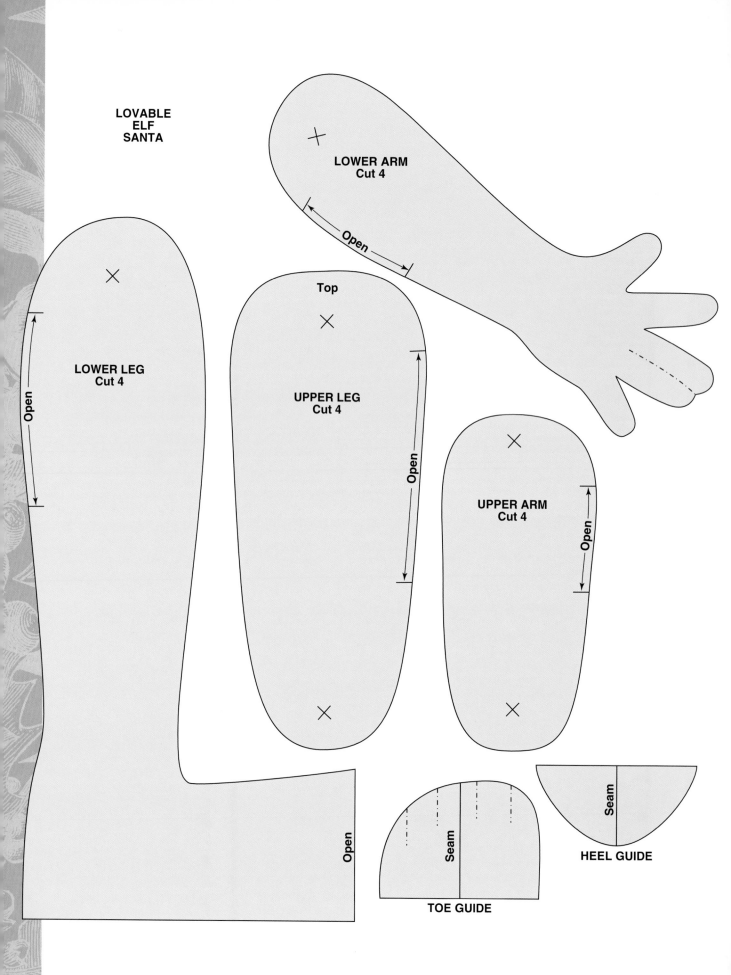

LOVABLE
ELF
SANTA

LOWER ARM
Cut 4

Open

LOWER LEG
Cut 4

Open

Top

UPPER LEG
Cut 4

Open

UPPER ARM
Cut 4

Open

Open

Seam

TOE GUIDE

Seam

HEEL GUIDE

314

candy cane scarf set

As shown on page 293. Knitting abbreviations are on page 320.

Size

For children ages 5–10 years

Skill level

For the intermediate knitter

Materials for the set

Lily's Sugar 'n Cream yarn: four skeins red (95) and three skeins eggshell (05)

Sizes 5 and 7 straight knitting needles or size to obtain gauge below

Size 5 double-pointed knitting needles (dpn)

Yarn needle; one small stitch holder

Cable needle (cn)

Gauge

In stockinette stitch (st st) with larger needles, 17 sts and 25 rows = 4 inches

CABLE PATTERN: Row 1 (RS): P 2; place next 3 sts onto cn and hold at back of work, k 3 sts, k 3 sts from cn; slip next 3 sts onto cn and hold at front of work, k 3 sts, k 3 sts from cn; p 2.

Row 2: K 2, p 12, k 2.

Row 3: P 2, k 12, p 2.

Rows 4–9: Rep rows 2–3.

Row 10: Rep Row 2.

Instructions

MITTENS: **Right Hand:** With smaller straight needles and red, cast on 31 sts.

For ribbing, Row 1 (RS): K 1, * p 1, k 1; rep from * across. Row 2: P 1, * k 1, p 1; rep from * across. Rep rows 1–2 to 2½ inches from beginning, ending with Row 2 and inc 4 sts evenly spaced on the last row = 35 sts.

Change to the larger straight needles. Row 1 (RS): K 1, p 2, k 12, p 2, k 18. Row 2: P 1, k 2, p 12, k 2, p 18.

Change to white; k 1, work Row 1 of Cable Pat on next 16 sts, k 18.

Row 2: P 18, Cable Pat on 16 sts, p 1.

Rows 3–4: Work in est pat.

Row 5: K 1, Cable Pat on 16 sts, (slip horizontal running thread between last st and next st onto left needle, k in back lp of this new st = M 1 made), k 2, M 1, k to end.

Row 6: P 20, Cable Pat on 16 sts, p 1.

Row 7: K 1, Cable 16, M 1, k 4, M 1, k to end.

Row 8: P 22, Cable 16, p 1.

Row 9: K 1, Cable 16, M 1, k 6, M 1, k to end.

Row 10: P 24, Cable 16, p 1.

Change to red; k 1, work Row 1 of Cable Pat on next 16 sts, place next 8 sts onto a small holder, k 16. Cont on these 33 sts in cable and striped pat for one red and one white stripe. With red, work as est for 6 rows.

For shaping, Row 1: * K2tog, k 1; rep from * across. Row 2: P 22. Row 3: * K 1, k2tog across, ending k 1. Row 4: P 15.

For top, leaving a long tail for sewing, cut yarn. Thread tail into yarn needle and back through rem 15 sts; pull up to tightly close opening. Using matching yarn colors, join sides.

To complete thumb, arrange sts from holder onto 3 dpn. Join

white and k 8; pick up and k 3 sts along top edge. K around and around for 7 rnds. (K2tog, k 1) around, ending k2tog = 7 sts. K 1 rnd. K 1, (k2tog) around = 4 sts. Finish as for the mitten top.

Left Hand: Work as for the Right Hand through completion of ribbing. Change to larger straight needles. Row 1 (RS): K 18, p 2, k 12, p 2, k 1. Reversing Cable Pat and thumb, work as for the Right Hand.

HAT: With larger straight needles and red, cast on 86 sts.

Row 1 (WS): P 1, (k 1, p 1) across next 34 sts, k 2, p 12, k 2, (p 1, k 1) across the next 34 sts, p 1.

Row 2: K 1, (p 1, k 1) across next 34 sts, Row 1 of Cable Pat on 16 sts, (k 1, p 1) on 34 sts, k 1.

Row 3: Rep Row 1.

Row 4: K 35, Row 3 of Cable Pat on 16 sts, k 35.

Row 5: P 35, Row 4 of Cable Pat on 16 sts, p 35.

Cont est pat through completion of Cable Pat, Row 10; cut red and join white. Working center 16 sts in Cable Pat and 35 sts along edge side in st st work one white stripe and one red. Change to white and work 6 rows of Cable Pat.

For crown shaping, with white (k2tog, k 1) across, ending k2tog. P 57. K 1, (k2tog) across. P 29. Change to red, k 1, (k2tog) across. P 15. K 1, (k2tog) across. P 8. Leaving a sewing tail, cut yarn. Thread tail through rem sts; pull tightly to close top. Using matching yarn colors, sew back seam.

For tassel (make two), cut 17 red strands each measuring 14 inches. Holding strands together, tie a separate strand of red tightly around center. Fold strands in half and tie another red strand tightly

candy cane scarf set — *continued*

½-inch from top. Attach to the top of the hat.
SCARF: With larger straight needles and red, cast on 60 sts. P 22, k 2, p 12, k 2, p 22. Keeping 22 sts along edge, edge in st st and beginning with Row 1 of Cable Pat on center 16 sts, work 10 rows red and 10 rows white for 23 stripes. Bind off all sts. Using matching yarn colors, sew the back seam.

For fringe, cut 7 strands of red each 16 inches. Holding strands together, fold in half to form loop. Pull loop through center of cable; draw ends through loop; pull up to form a knot. Alternating colors, add four more bundles of fringe along side of center bundle of fringe. Repeat for opposite edge.

gingerbread noah's ark and animals

As shown on pages 294–295, ark measures 4×12×8 inches.

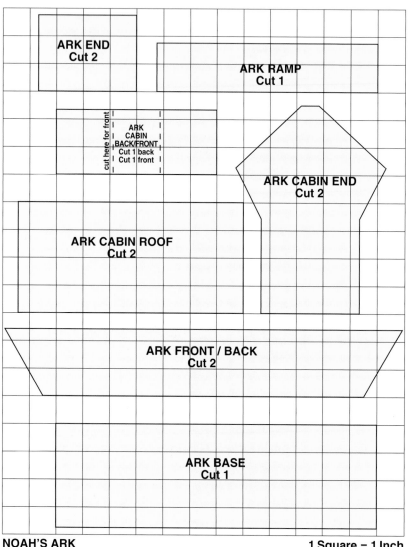

NOAH'S ARK   **1 Square = 1 Inch**

Materials

Tracing paper
Clear adhesive plastic (optional)
Gingerbread recipe, opposite
2 to 2½-inch Animal cookie cutters (we used Wilton brand cutters)
Pastry bags, couplers, and tips (we used small round and star tips)
Candy-coated fruit-flavored pieces
Candy canes
Striped round peppermint candies
Waxed paper or aluminum foil
Royal Icing recipe, opposite

Instructions

To make ark, enlarge the patterns, *left,* onto tracing paper. If desired, cover both sides of the pattern pieces with clear adhesive plastic. This will protect the patterns so they can be used again.

Using a floured rolling pin, roll out the cookie dough ⅛- to ¼-inch thick on the back of an ungreased 15×10×1-inch baking pan. Place the patterns 1 inch apart on the dough; cut around the patterns with a sharp knife. Remove excess dough.

Bake pieces in a 375° oven for 10 to 12 minutes. While cookie pieces are still very warm, place patterns on cookies and trim excess cookie as necessary. For easier assembly, cookies should be cut as exact as possible. Return cookies to oven for 2 to 3 minutes. Cool for 2 minutes. Loosen from baking pan with spatula. When nearly cool, transfer to wire rack to cool completely. Repeat until all pattern pieces have been baked.

To make animal cookies, roll out dough 1/8- to 1/4-inch thick on a lightly floured surface. Use animal cutters to cut out cookies. To make stands for cookies, cut out triangles from some of the rolled dough using a sharp knife. Triangles should be 2 inches tall.

Place shapes 1 inch apart on a lightly greased baking sheet. Bake in a 375° oven for 8 to 9 minutes or until edges are lightly browned. Remove to a wire rack to cool.

To decorate ark and animals, fit pastry bags with couplers and tips. Fill with Royal Icing and decorate shapes. If tips dry shut during decorating, wipe with a damp cloth. Attach fruit-flavored candy pieces while icing is still wet. Candy canes and peppermint candies are added after assembly. Let pieces dry for several hours or overnight before assembling. Prepared Royal Icing may be held overnight in refrigerator; beat with an electric mixer again until very stiff.

To assemble ark, use glass measuring cups to hold pieces in place. Position ark base on a piece of waxed paper. Pipe icing on one long edge. Immediately attach one ark side. Hold in place with measuring cups. Meanwhile,

attach front and back of ark cabin to base, then attach other side of ark to ark base, piping more icing where pieces join. When these pieces are set (about 20 minutes) continue with ark ends, cabin ends, and cabin roof. (Cabin roof may take longer to set.) Attach candy canes and peppermint candies as a finishing touch to ark.

Attach cookies to their stands, using more icing. Let dry completely, cookie face down, before standing upright.

Gingerbread Recipe:
Note: As shown on pages 294–295. For Noah's ark and animals, make recipe twice; don't double it.

Ingredients
- 1/2 cup butter or margarine, softened
- 1/2 cup shortening
- 1 cup sugar
- 1 1/2 teaspoons ground ginger
- 1 1/2 teaspoons ground allspice
- 1 teaspoon baking soda
- 1/2 teaspoon salt
- 1 egg
- 1/2 cup molasses
- 2 tablespoons lemon juice
- 3 cups all-purpose flour
- 1 cup whole wheat flour

Method
In large mixing bowl, beat butter or margarine and shortening with electric mixer on medium to high speed for 30 seconds. Add sugar, ginger, allspice, soda, and salt; beat until combined. Add egg, molasses, and lemon juice; beat until combined. Beat in as much of the all-purpose flour as you can with mixer. Stir in any remaining flour and whole wheat

flour with a wooden spoon. Divide the dough in half; wrap halves in clear plastic wrap. Chill 3 hours.

Royal Icing:
Note: As shown on pages 294–295. For Noah's ark and animals, make recipe twice; don't double it.

Ingredients
- 3 tablespoons meringue powder
- 1/3 cup warm water
- 1 16-ounce package powdered sugar, sifted (4 1/2 cups)
- 1 teaspoon vanilla
- 1/2 teaspoon cream of tartar
  Paste food coloring

Method
In bowl, combine meringue powder, water, powdered sugar, vanilla, and cream of tartar. Beat with mixer on low speed until combined, then on high for 7 to 10 minutes. Use at once.

Divide icing; tint with paste food coloring. When not using icing, keep it covered with clear plastic wrap to prevent it from drying out. Makes 3 cups.

index